DATE DUE

OCT 2 9 2008		
NOV 1 9 2008		
MAR 2 4 2008		
DEC 1 1 2010		
JAN 0 6 2011		
NOV 1 5 2011		
MAR 0 7 2012		
AUG 2 6 2013		
SEP 3 0 2013		
DEC 2 7 2013		
FE 1 7 '15		
JUL 1 8 2016		

A Publication of **Renaissance Press**

Amelia Rules! Volume Four:
When the Past Is a Present

Renaissance Press
PO Box 5060
Harrisburg, PA 17110

www.ameliarules.com

ISBN 978-09712169-9-0 (softcover)
ISBN 978-09712169-8-3 (hardcover)

First Renaissance Press edition 2008
10 9 8 7 6 5 4 3 2 1

Editor: Michael Cohen
Marketing and Promotion: Karen Gownley
Director of Publishing and Operations: Harold Buchholz
Brand Manager: Ben Haber

Printed in Korea

Other Books in This Series:

Amelia Rules! The Whole World's Crazy
ISBN 978-0-9712169-2-1 (softcover)
ISBN 978-0-9712169-3-8 (hardcover)
Amelia Rules! What Makes You Happy
ISBN 978-0-9712169-4-5 (softcover)
ISBN 978-0-9712169-5-2 (hardcover)
Amelia Rules! Superheroes
ISBN 978-0-9712169-6-9 (softcover)
ISBN 978-0-9712169-7-6 (hardcover)

To order additional volumes from Renaissance Press, visit us at ameliarules.com
Also available in fine bookstores and comic shops everywhere
To find the comic shop nearest you call 1-888-comicbook

AMELIA RULES!

When the Past is a Present

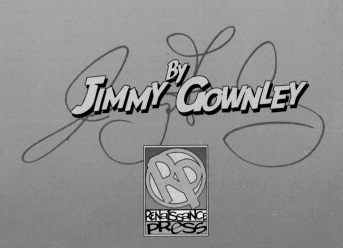

BY JIMMY GOWNLEY

RENAISSANCE PRESS

·a Renaissance Press book·

DEDICATION

This book is dedicated to:

Kerensa Bartlett, Hailey Cook, Ethan Gourlay,
James Elmour, Frances Cooke, and everyone at
Small Pond Productions. And especially to
Kasey Perkins who brought Amelia McBride
to life before my very eyes.

That's what magic is.

INTRODUCTION

A few years ago I was appearing at my first convention panel at
San Diego's Comic-Con. As enjoyable as it was to wander the
cavernous aisles of my comic book heroes, I couldn't help but wish my
kids were there to enjoy it with me. Being the good geek father that I
am, I tried to raise my children with a healthy dose of Batman,
Superman, Spider-Man, etc. My five year-old twin sons were hooked.
But, alas, my eight year-old daughter Eden never quite warmed to the
exploits of these "-men." She couldn't relate. They weren't real.

And then I met Amelia. Or more accurately, I met Jimmy Gownley
and his wife Karen when I stumbled upon and flipped through issues
of *Amelia Rules!* at their Comic-Con booth. The artwork was clean
and pleasurable, the writing was smart and genuine. And most
importantly, Amelia was a girl after my daughter's own heart: a girl
roughly the same age, a transplanted New Yorker. And while Eden
didn't come from a broken home, she had many friends who did.
Amelia was real.

Jimmy and Karen, being fans of my work, generously gave me several
issues to take home with me. Eden lapped them up, loving every one
of them, hungry for more. So thank you, Amelia, and congratulations,
Jimmy. Because of you, my daughter and I now have a comic book we
can geek out over together.

David Fury
Writer, Producer
Buffy the Vampire Slayer, Lost, Angel, 24

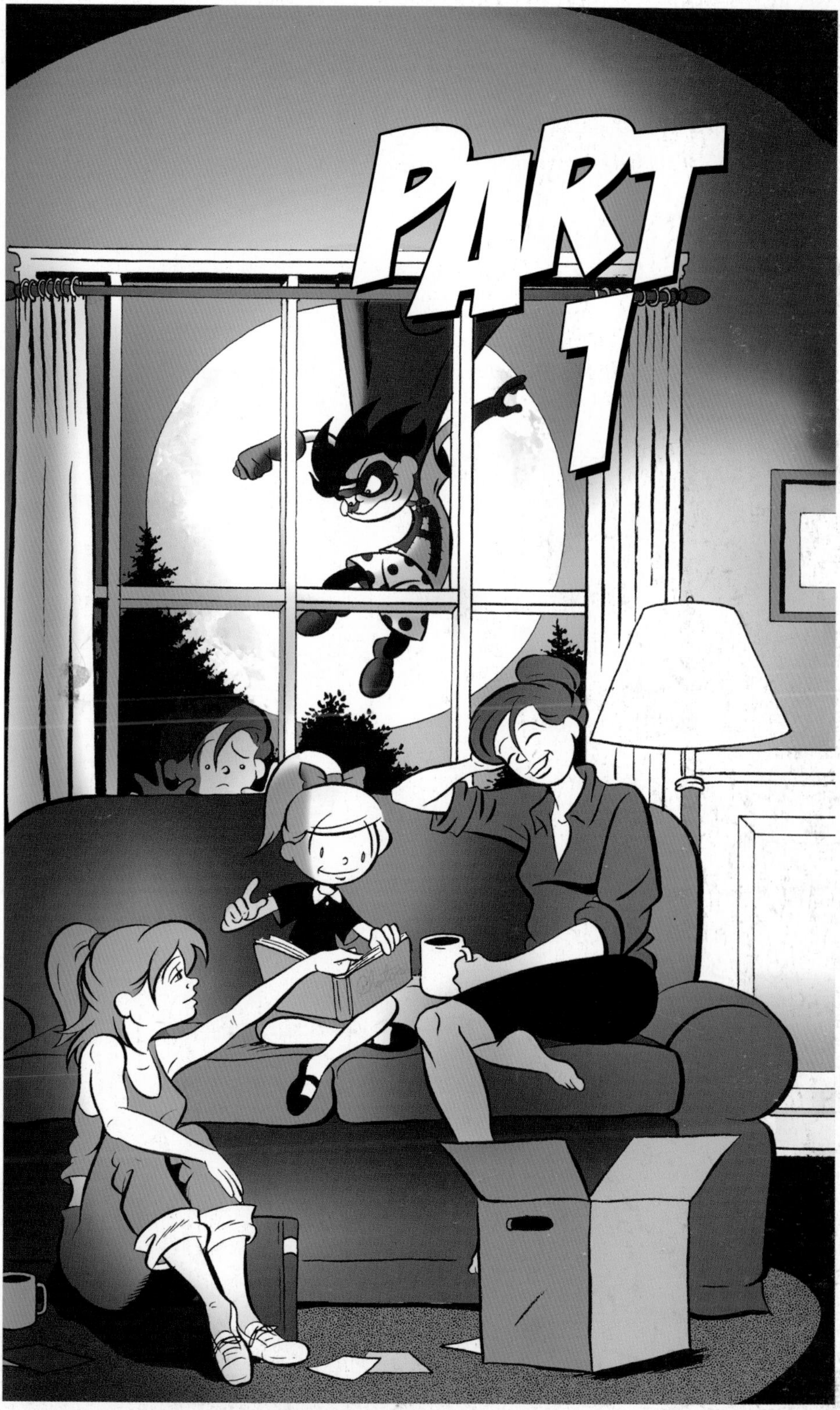
PART 1

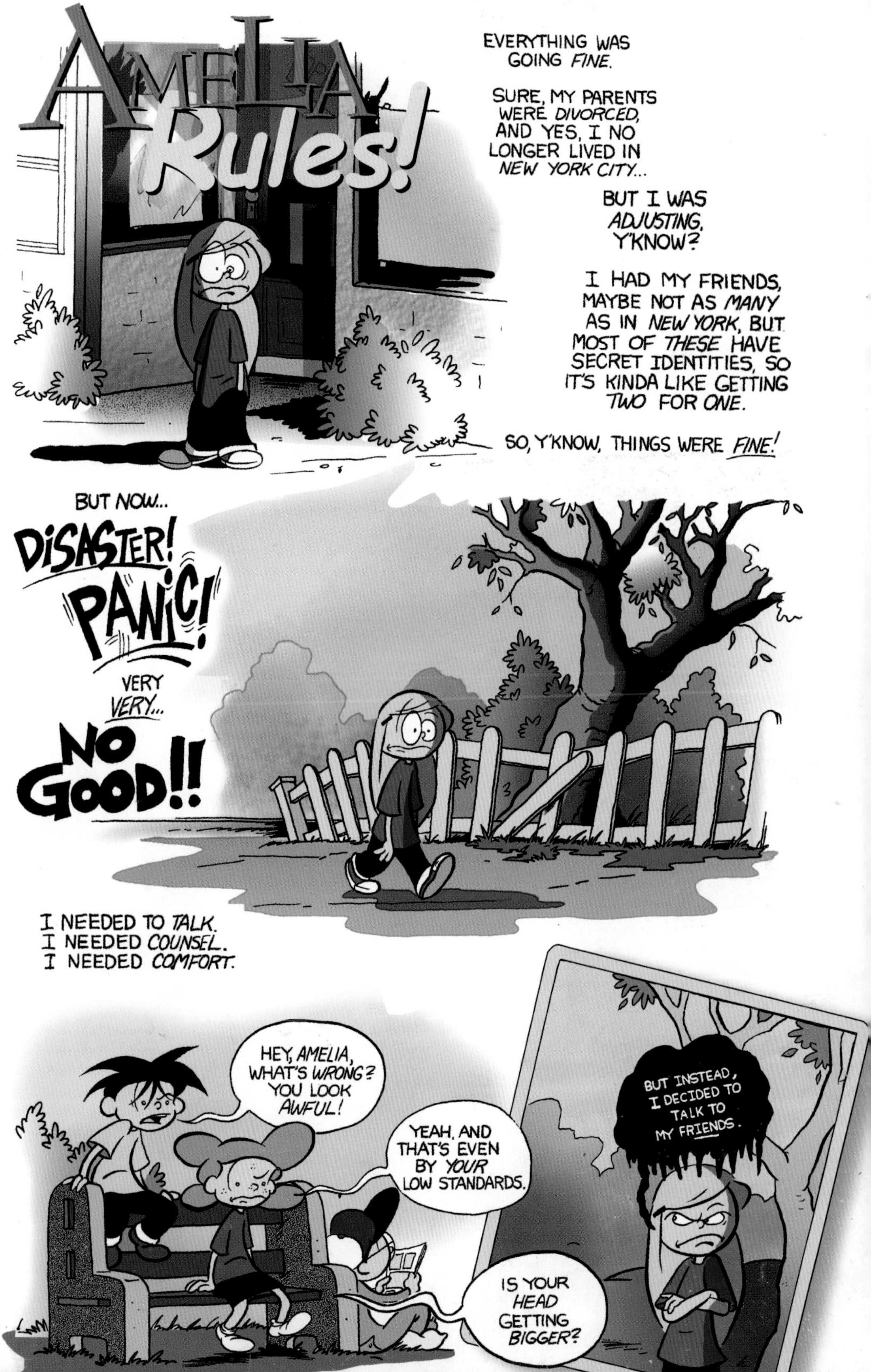

AMELIA Rules!
EVERYTHING WAS GOING FINE.
SURE, MY PARENTS WERE DIVORCED, AND YES, I NO LONGER LIVED IN NEW YORK CITY...
BUT I WAS ADJUSTING, Y'KNOW?
I HAD MY FRIENDS, MAYBE NOT AS MANY AS IN NEW YORK, BUT MOST OF THESE HAVE SECRET IDENTITIES, SO IT'S KINDA LIKE GETTING TWO FOR ONE.
SO, Y'KNOW, THINGS WERE FINE!
BUT NOW...
DISASTER!
PANIC!
VERY VERY...
NO GOOD!!
I NEEDED TO TALK.
I NEEDED COUNSEL.
I NEEDED COMFORT.
HEY, AMELIA, WHAT'S WRONG? YOU LOOK AWFUL!
YEAH, AND THAT'S EVEN BY YOUR LOW STANDARDS.
IS YOUR HEAD GETTING BIGGER?
BUT INSTEAD, I DECIDED TO TALK TO MY FRIENDS.

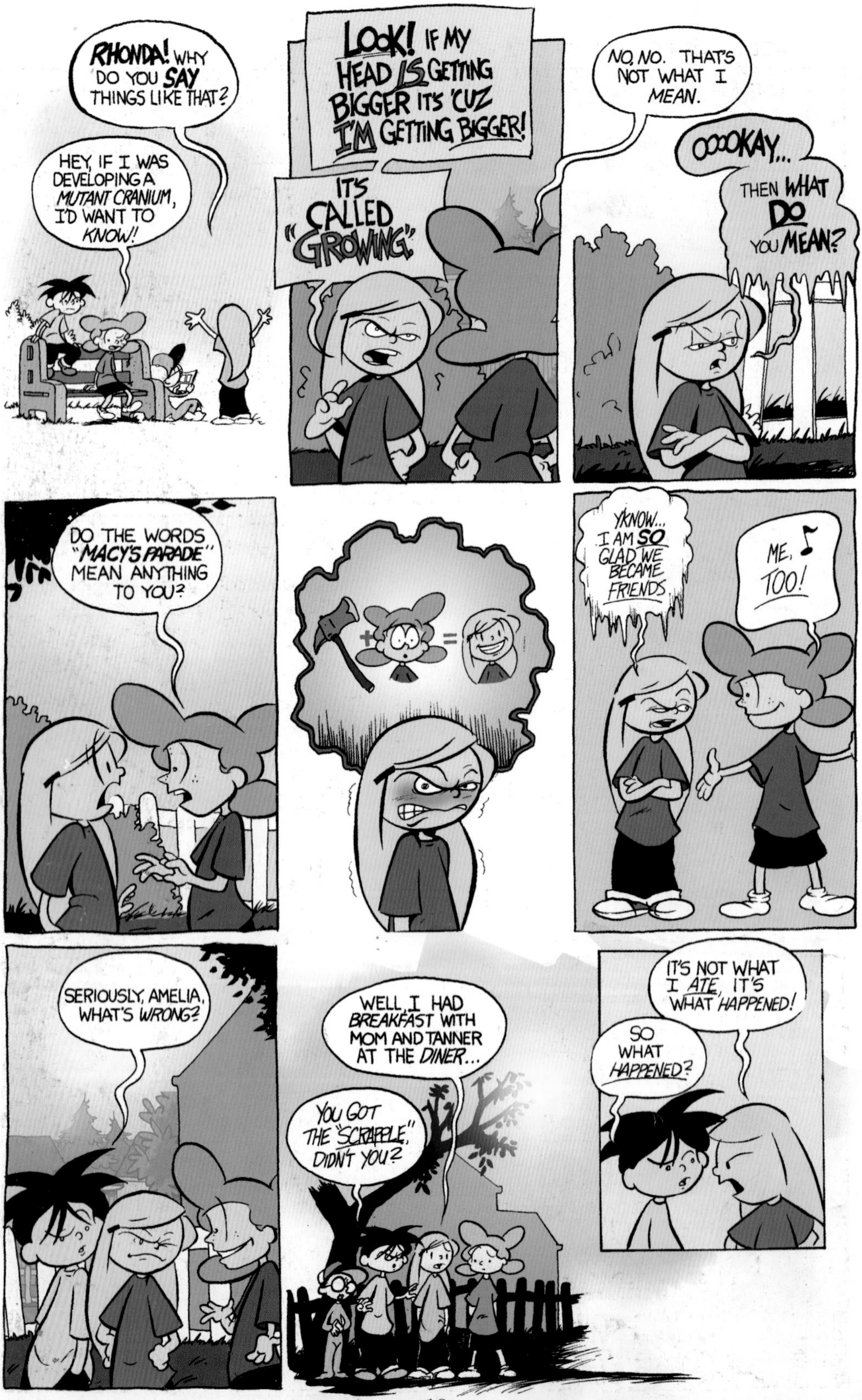
RHONDA! WHY DO YOU SAY THINGS LIKE THAT?
HEY, IF I WAS DEVELOPING A MUTANT CRANIUM, I'D WANT TO KNOW!
LOOK! IF MY HEAD IS GETTING BIGGER IT'S 'CUZ I'M GETTING BIGGER!
IT'S CALLED "GROWING."
NO, NO. THAT'S NOT WHAT I MEAN.
OOOOKAY...
THEN WHAT DO YOU MEAN?
DO THE WORDS "MACY'S PARADE" MEAN ANYTHING TO YOU?
Y'KNOW... I AM SO GLAD WE BECAME FRIENDS.
ME, TOO!
SERIOUSLY, AMELIA, WHAT'S WRONG?
WELL, I HAD BREAKFAST WITH MOM AND TANNER AT THE DINER...
YOU GOT THE "SCRAPPLE," DIDN'T YOU?
SO WHAT HAPPENED?
IT'S NOT WHAT I ATE, IT'S WHAT HAPPENED!

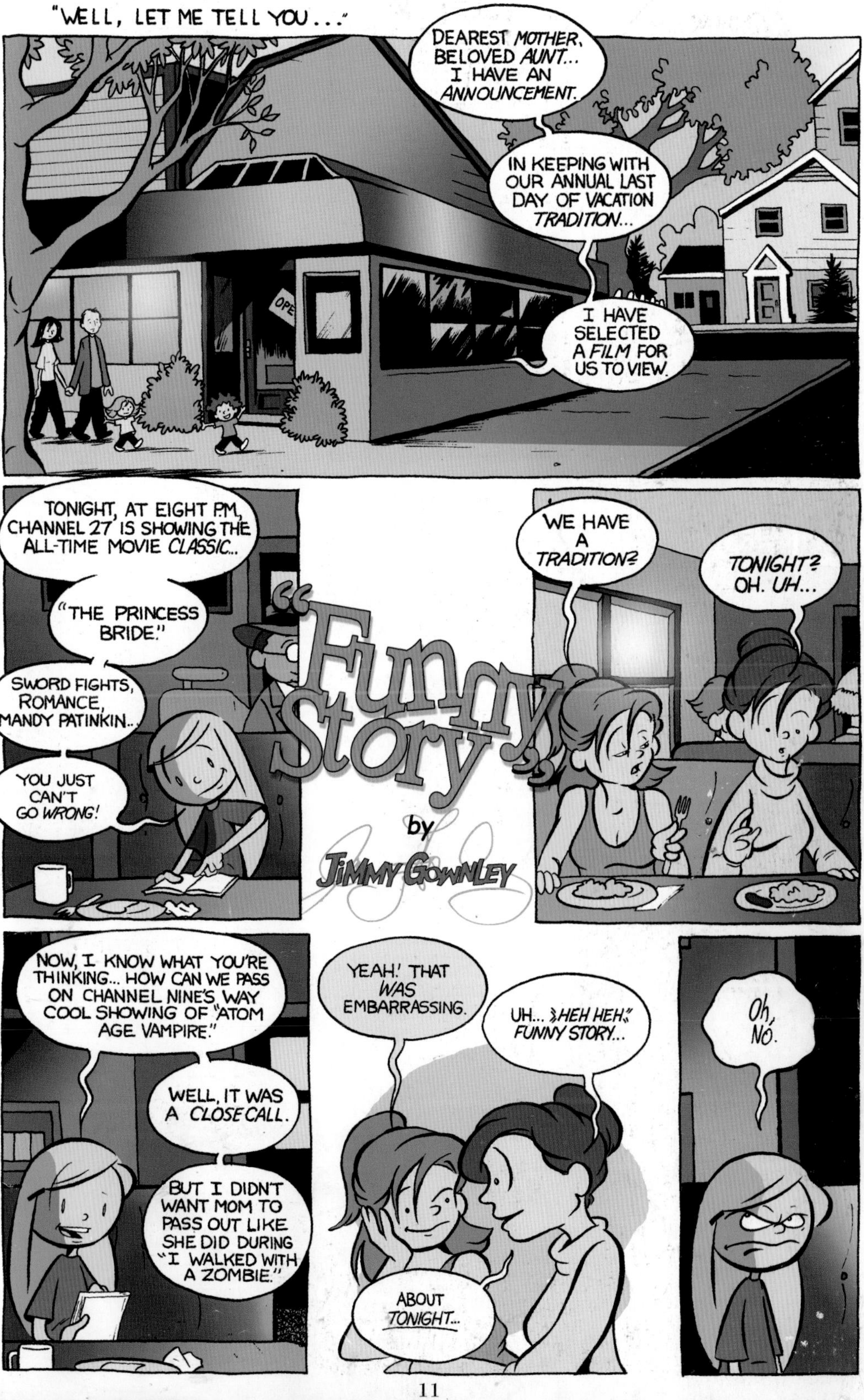
"WELL, LET ME TELL YOU..."
DEAREST MOTHER, BELOVED AUNT... I HAVE AN ANNOUNCEMENT.
IN KEEPING WITH OUR ANNUAL LAST DAY OF VACATION TRADITION...
I HAVE SELECTED A FILM FOR US TO VIEW.
OPE
TONIGHT, AT EIGHT P.M., CHANNEL 27 IS SHOWING THE ALL-TIME MOVIE CLASSIC...
"THE PRINCESS BRIDE."
SWORD FIGHTS, ROMANCE, MANDY PATINKIN...
YOU JUST CAN'T GO WRONG!
"Funny Story"
by
JIMMY GOWNLEY
WE HAVE A TRADITION?
TONIGHT? OH. UH...
NOW, I KNOW WHAT YOU'RE THINKING... HOW CAN WE PASS ON CHANNEL NINE'S WAY COOL SHOWING OF "ATOM AGE VAMPIRE."
WELL, IT WAS A CLOSE CALL.
BUT I DIDN'T WANT MOM TO PASS OUT LIKE SHE DID DURING "I WALKED WITH A ZOMBIE."
YEAH! THAT WAS EMBARRASSING.
UH... "HEH HEH," FUNNY STORY...
ABOUT TONIGHT...
Oh, No.

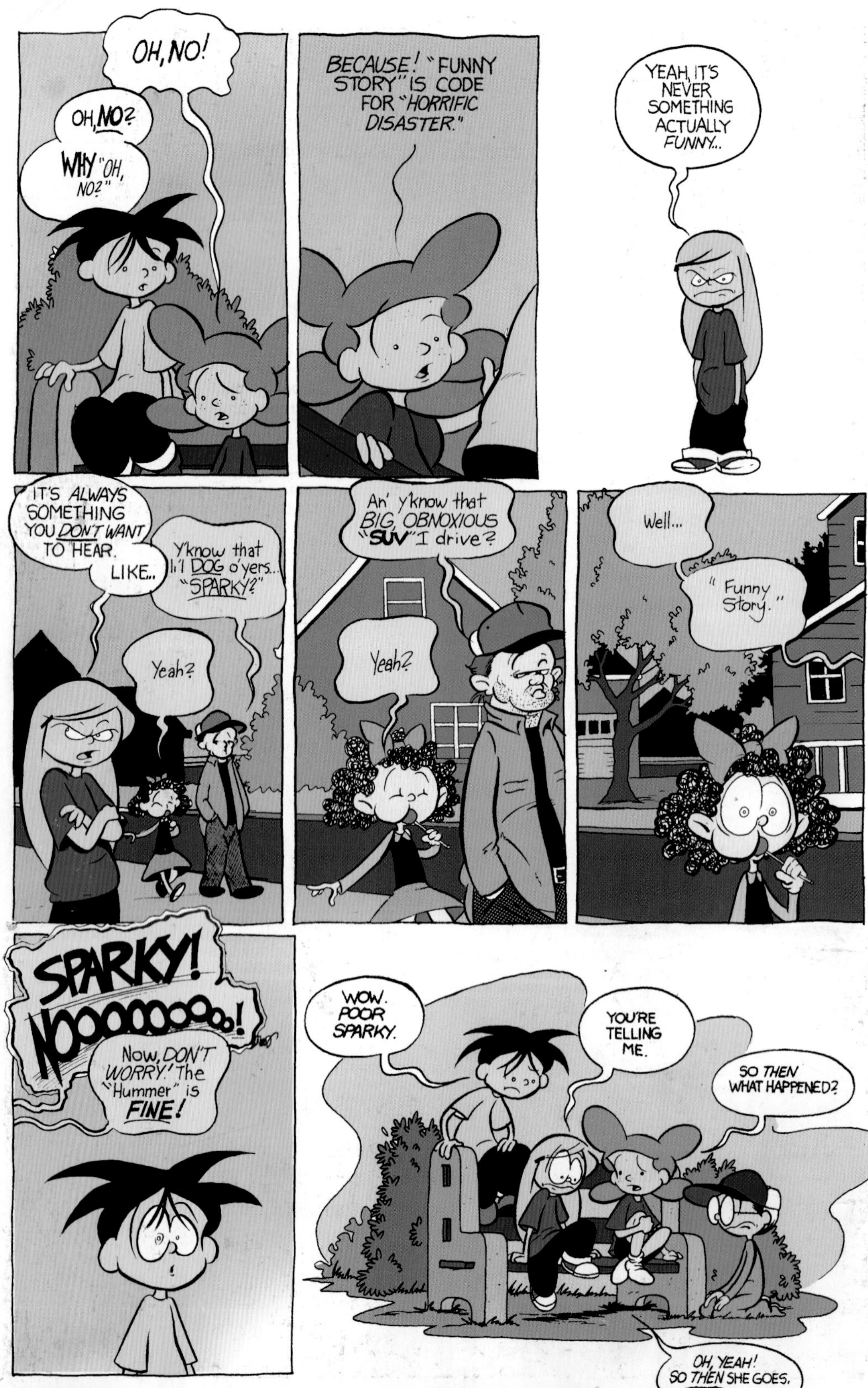
OH, NO!
OH, NO?
WHY "OH, NO?"
BECAUSE! "FUNNY STORY" IS CODE FOR "HORRIFIC DISASTER."
YEAH, IT'S NEVER SOMETHING ACTUALLY FUNNY...
IT'S ALWAYS SOMETHING YOU DON'T WANT TO HEAR.
LIKE...
Y'know that li'l DOG o'yers... "SPARKY?"
Yeah?
An' y'know that BIG, OBNOXIOUS "SUV" I drive?
Yeah?
Well...
"Funny Story."
SPARKY! NOOOOOOOoo!
Now, DON'T WORRY! The "Hummer" is FINE!
WOW. POOR SPARKY.
YOU'RE TELLING ME.
SO THEN WHAT HAPPENED?
OH, YEAH! SO THEN SHE GOES,

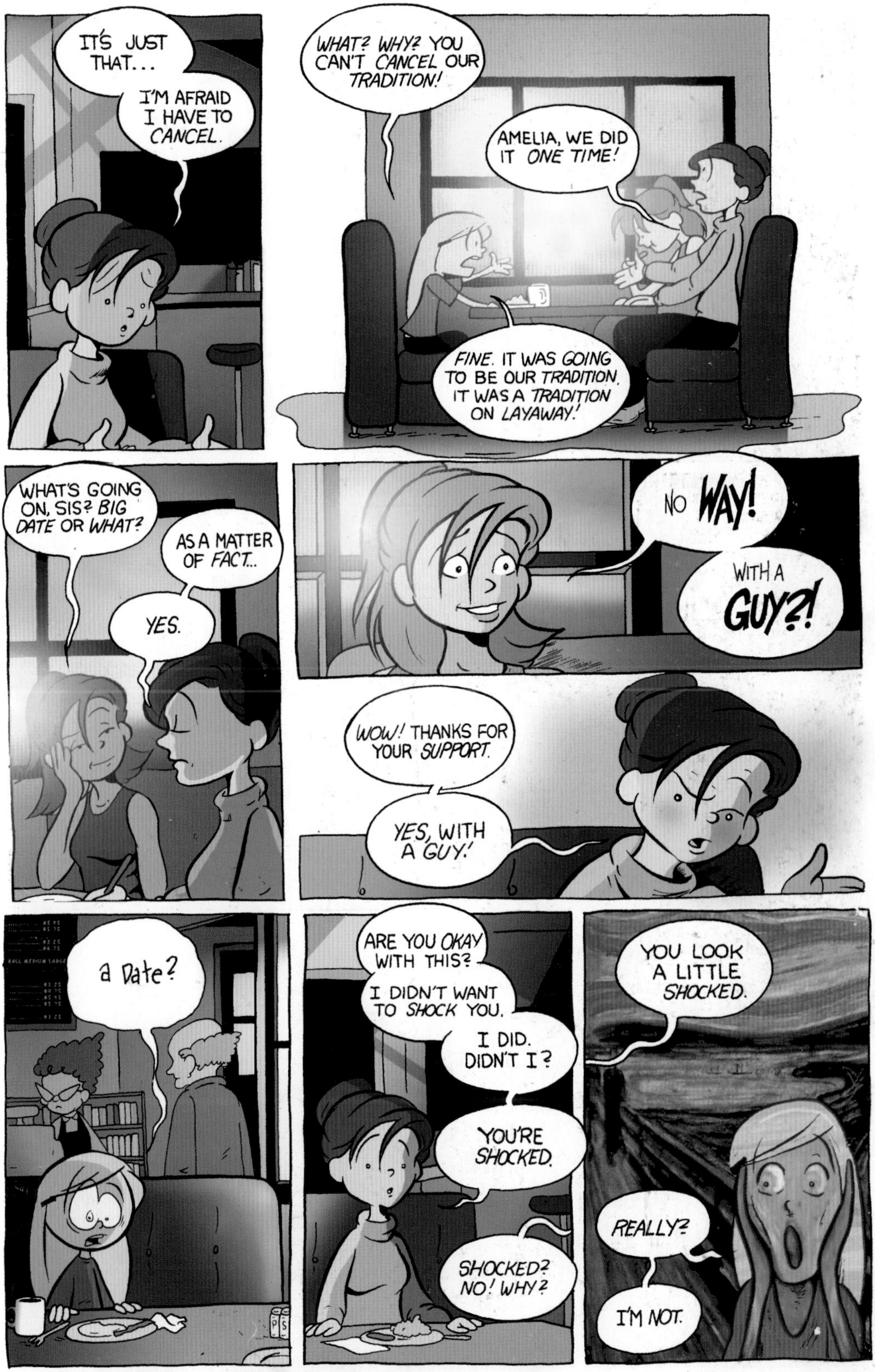
IT'S JUST THAT...
I'M AFRAID I HAVE TO CANCEL.
WHAT? WHY? YOU CAN'T CANCEL OUR TRADITION!
AMELIA, WE DID IT ONE TIME!
FINE. IT WAS GOING TO BE OUR TRADITION. IT WAS A TRADITION ON LAYAWAY!
WHAT'S GOING ON, SIS? BIG DATE OR WHAT?
AS A MATTER OF FACT...
YES.
NO WAY!
WITH A GUY?!
WOW! THANKS FOR YOUR SUPPORT.
YES, WITH A GUY!
a Date?
ARE YOU OKAY WITH THIS?
I DIDN'T WANT TO SHOCK YOU.
I DID. DIDN'T I?
YOU'RE SHOCKED.
SHOCKED? NO! WHY?
YOU LOOK A LITTLE SHOCKED.
REALLY?
I'M NOT.

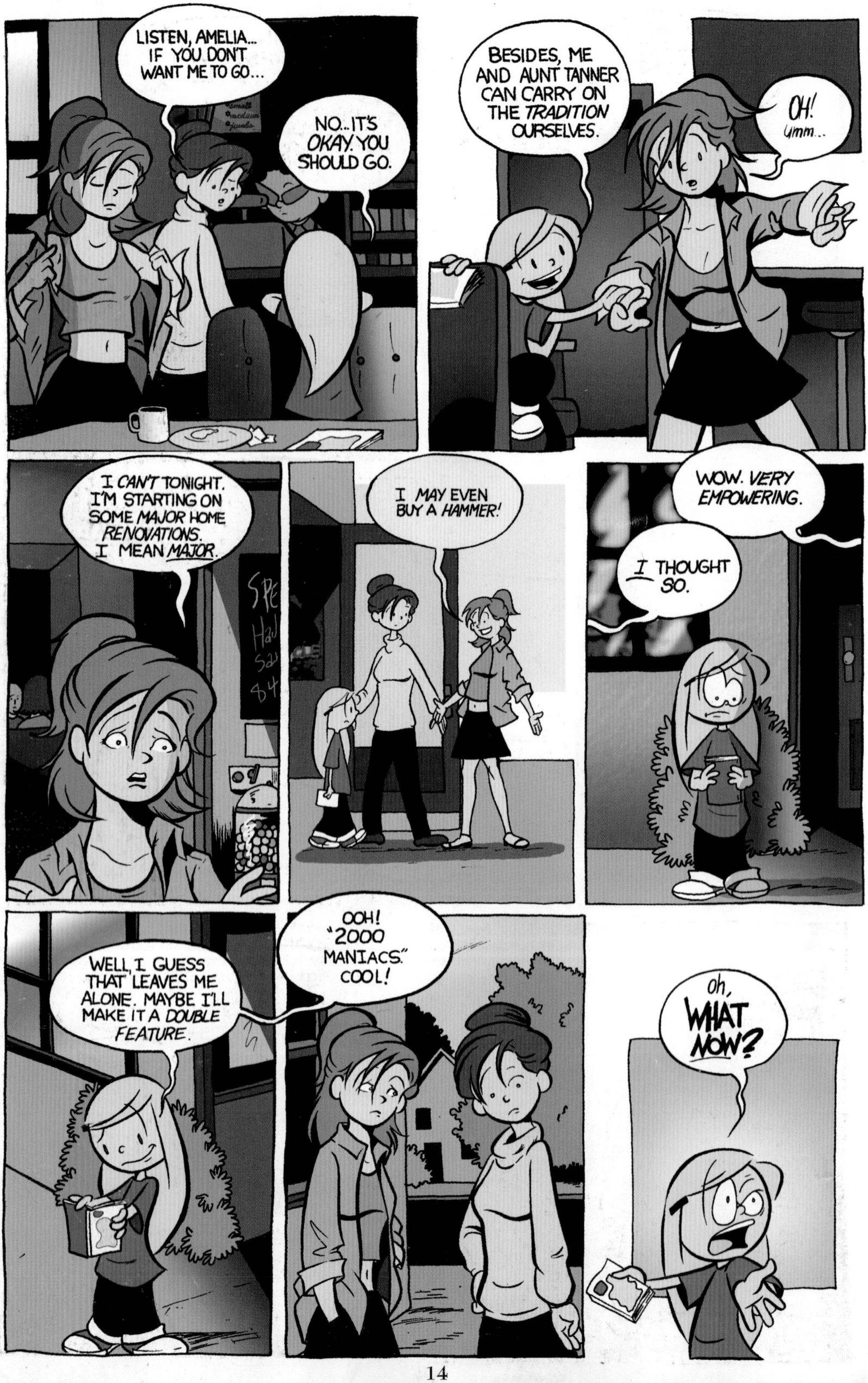
LISTEN, AMELIA... IF YOU DON'T WANT ME TO GO...
NO...IT'S OKAY. YOU SHOULD GO.
BESIDES, ME AND AUNT TANNER CAN CARRY ON THE TRADITION OURSELVES.
OH! Umm...
I CAN'T TONIGHT. I'M STARTING ON SOME MAJOR HOME RENOVATIONS. I MEAN MAJOR.
I MAY EVEN BUY A HAMMER!
WOW. VERY EMPOWERING.
I THOUGHT SO.
WELL, I GUESS THAT LEAVES ME ALONE. MAYBE I'LL MAKE IT A DOUBLE FEATURE.
OOH! "2000 MANIACS." COOL!
Oh, WHAT NOW?

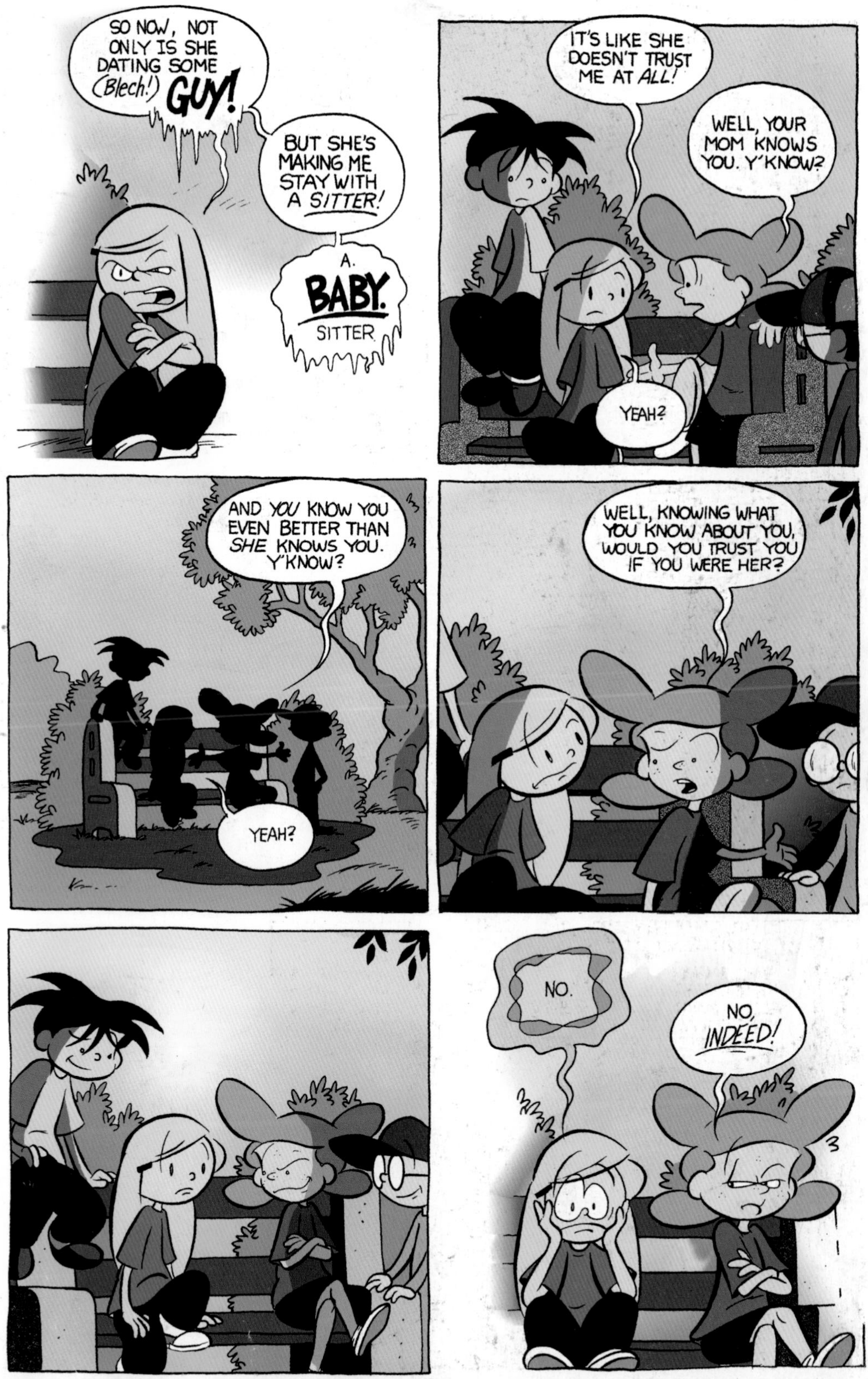

SO NOW, NOT ONLY IS SHE DATING SOME (Blech!) GUY!
BUT SHE'S MAKING ME STAY WITH A SITTER!
A. BABY. SITTER
IT'S LIKE SHE DOESN'T TRUST ME AT ALL!
WELL, YOUR MOM KNOWS YOU. Y'KNOW?
YEAH?
AND YOU KNOW YOU EVEN BETTER THAN SHE KNOWS YOU. Y'KNOW?
YEAH?
WELL, KNOWING WHAT YOU KNOW ABOUT YOU, WOULD YOU TRUST YOU IF YOU WERE HER?
NO.
NO, INDEED!

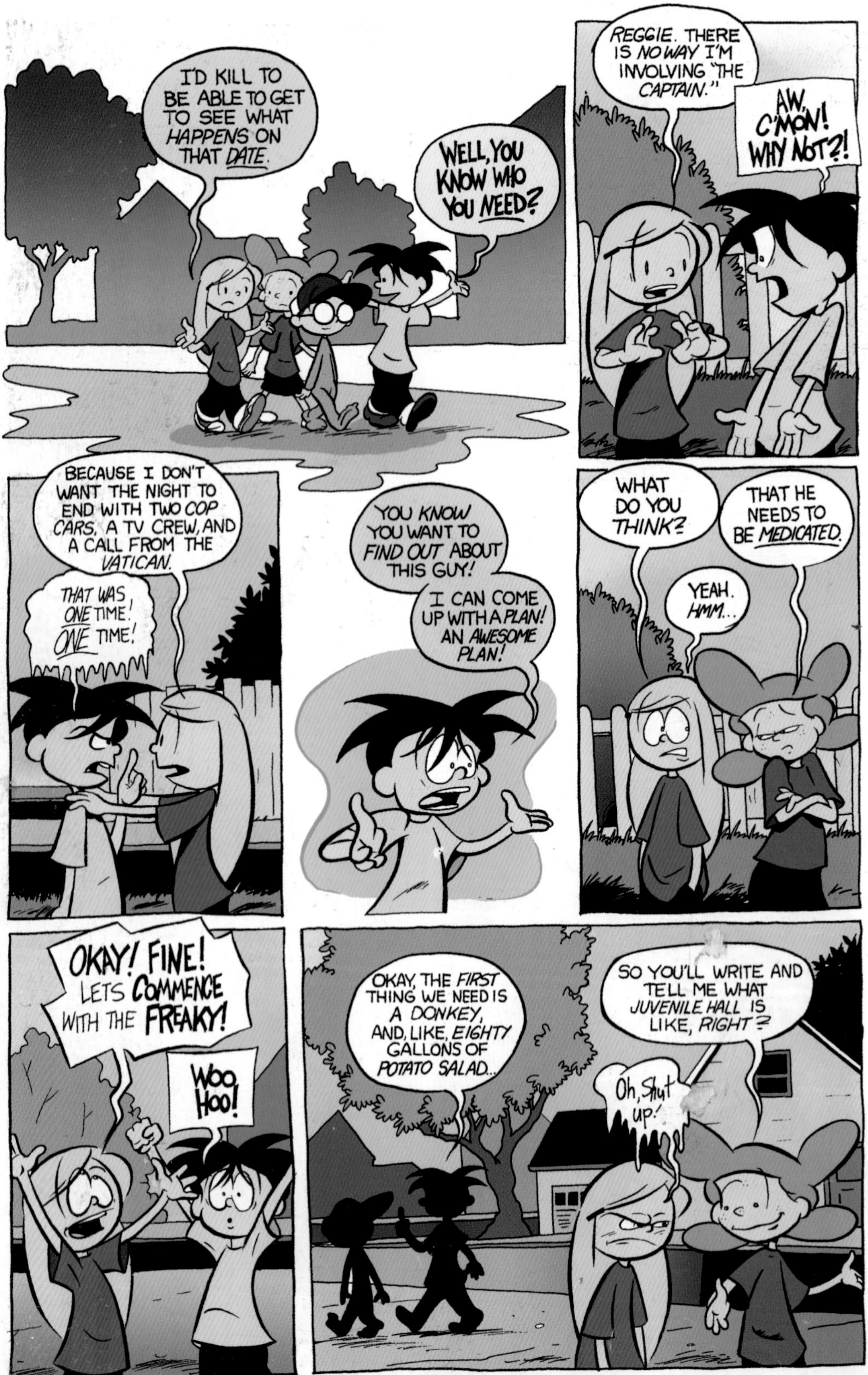
I'D KILL TO BE ABLE TO GET TO SEE WHAT HAPPENS ON THAT DATE.
WELL, YOU KNOW WHO YOU NEED?
REGGIE. THERE IS NO WAY I'M INVOLVING "THE CAPTAIN."
AW, C'MON! WHY NOT?!
BECAUSE I DON'T WANT THE NIGHT TO END WITH TWO COP CARS, A TV CREW, AND A CALL FROM THE VATICAN.
THAT WAS ONE TIME! ONE TIME!
YOU KNOW YOU WANT TO FIND OUT ABOUT THIS GUY!
I CAN COME UP WITH A PLAN! AN AWESOME PLAN!
WHAT DO YOU THINK?
THAT HE NEEDS TO BE MEDICATED.
YEAH. HMM...
OKAY! FINE! LETS COMMENCE WITH THE FREAKY!
WOO HOO!
OKAY, THE FIRST THING WE NEED IS A DONKEY, AND, LIKE, EIGHTY GALLONS OF POTATO SALAD...
SO YOU'LL WRITE AND TELL ME WHAT JUVENILE HALL IS LIKE, RIGHT?
Oh, Shut up!

Y'KNOW, THE WORST PART IS THAT WITH NO NOTICE, THERE WILL ONLY BE ONE SITTER *AVAILABLE*...

"KRAZY" KATE KADINGO!

Did Someone mention (gulp!) "Krazy" KATE?!

SHE'S PROBABLY GONNA *BABYSIT* FOR AMELIA TONIGHT.

OH! Poor Miss Amelia!

That's bad NEWS, kid

"She sat for my Cousin once, and it was so *HORRIFYING* that he lost the ability to *SPEAK!*"

"To this *DAY*, the only time he *TALKS* is to *SWEAR* at *PASSERSBY* in *LITHUANIAN*."

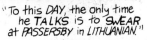

GAUSI MUŠÉ PER ŠIKNA!

On the *PLUS* side, though, *CHICKS* seem to *DIG* him.

She sat for *ME* once.

"The whole thing was so *ICKY WICKY* that it would've sent me into *INTENSIVE THERAPY*."

That is, if I wasn't going ALREADY.

SO WHAT ARE YOU GUYS SAYING?

JUST THAT WHEN YOUR MOM GETS BACK FROM HER DATE...

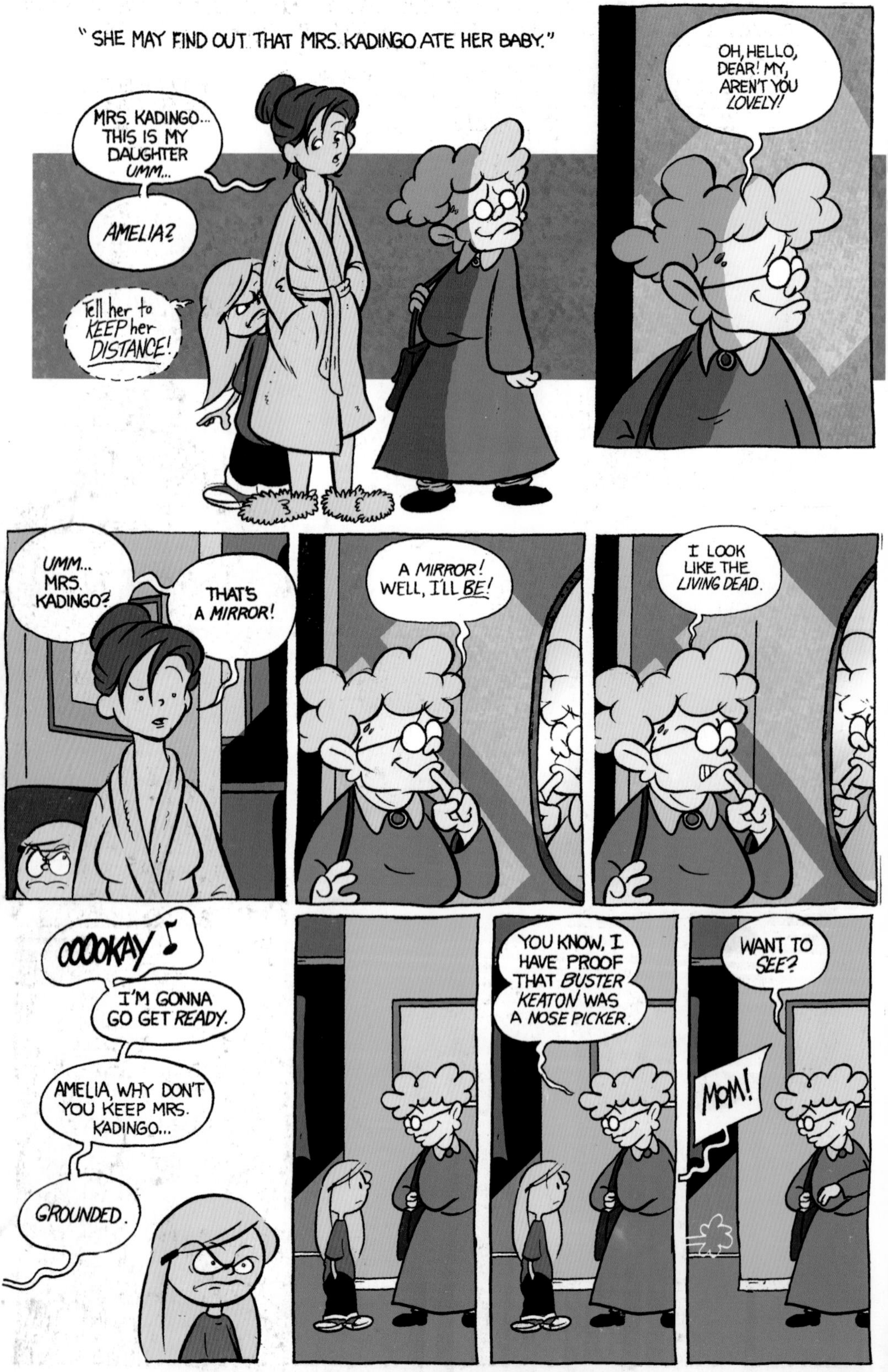

" SHE MAY FIND OUT THAT MRS. KADINGO ATE HER BABY."
MRS. KADINGO... THIS IS MY DAUGHTER UMM...
AMELIA?
Tell her to KEEP her DISTANCE!
OH, HELLO, DEAR! MY, AREN'T YOU LOVELY!
UMM... MRS. KADINGO?
THAT'S A MIRROR!
A MIRROR! WELL, I'LL BE!
I LOOK LIKE THE LIVING DEAD.
OOOOKAY
I'M GONNA GO GET READY.
AMELIA, WHY DON'T YOU KEEP MRS. KADINGO...
GROUNDED.
YOU KNOW, I HAVE PROOF THAT BUSTER KEATON WAS A NOSE PICKER.
MOM!
WANT TO SEE?

SO, BEING TOTALLY ***GROSSED OUT***, I WENT UPSTAIRS TO WATCH MOM GET READY. LOOKING IN THE MIRROR, I DIDN'T SEE THE ***LIVING DEAD***, BUT I FELT LIKE THE ***WALKING WOUNDED***.

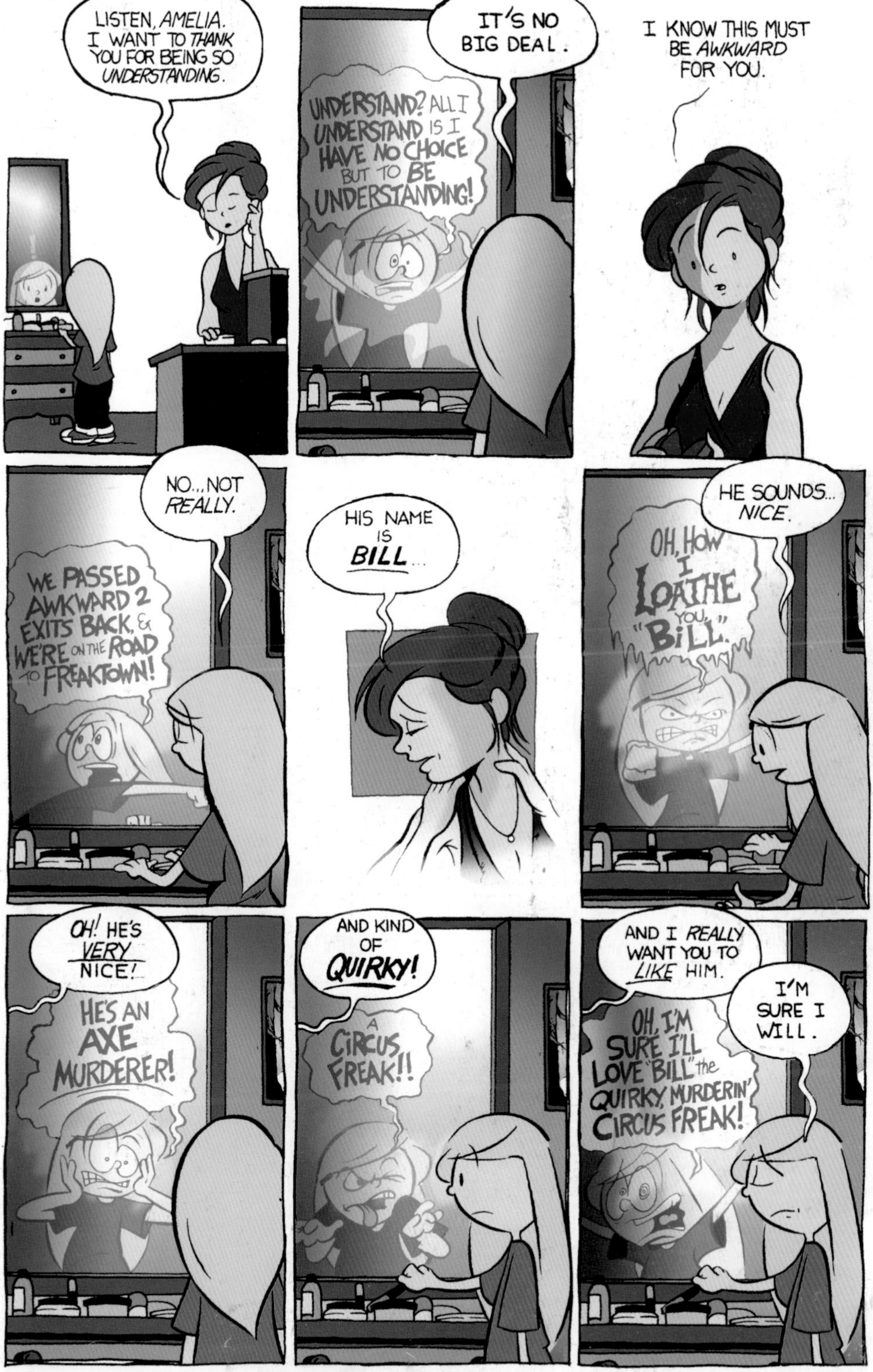
LISTEN, AMELIA. I WANT TO THANK YOU FOR BEING SO UNDERSTANDING.
IT'S NO BIG DEAL.
UNDERSTAND? ALL I UNDERSTAND IS I HAVE NO CHOICE BUT TO BE UNDERSTANDING!
I KNOW THIS MUST BE AWKWARD FOR YOU.
NO... NOT REALLY.
WE PASSED AWKWARD 2 EXITS BACK, & WE'RE ON THE ROAD TO FREAKTOWN!
HIS NAME IS BILL...
HE SOUNDS... NICE.
OH, HOW I LOATHE YOU, "BILL."
OH! HE'S VERY NICE!
HE'S AN AXE MURDERER!
AND KIND OF QUIRKY!
A CIRCUS FREAK!!
AND I REALLY WANT YOU TO LIKE HIM.
OH, I'M SURE I'LL LOVE "BILL" the QUIRKY, MURDERIN' CIRCUS FREAK!
I'M SURE I WILL.

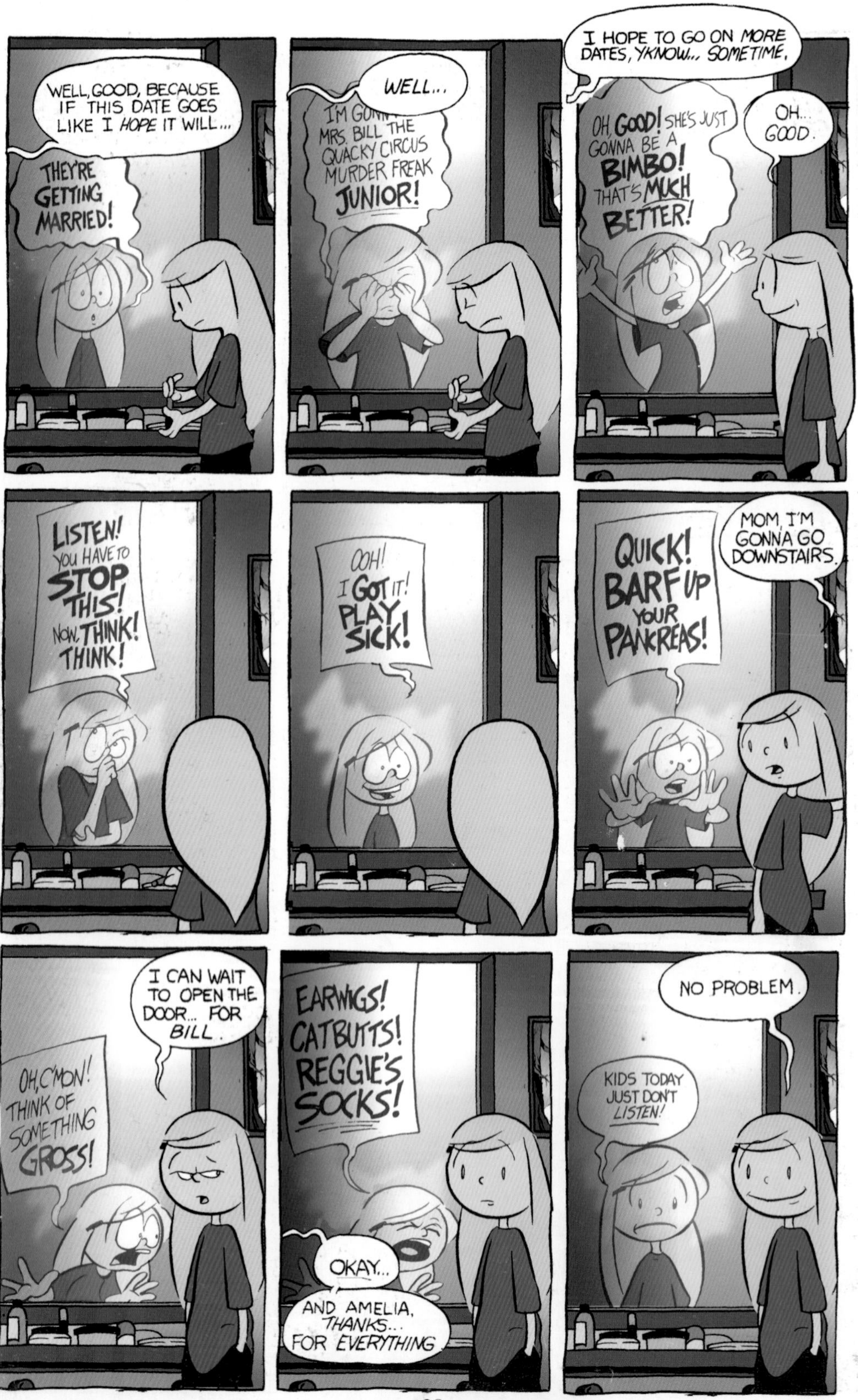
WELL, GOOD, BECAUSE IF THIS DATE GOES LIKE I HOPE IT WILL...
THEY'RE GETTING MARRIED!
WELL...
I'M GONNA BE MRS. BILL THE QUACKY CIRCUS MURDER FREAK JUNIOR!
I HOPE TO GO ON MORE DATES, Y'KNOW... SOMETIME.
OH, GOOD! SHE'S JUST GONNA BE A BIMBO! THAT'S MUCH BETTER!
OH... GOOD.
LISTEN! YOU HAVE TO STOP THIS! NOW, THINK! THINK!
OOH! I GOT IT! PLAY SICK!
QUICK! BARF UP YOUR PANKREAS!
MOM, I'M GONNA GO DOWNSTAIRS.
I CAN WAIT TO OPEN THE DOOR... FOR BILL.
OH, C'MON! THINK OF SOMETHING GROSS!
EARWIGS! CATBUTTS! REGGIE'S SOCKS!
OKAY...
AND AMELIA, THANKS... FOR EVERYTHING
NO PROBLEM.
KIDS TODAY JUST DON'T LISTEN!

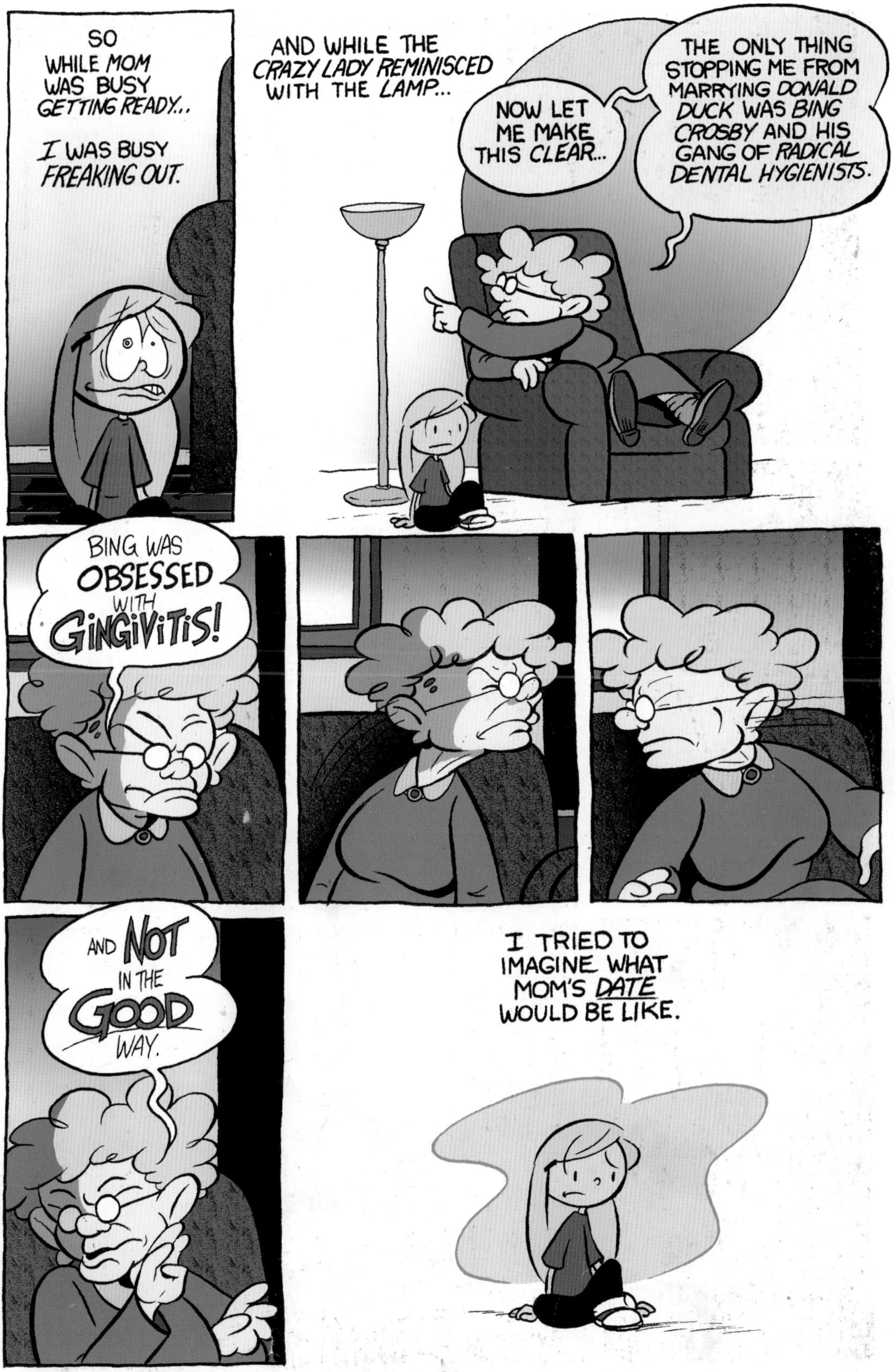
SO WHILE MOM WAS BUSY GETTING READY...
I WAS BUSY FREAKING OUT.
AND WHILE THE CRAZY LADY REMINISCED WITH THE LAMP...
NOW LET ME MAKE THIS CLEAR...
THE ONLY THING STOPPING ME FROM MARRYING DONALD DUCK WAS BING CROSBY AND HIS GANG OF RADICAL DENTAL HYGIENISTS.
BING WAS OBSESSED WITH GINGIVITIS!
AND NOT IN THE GOOD WAY.
I TRIED TO IMAGINE WHAT MOM'S DATE WOULD BE LIKE.

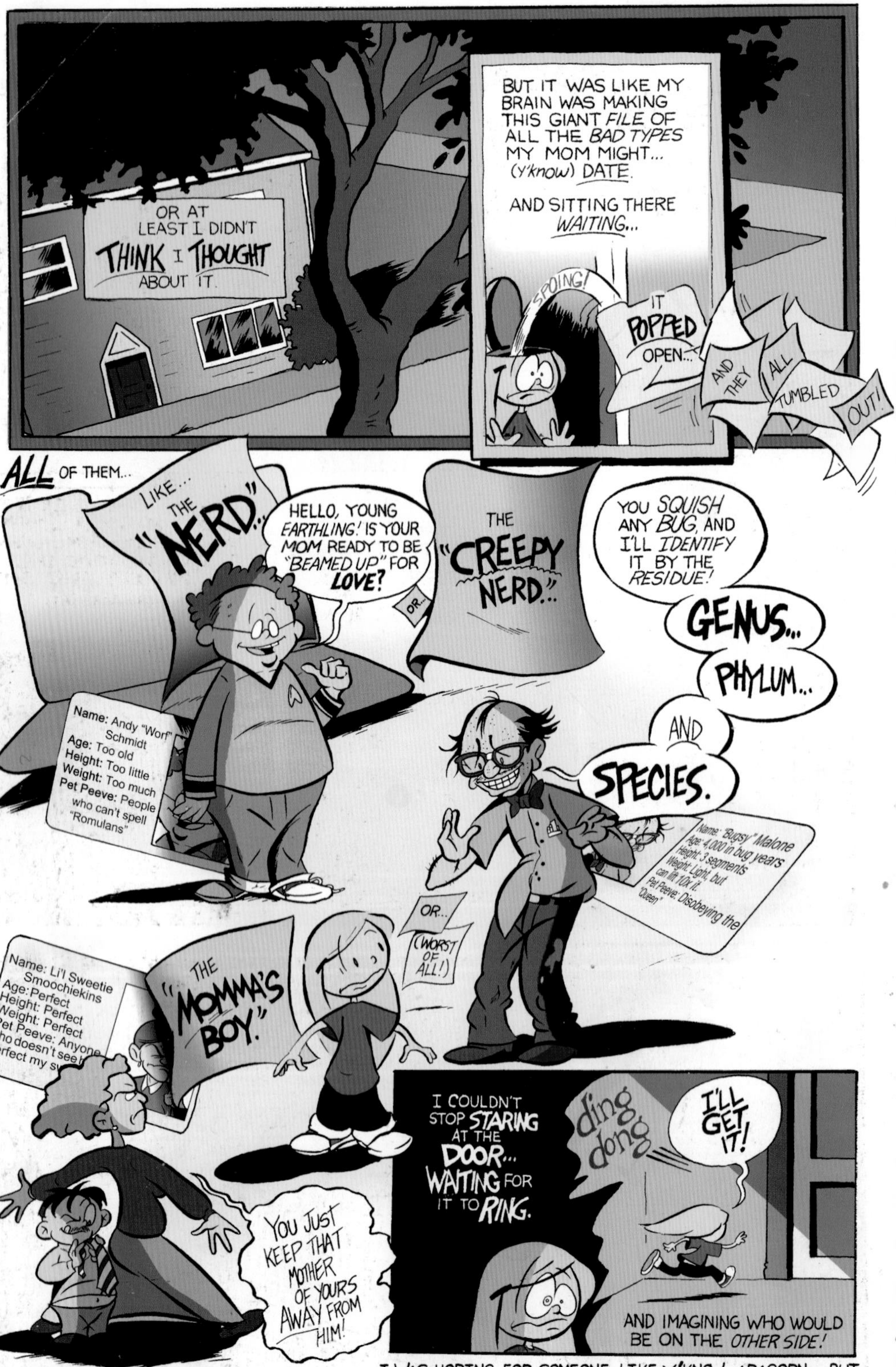
OR AT LEAST I DIDN'T THINK I THOUGHT ABOUT IT.
BUT IT WAS LIKE MY BRAIN WAS MAKING THIS GIANT FILE OF ALL THE BAD TYPES MY MOM MIGHT... (Y'know) DATE.
AND SITTING THERE WAITING...
SPOING!
IT POPPED OPEN...
AND THEY ALL TUMBLED OUT!
ALL OF THEM...
LIKE... THE "NERD"...
HELLO, YOUNG EARTHLING! IS YOUR MOM READY TO BE "BEAMED UP" FOR LOVE?
Name: Andy "Worf" Schmidt
Age: Too old
Height: Too little
Weight: Too much
Pet Peeve: People who can't spell "Romulans"
OR...
THE "CREEPY NERD"...
YOU SQUISH ANY BUG, AND I'LL IDENTIFY IT BY THE RESIDUE!
GENUS...
PHYLUM...
AND
SPECIES.
Name: "Bugsy" Malone
Age: 4,000 in bug years
Height: 3 segments
Weight: Light, but can lift 10x it.
Pet Peeve: Disobeying the "Queen"
OR...
(WORST OF ALL!)
THE "MOMMA'S BOY."
Name: Li'l Sweetie Smoochiekins
Age: Perfect
Height: Perfect
Weight: Perfect
Pet Peeve: Anyone who doesn't see
perfect my s
YOU JUST KEEP THAT MOTHER OF YOURS AWAY FROM HIM!
I COULDN'T STOP STARING AT THE DOOR... WAITING FOR IT TO RING.
ding dong
I'LL GET IT!
AND IMAGINING WHO WOULD BE ON THE OTHER SIDE!
I WAS HOPING FOR SOMEONE LIKE, Y'KNOW... ARAGORN, BUT...

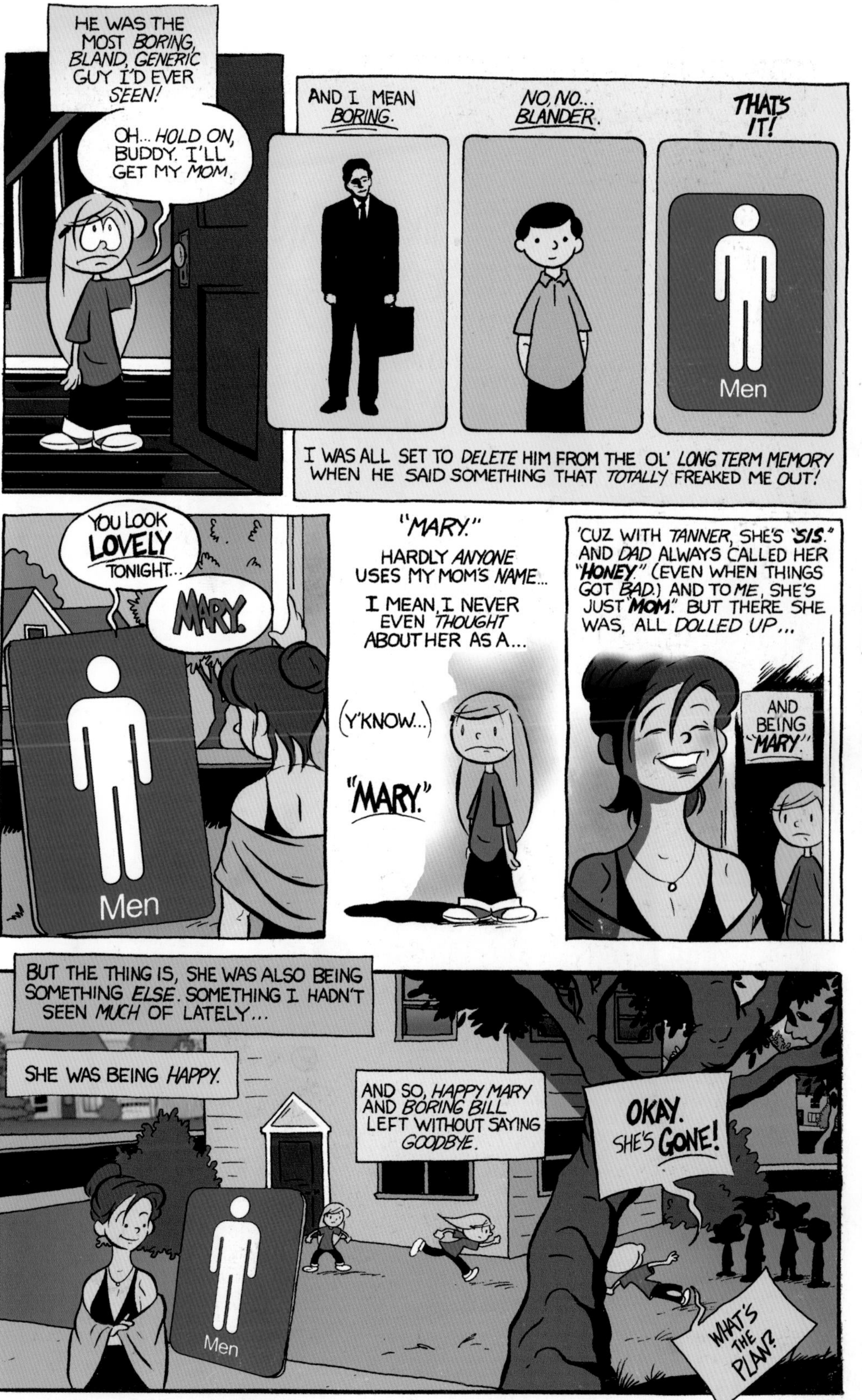
HE WAS THE MOST BORING, BLAND, GENERIC GUY I'D EVER SEEN!
OH... HOLD ON, BUDDY. I'LL GET MY MOM.
AND I MEAN BORING.
NO, NO... BLANDER.
THAT'S IT!
Men
I WAS ALL SET TO DELETE HIM FROM THE OL' LONG TERM MEMORY WHEN HE SAID SOMETHING THAT TOTALLY FREAKED ME OUT!
YOU LOOK LOVELY TONIGHT...
MARY.
Men
"MARY."
HARDLY ANYONE USES MY MOM'S NAME...
I MEAN, I NEVER EVEN THOUGHT ABOUT HER AS A...
(Y'KNOW...)
"MARY."
'CUZ WITH TANNER, SHE'S "SIS." AND DAD ALWAYS CALLED HER "HONEY." (EVEN WHEN THINGS GOT BAD.) AND TO ME, SHE'S JUST "MOM." BUT THERE SHE WAS, ALL DOLLED UP...
AND BEING "MARY."
BUT THE THING IS, SHE WAS ALSO BEING SOMETHING ELSE. SOMETHING I HADN'T SEEN MUCH OF LATELY...
SHE WAS BEING HAPPY.
AND SO, HAPPY MARY AND BORING BILL LEFT WITHOUT SAYING GOODBYE.
OKAY. SHE'S GONE!
Men
WHAT'S THE PLAN?

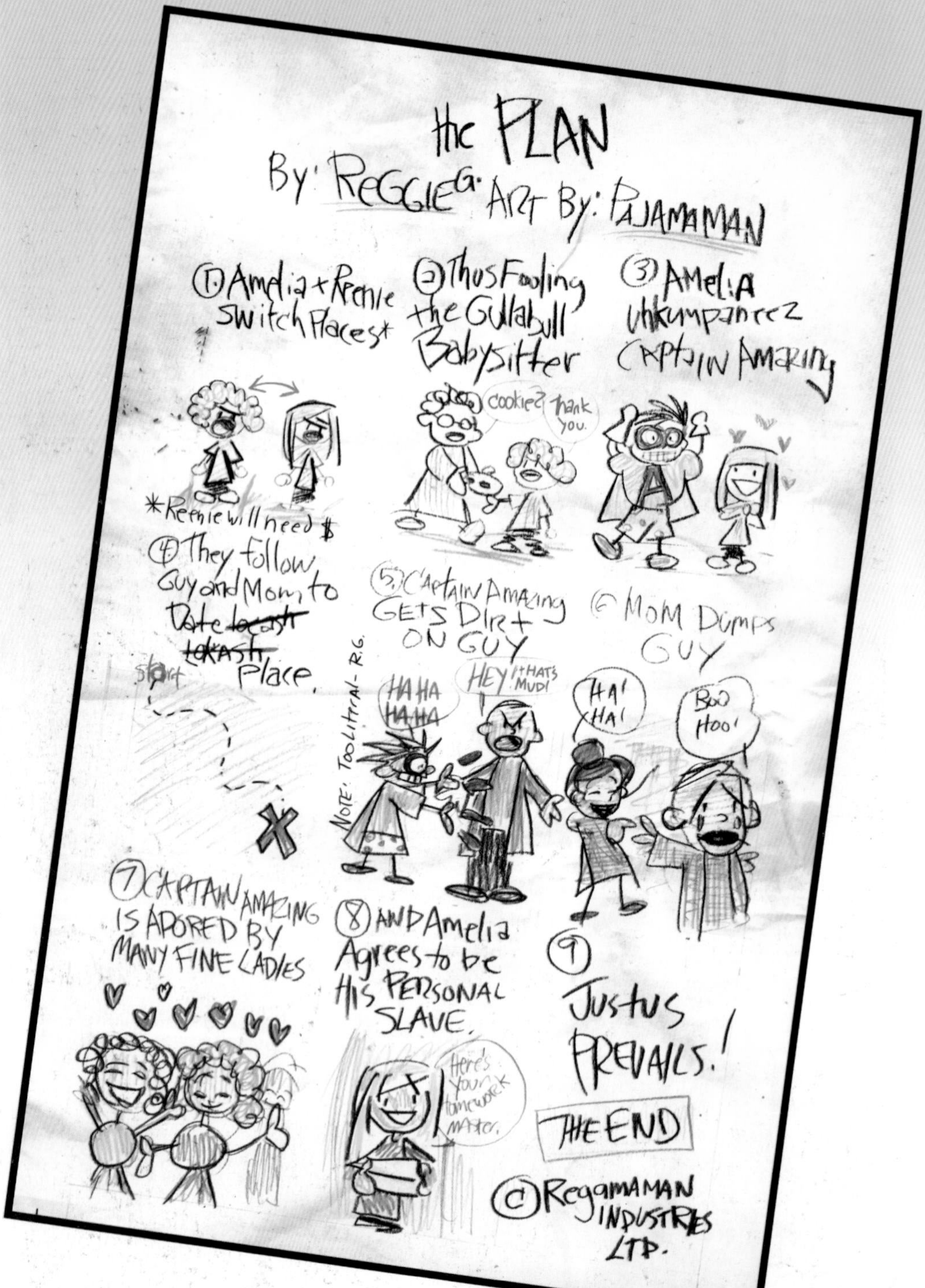
the PLAN
By: REGGIE G. Art By: PAJAMAMAN
1. Amelia + Reenie switch places*
2. Thus Fooling the Gullabull Babysitter
cookie?
Thank you.
3. AMeliA unkumpaneez CAPtain Amazing
*Reenie will need $
4. They follow Guy and Mom to Place.
start
5. CAPtAIN Amazing GETS DIRT ON GUY
NOTE: TOOLITTRAL - R.G.
HA HA HA HA
HEY! THAT'S MUD!
6. MOM DUMPS GUY
HA! HA!
Boo Hoo!
7. CAPTAIN AMAZING IS ADORED BY MANY FINE LADIES
8. AND Amelia Agrees to be His PERSONAL SLAVE.
Here's your homework master.
9. JUSTUS PREVAILS!
THE END
© Regamaman INDUSTRIES LTD.

OKAY, SO MAYBE IT WAS A DUMB PLAN, BUT SINCE I HAD NO DESIRE TO BE "SAT" BY "KRAZY KATE", I TRADED SHIRTS WITH RHONDA'S SISTER AND SENT HER INSIDE, LEAVING ME FREE TO CAVORT WITH THE INFAMOUS CAPTAIN AMAZING.

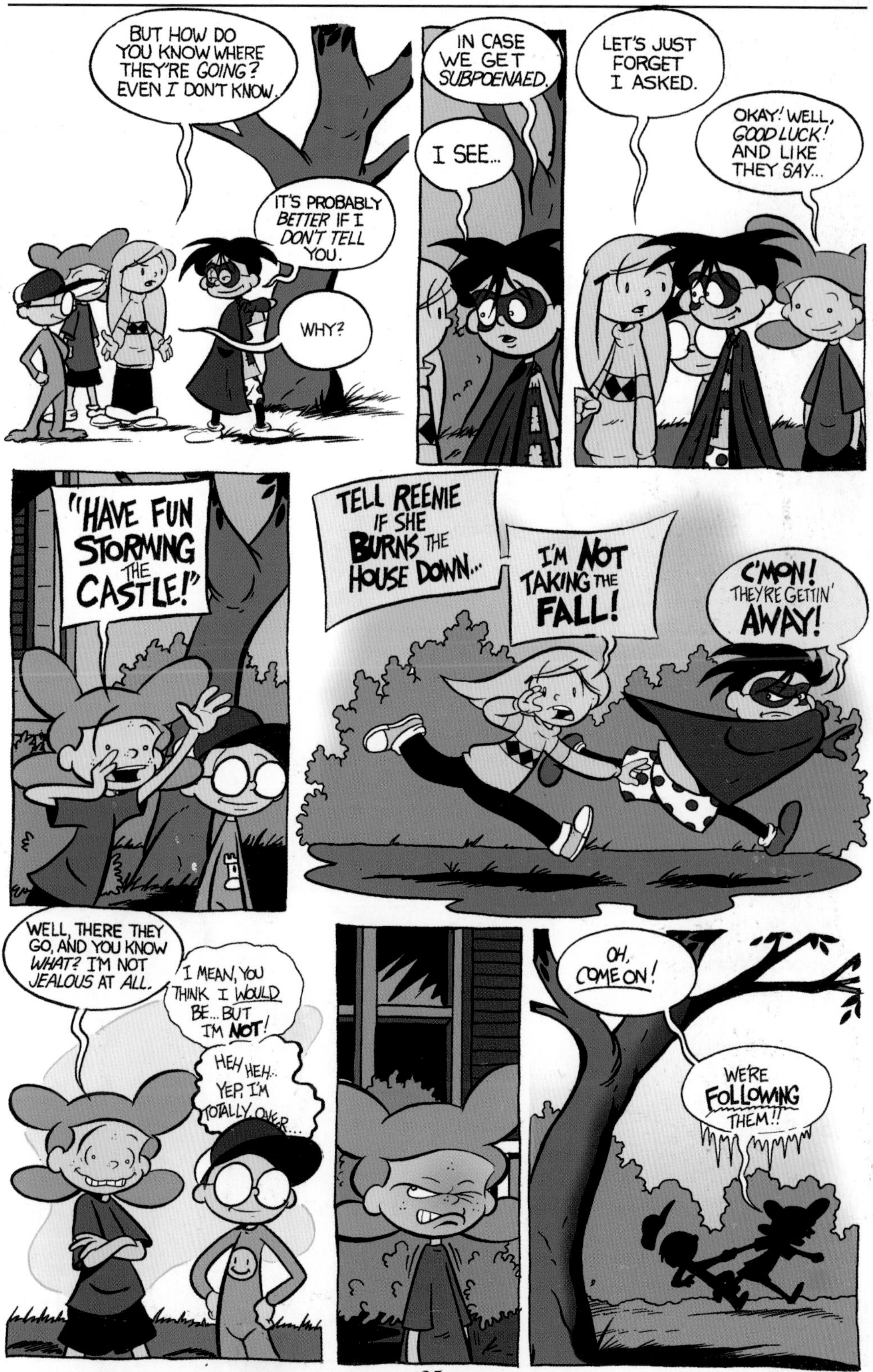

BUT HOW DO YOU KNOW WHERE THEY'RE GOING? EVEN I DON'T KNOW.
IT'S PROBABLY BETTER IF I DON'T TELL YOU.
WHY?
IN CASE WE GET SUBPOENAED.
I SEE...
LET'S JUST FORGET I ASKED.
OKAY! WELL, GOOD LUCK! AND LIKE THEY SAY...
"HAVE FUN STORMING THE CASTLE!"
TELL REENIE IF SHE BURNS THE HOUSE DOWN...
I'M NOT TAKING THE FALL!
C'MON! THEY'RE GETTIN' AWAY!
WELL, THERE THEY GO, AND YOU KNOW WHAT? I'M NOT JEALOUS AT ALL.
I MEAN, YOU THINK I WOULD BE... BUT I'M NOT!
HEH HEH... YEP, I'M TOTALLY OVER-R...
OH, COME ON!
WE'RE FOLLOWING THEM!!

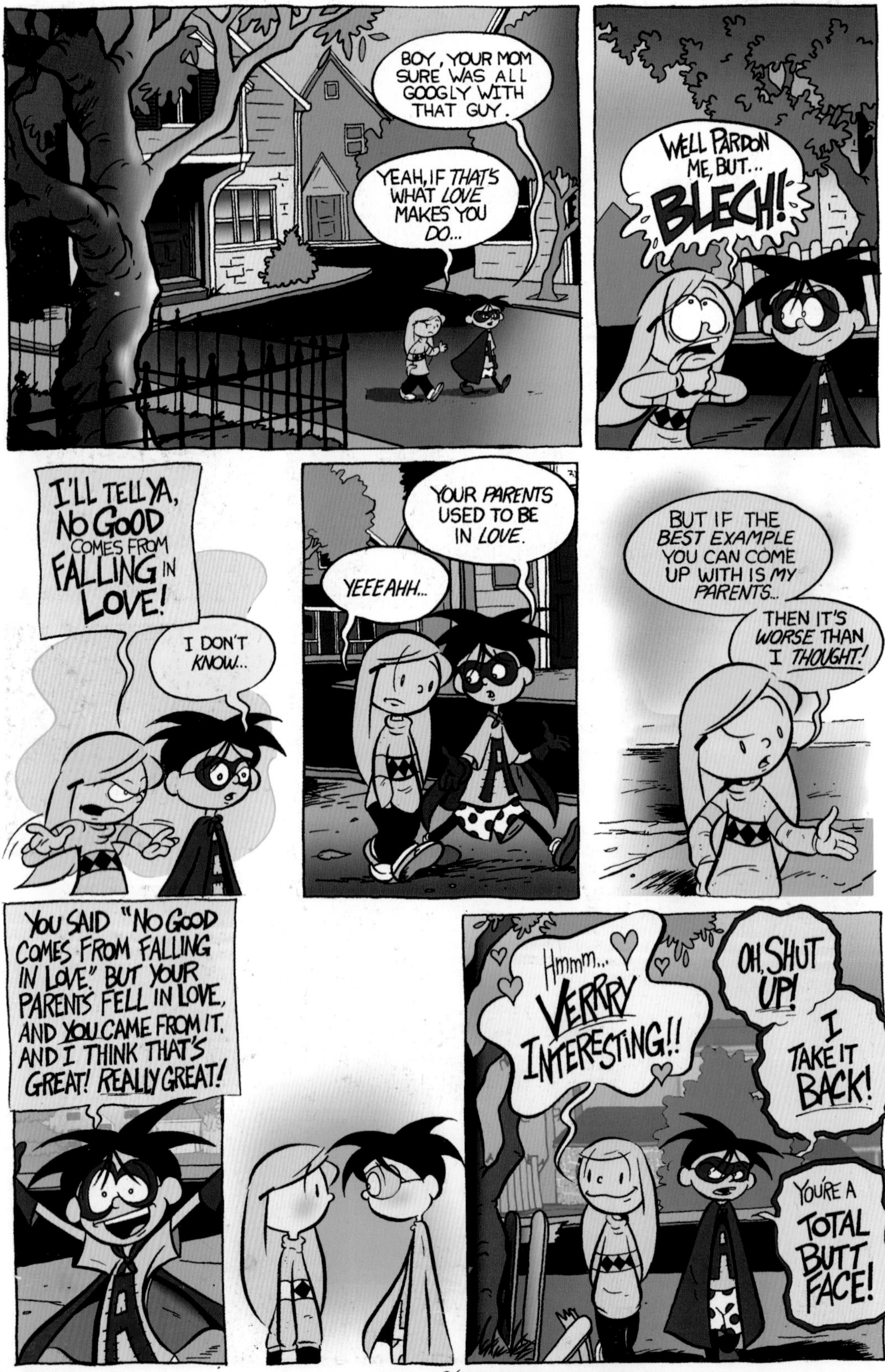
BOY, YOUR MOM SURE WAS ALL GOOGLY WITH THAT GUY.
YEAH, IF THAT'S WHAT LOVE MAKES YOU DO...
WELL PARDON ME, BUT... BLECH!
I'LL TELL YA, NO GOOD COMES FROM FALLING IN LOVE!
I DON'T KNOW...
YOUR PARENTS USED TO BE IN LOVE.
YEEEAHH...
BUT IF THE BEST EXAMPLE YOU CAN COME UP WITH IS MY PARENTS...
THEN IT'S WORSE THAN I THOUGHT!
YOU SAID "NO GOOD COMES FROM FALLING IN LOVE." BUT YOUR PARENTS FELL IN LOVE, AND YOU CAME FROM IT. AND I THINK THAT'S GREAT! REALLY GREAT!
Hmmm... VERRRY INTERESTING!!
OH, SHUT UP!
I TAKE IT BACK!
YOU'RE A TOTAL BUTT FACE!

IN "THE PRINCESS BRIDE," BUTTERCUP WAITS FIVE YEARS FOR HER *TRUE LOVE* TO RETURN.

BUT ISN'T THAT A *TAD EXTREME?*

I MEAN, WHAT MADE HER DECIDE WESLEY WAS HER *TRUE LOVE,* ANYWAY? WAS IT BECAUSE HE LET HER BOSS HIM *AROUND* ALL THE *TIME?*

BECAUSE I CAN GET *BEHIND THAT.*

Y'KNOW?

HERE IT *IS...* THE **SCENE** OF THE **CRIME.**

I WONDER IF MOM THINKS "*BILL*" IS **HER** ONE TRUE LOVE? DID SHE USED TO THINK *DAD* WAS IT? WHY DOESN'T SHE ANY *MORE?*

Y'KNOW, I BET SHE DOESN'T KNOW ANYTHING MORE ABOUT LOVE THAN *I* DO, AND I KNOW **ZILCH.**

OKAY, MAYBE I DON'T KNOW MUCH ABOUT *LOVE,* BUT I *HOPE* TRUE LOVE SPRINGS FOR MORE THAN A **TURKEY CLUB...**

WAIT A...!

THAT'S THE **SAME DUMP** WE ATE **BREAKFAST** AT!

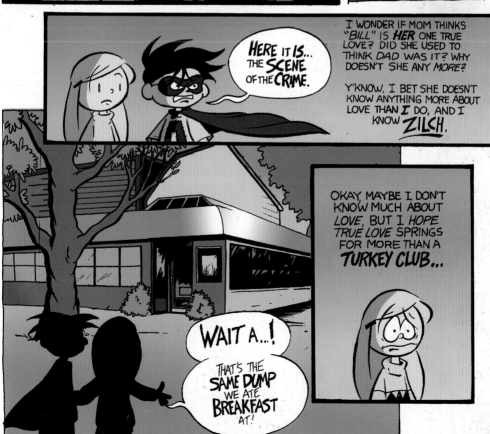

OTHERWISE, WHY IS EVERYBODY TRYING SO HARD TO FIND IT?

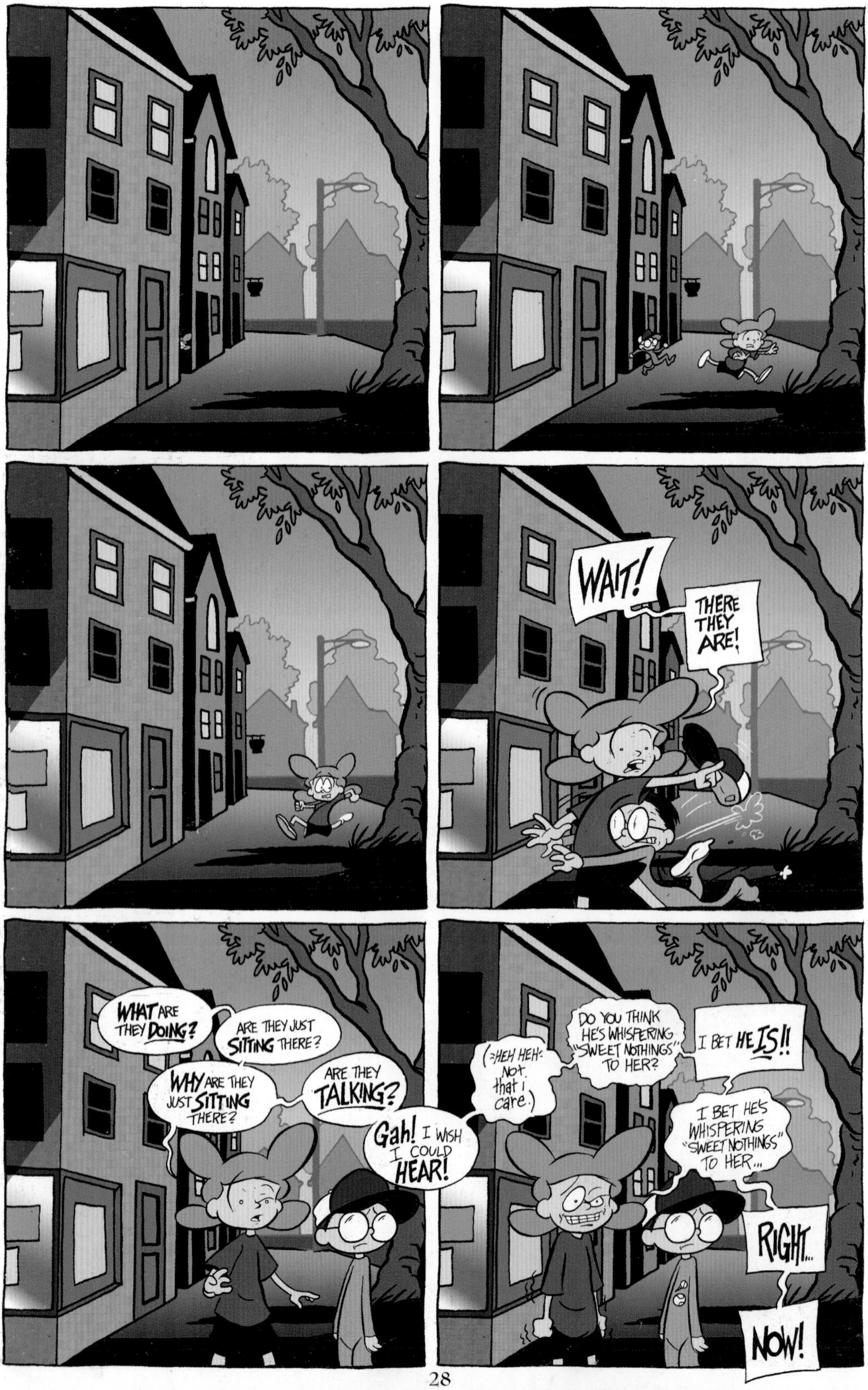

WAIT!
THERE THEY ARE!
WHAT ARE THEY DOING?
ARE THEY JUST SITTING THERE?
WHY ARE THEY JUST SITTING THERE?
ARE THEY TALKING?
Gah! I WISH I COULD HEAR!
(HEH HEH- Not that i care.)
DO YOU THINK HE'S WHISPERING "SWEET NOTHINGS" TO HER?
I BET HE IS!!
I BET HE'S WHISPERING "SWEET NOTHINGS" TO HER...
RIGHT...
NOW!

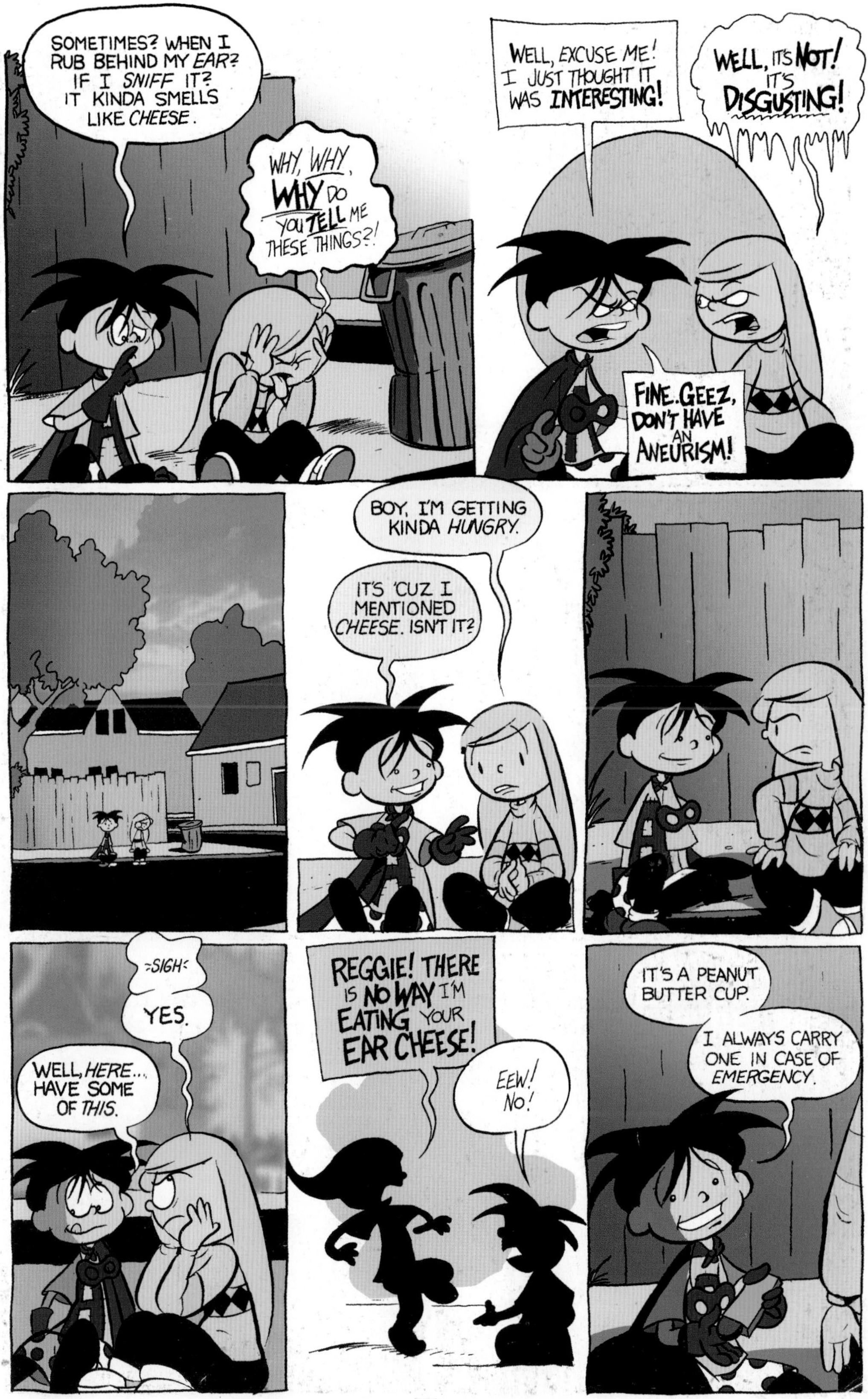
SOMETIMES? WHEN I RUB BEHIND MY EAR? IF I SNIFF IT? IT KINDA SMELLS LIKE CHEESE.
WHY, WHY, WHY DO YOU TELL ME THESE THINGS?!
WELL, EXCUSE ME! I JUST THOUGHT IT WAS INTERESTING!
WELL, IT'S NOT! IT'S DISGUSTING!
FINE. GEEZ, DON'T HAVE AN ANEURISM!
BOY, I'M GETTING KINDA HUNGRY.
IT'S 'CUZ I MENTIONED CHEESE. ISN'T IT?
=SIGH=
YES.
WELL, HERE... HAVE SOME OF THIS.
REGGIE! THERE IS NO WAY I'M EATING YOUR EAR CHEESE!
EEW! NO!
IT'S A PEANUT BUTTER CUP.
I ALWAYS CARRY ONE IN CASE OF EMERGENCY.

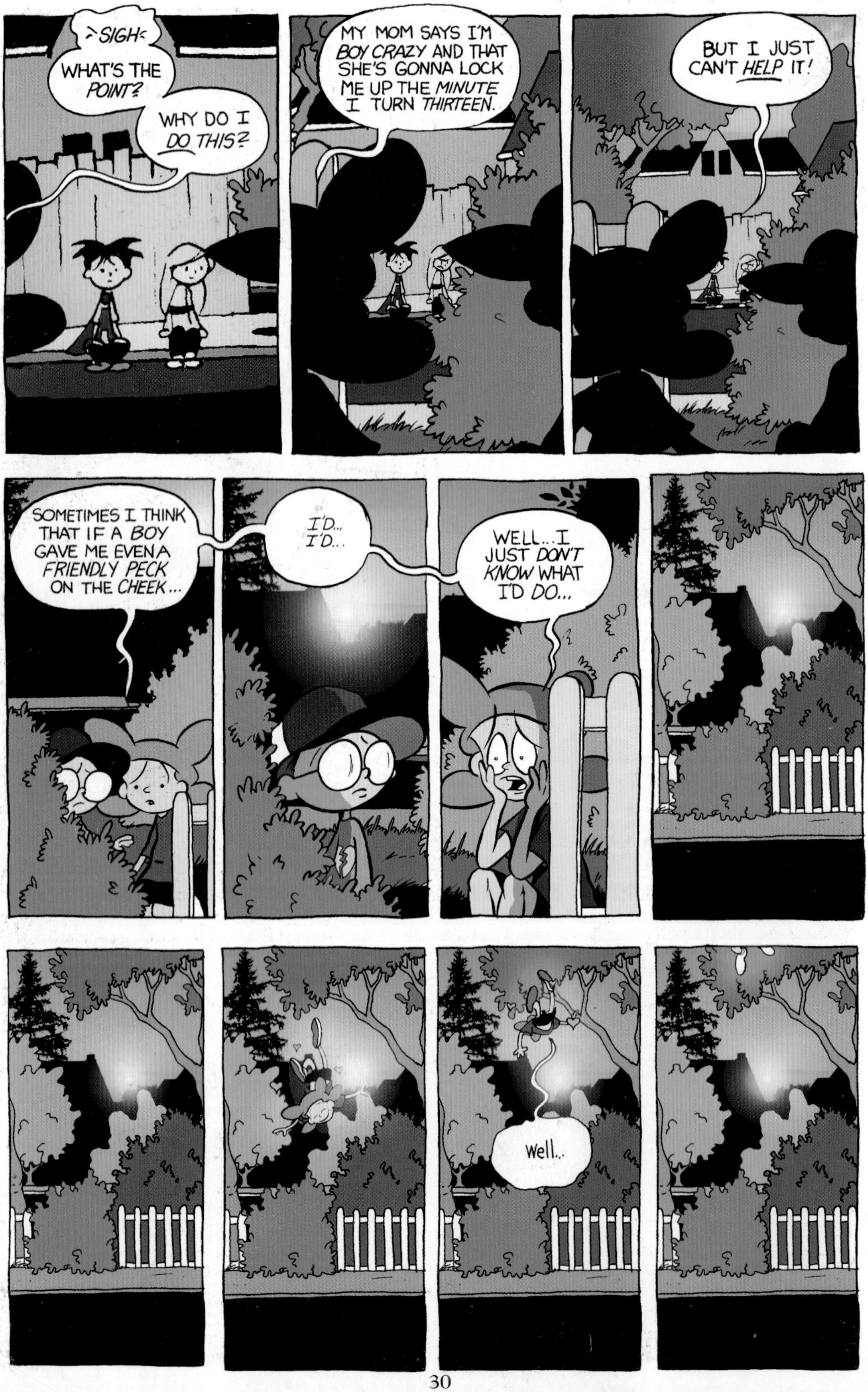

~SIGH~
WHAT'S THE POINT?
WHY DO I DO THIS?
MY MOM SAYS I'M BOY CRAZY AND THAT SHE'S GONNA LOCK ME UP THE MINUTE I TURN THIRTEEN.
BUT I JUST CAN'T HELP IT!
SOMETIMES I THINK THAT IF A BOY GAVE ME EVEN A FRIENDLY PECK ON THE CHEEK...
I'D... I'D...
WELL... I JUST DON'T KNOW WHAT I'D DO...
Well..

THAT ANSWERS *THAT* QUESTION.

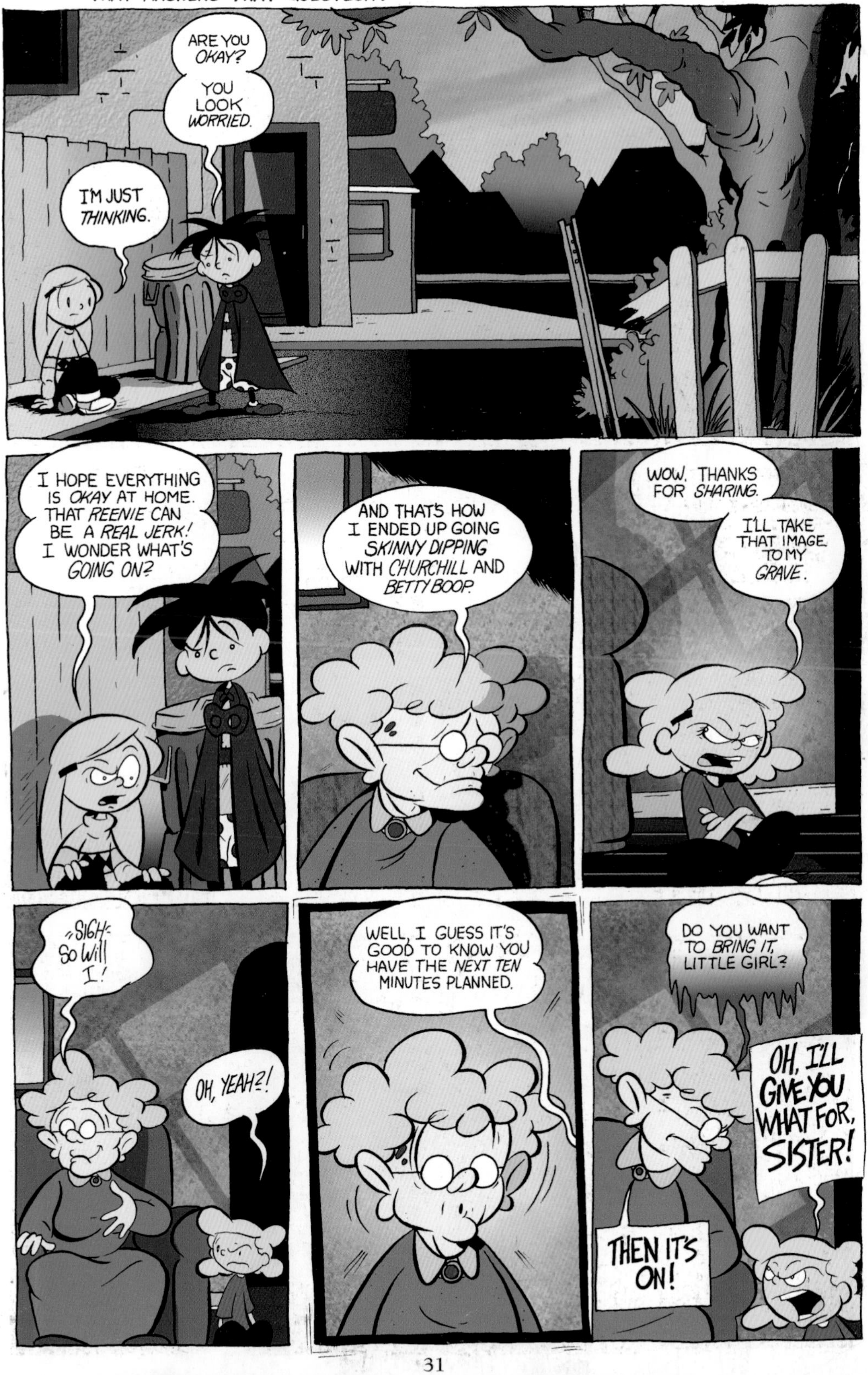

ARE YOU *OKAY?*
YOU LOOK *WORRIED.*
I'M JUST *THINKING.*
I HOPE EVERYTHING IS *OKAY* AT HOME. THAT *REENIE* CAN BE A *REAL JERK!* I WONDER WHAT'S *GOING ON?*
AND THAT'S HOW I ENDED UP GOING *SKINNY DIPPING* WITH *CHURCHILL* AND *BETTY BOOP.*
WOW. THANKS FOR *SHARING.*
I'LL TAKE THAT IMAGE TO MY *GRAVE.*
-SIGH- So Will I!
OH, YEAH?!
WELL, I GUESS IT'S GOOD TO KNOW YOU HAVE THE *NEXT TEN* MINUTES PLANNED.
DO YOU WANT TO *BRING IT,* LITTLE GIRL?
OH, I'LL GIVE YOU WHAT FOR, SISTER!
THEN IT'S ON!

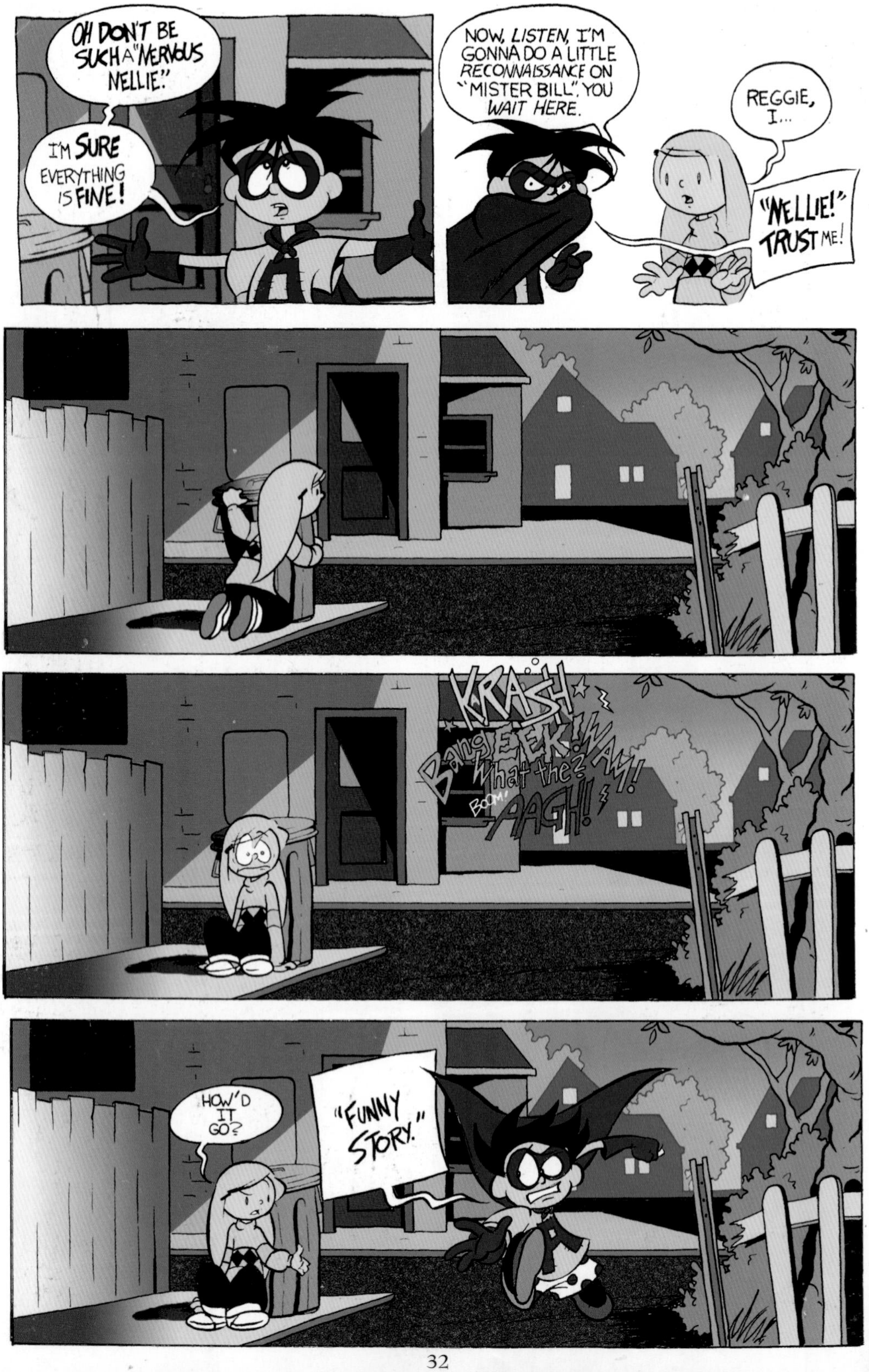
OH DON'T BE SUCH A "NERVOUS NELLIE."
I'M SURE EVERYTHING IS FINE!
NOW, LISTEN, I'M GONNA DO A LITTLE RECONNAISSANCE ON "MISTER BILL". YOU WAIT HERE.
REGGIE, I...
"NELLIE!" TRUST ME!
KRASH
Bang
EEK!
WAM!
What the?
BOOM!
AAGH!
HOW'D IT GO?
"FUNNY STORY."

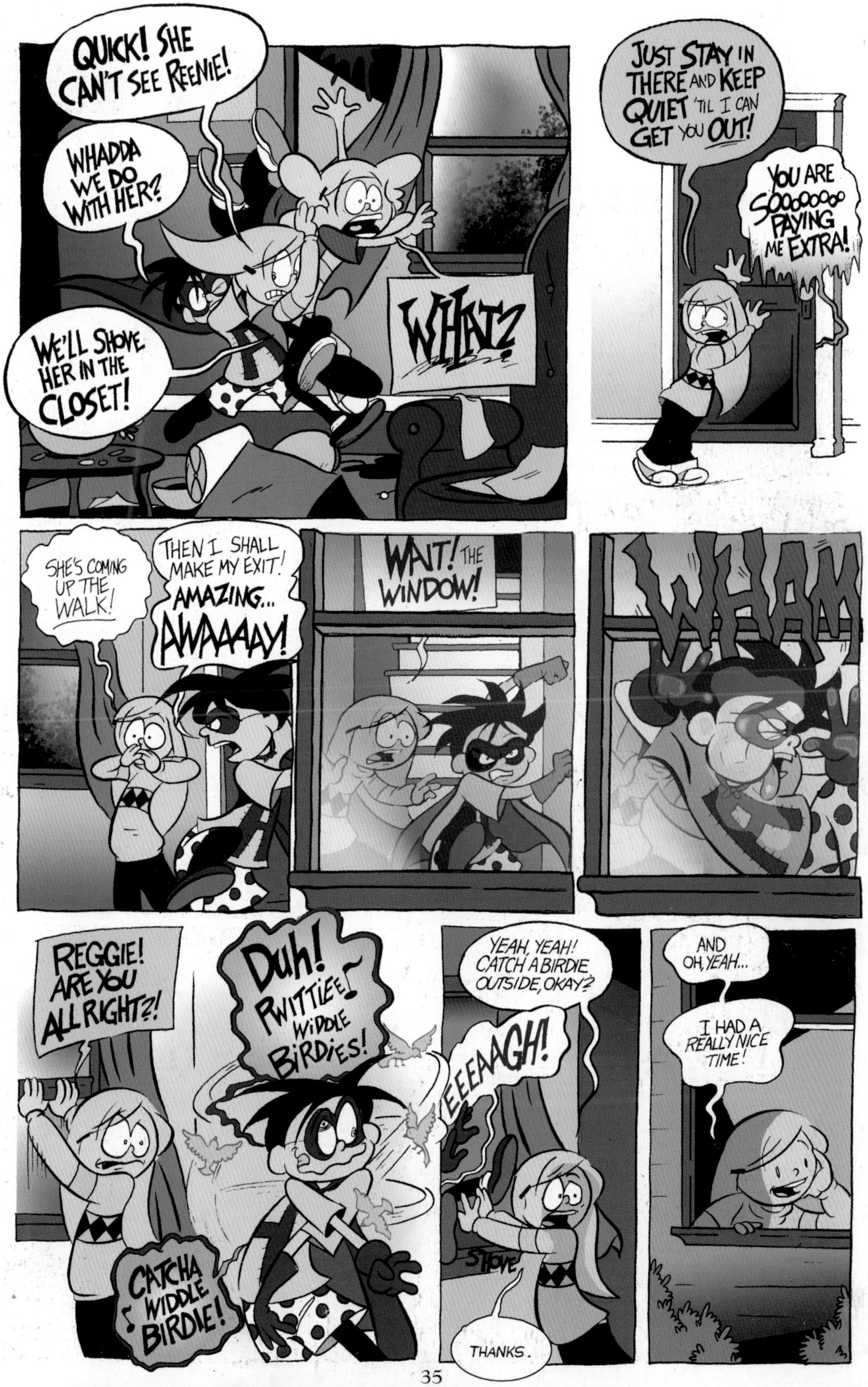
QUICK! SHE CAN'T SEE REENIE!
WHADDA WE DO WITH HER?
WE'LL SHOVE HER IN THE CLOSET!
WHAT?
JUST STAY IN THERE AND KEEP QUIET 'TIL I CAN GET YOU OUT!
YOU ARE SOOOOOOOO PAYING ME EXTRA!
SHE'S COMING UP THE WALK!
THEN I SHALL MAKE MY EXIT! AMAZING... AWAAAAAY!
WAIT! THE WINDOW!
WHAM
REGGIE! ARE YOU ALL RIGHT?!
Duh! PWITTIEEE! WIDDLE BIRDIES!
CATCHA WIDDLE BIRDIE!
YEAH, YEAH! CATCH A BIRDIE OUTSIDE, OKAY?
EEEAAGH!
SHOVE
THANKS.
AND OH, YEAH...
I HAD A REALLY NICE TIME!

STEP ONE: **BECOME INNOCENT** - No matter how guilty you actually are, it is important that you act so blameless that you yourself believe you're innocent.

This works great if you are with someone who looks even more guilty than you.

STEP TWO: **SELL OUT YOUR FRIENDS** - This may seem cruel, but remember someday they'll do the same to you. That's what friends are for.

Then, run upstairs. Remove any evidence (or itchy sweaters), and let the eavesdropping begin.

STEP THREE: **UTILIZE DISTRACTION** - The first chance you get to change the subject, take it. Another opportunity might not come along.

*Please don't try this plan at home, and when you do try this plan at home, please leave my name out of it - Amelia Louise McBride

36

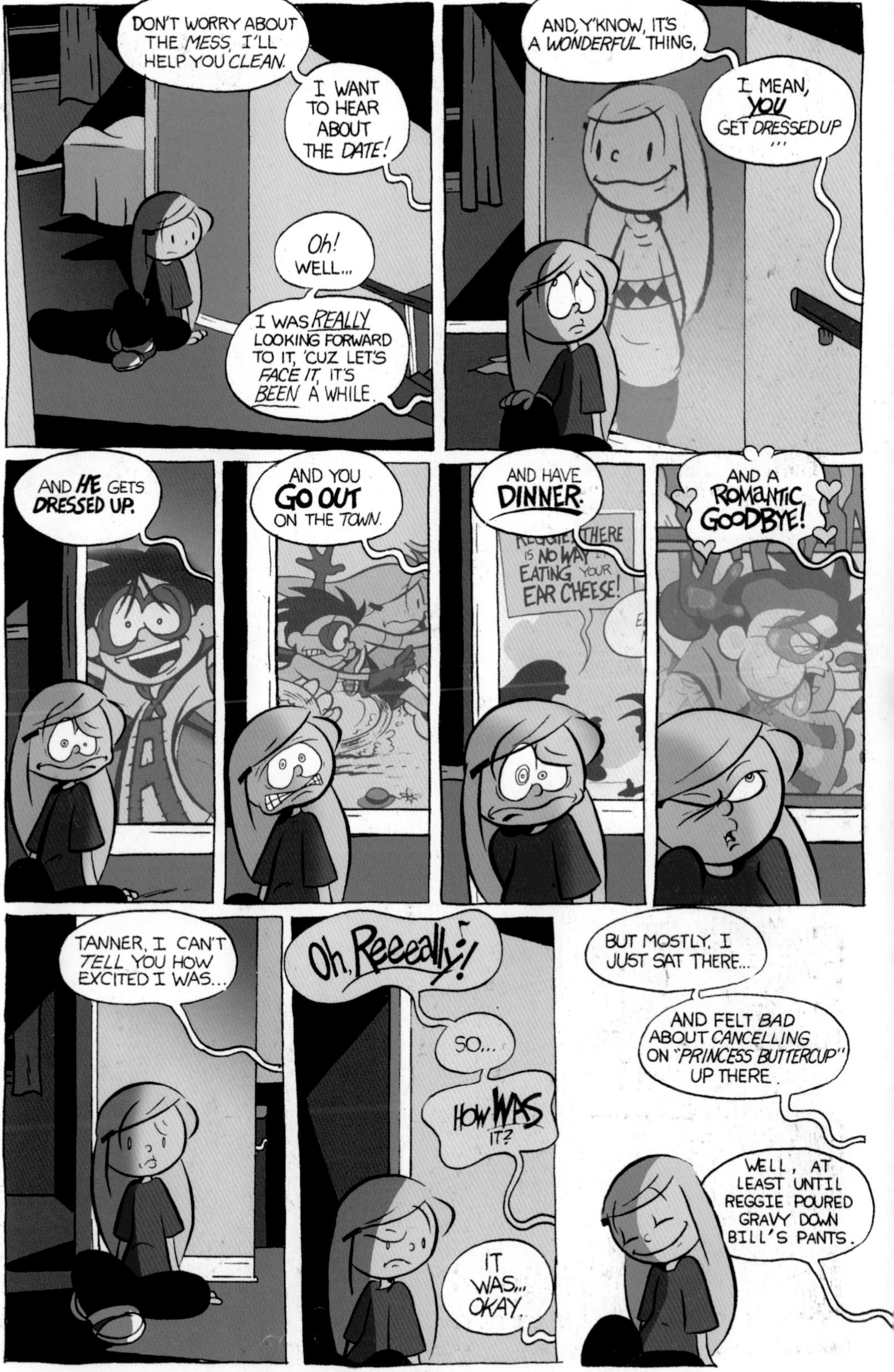
DON'T WORRY ABOUT THE MESS, I'LL HELP YOU CLEAN.
I WANT TO HEAR ABOUT THE DATE!
Oh! WELL...
I WAS REALLY LOOKING FORWARD TO IT, 'CUZ LET'S FACE IT, IT'S BEEN A WHILE.
AND, Y'KNOW, IT'S A WONDERFUL THING,
I MEAN, YOU GET DRESSED UP ...
AND HE GETS DRESSED UP.
AND YOU GO OUT ON THE TOWN.
AND HAVE DINNER.
REGGIE THERE IS NO WAY I'M EATING YOUR EAR CHEESE!
AND A ROMANTIC GOODBYE!
TANNER, I CAN'T TELL YOU HOW EXCITED I WAS...
Oh, Reeeally!
SO...
HOW WAS IT?
IT WAS... OKAY.
BUT MOSTLY, I JUST SAT THERE...
AND FELT BAD ABOUT CANCELLING ON "PRINCESS BUTTERCUP" UP THERE.
WELL, AT LEAST UNTIL REGGIE POURED GRAVY DOWN BILL'S PANTS.

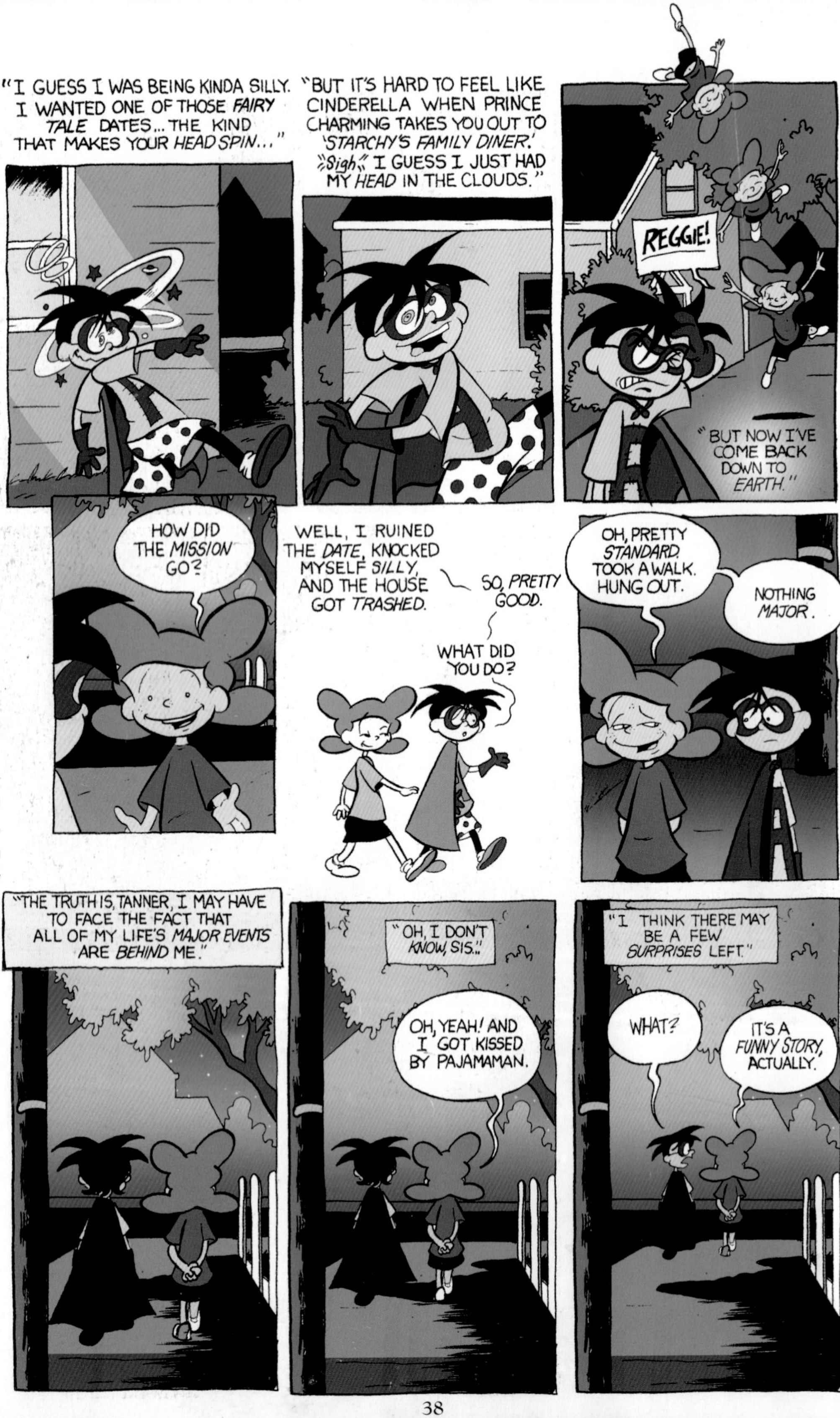
"I GUESS I WAS BEING KINDA SILLY. I WANTED ONE OF THOSE FAIRY TALE DATES... THE KIND THAT MAKES YOUR HEAD SPIN..."
"BUT IT'S HARD TO FEEL LIKE CINDERELLA WHEN PRINCE CHARMING TAKES YOU OUT TO 'STARCHY'S FAMILY DINER.' *Sigh* I GUESS I JUST HAD MY HEAD IN THE CLOUDS."
REGGIE!
"BUT NOW I'VE COME BACK DOWN TO EARTH."
HOW DID THE MISSION GO?
WELL, I RUINED THE DATE, KNOCKED MYSELF SILLY, AND THE HOUSE GOT TRASHED.
SO, PRETTY GOOD.
WHAT DID YOU DO?
OH, PRETTY STANDARD. TOOK A WALK. HUNG OUT.
NOTHING MAJOR.
"THE TRUTH IS, TANNER, I MAY HAVE TO FACE THE FACT THAT ALL OF MY LIFE'S MAJOR EVENTS ARE BEHIND ME."
"OH, I DON'T KNOW, SIS..."
OH, YEAH! AND I GOT KISSED BY PAJAMAMAN.
"I THINK THERE MAY BE A FEW SURPRISES LEFT."
WHAT?
IT'S A FUNNY STORY, ACTUALLY.

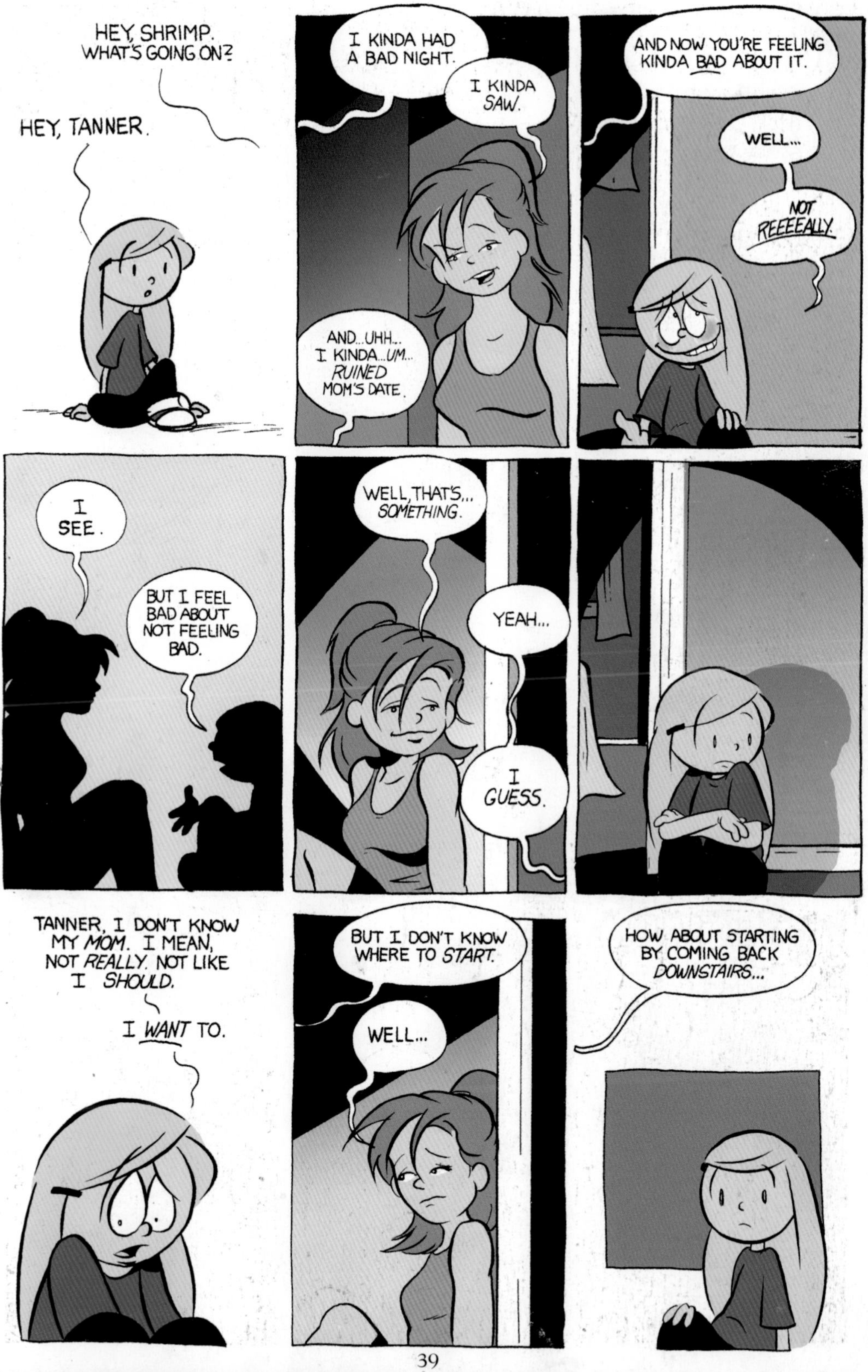
HEY, SHRIMP. WHAT'S GOING ON?
HEY, TANNER.
I KINDA HAD A BAD NIGHT.
I KINDA SAW.
AND...UHH... I KINDA...UM... RUINED MOM'S DATE.
AND NOW YOU'RE FEELING KINDA BAD ABOUT IT.
WELL...
NOT REEEEALLY.
I SEE.
BUT I FEEL BAD ABOUT NOT FEELING BAD.
WELL, THAT'S... SOMETHING.
YEAH...
I GUESS.
TANNER, I DON'T KNOW MY MOM. I MEAN, NOT REALLY. NOT LIKE I SHOULD.
I WANT TO.
BUT I DON'T KNOW WHERE TO START.
WELL...
HOW ABOUT STARTING BY COMING BACK DOWNSTAIRS...

40

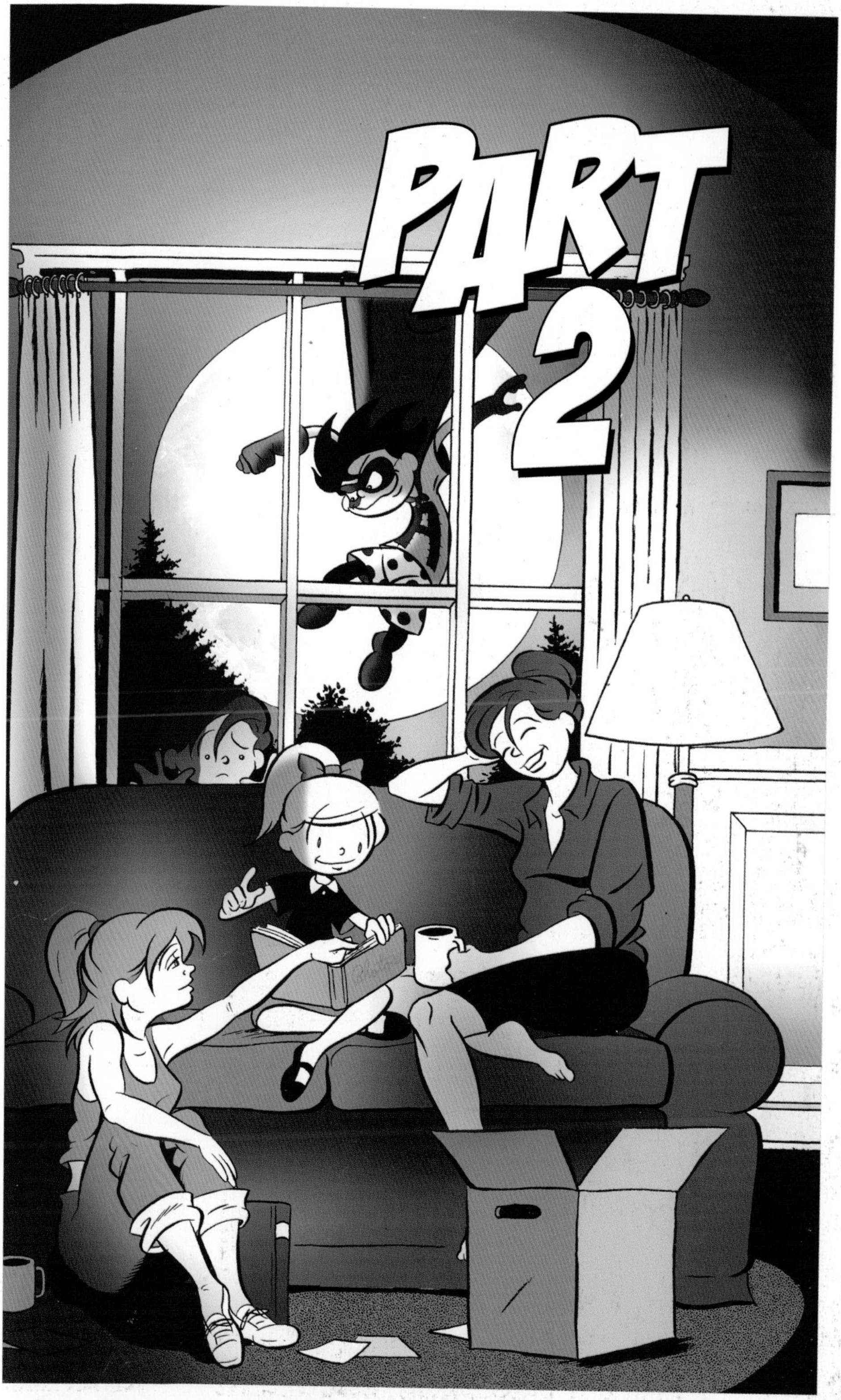
PART 2

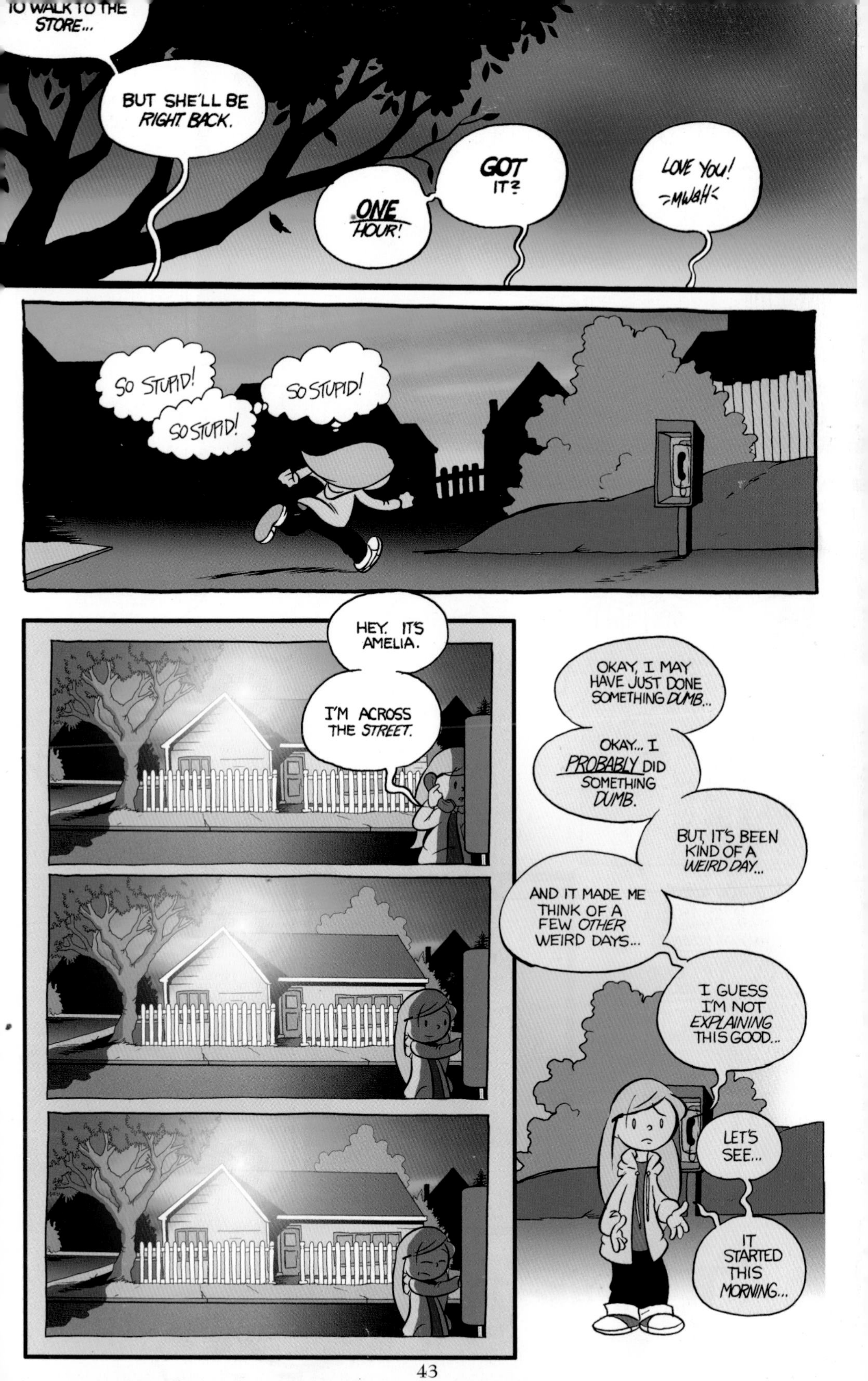

TO WALK TO THE STORE...
BUT SHE'LL BE RIGHT BACK.
ONE HOUR!
GOT IT?
LOVE YOU! =MWAH=
SO STUPID!
SO STUPID!
SO STUPID!
HEY. IT'S AMELIA.
I'M ACROSS THE STREET.
OKAY, I MAY HAVE JUST DONE SOMETHING DUMB...
OKAY... I PROBABLY DID SOMETHING DUMB.
BUT, IT'S BEEN KIND OF A WEIRD DAY...
AND IT MADE ME THINK OF A FEW OTHER WEIRD DAYS...
I GUESS I'M NOT EXPLAINING THIS GOOD...
LET'S SEE...
IT STARTED THIS MORNING...

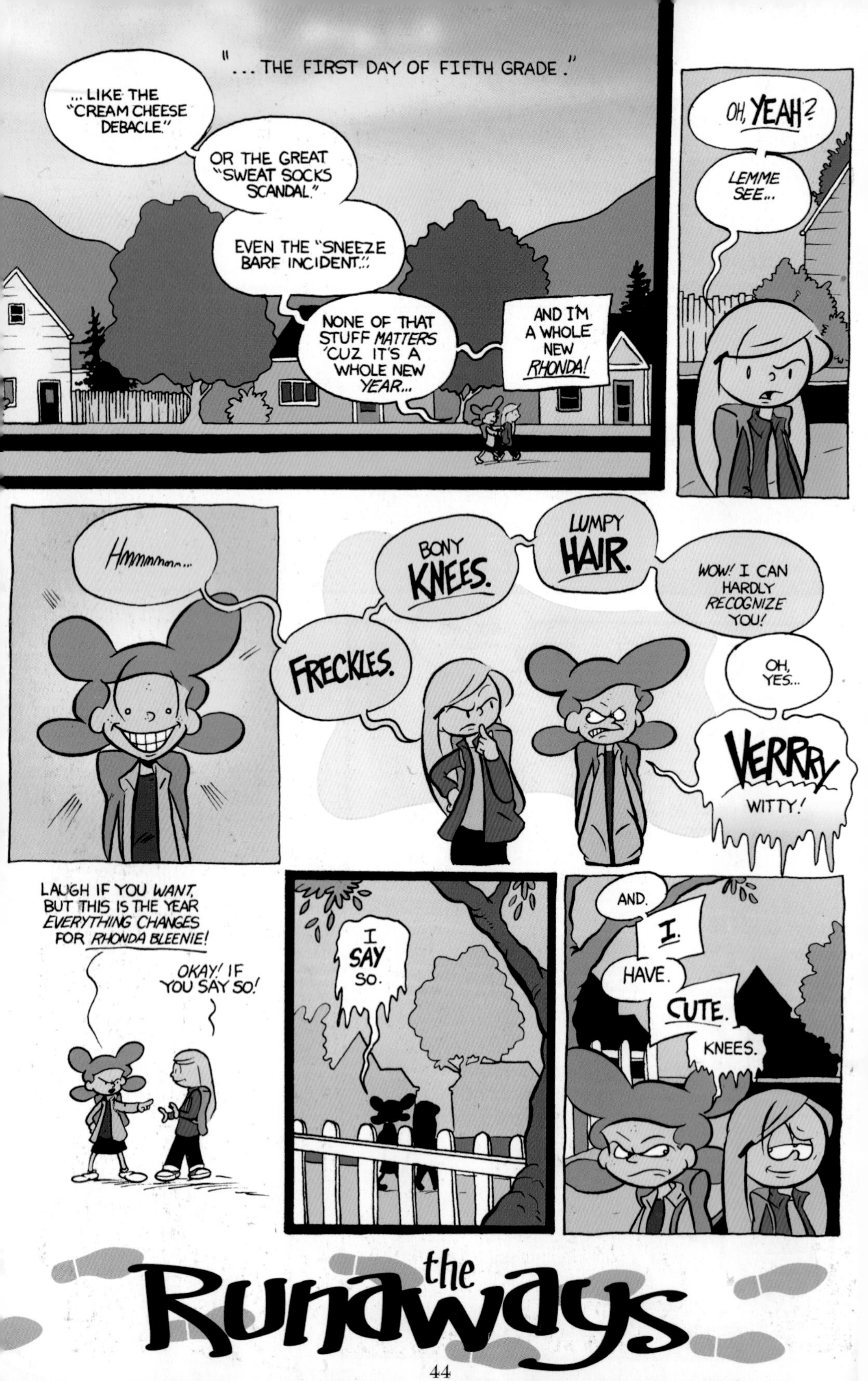
"... THE FIRST DAY OF FIFTH GRADE."
... LIKE THE "CREAM CHEESE DEBACLE."
OR THE GREAT "SWEAT SOCKS SCANDAL."
EVEN THE "SNEEZE BARF INCIDENT."
NONE OF THAT STUFF MATTERS 'CUZ IT'S A WHOLE NEW YEAR...
AND I'M A WHOLE NEW RHONDA!
OH, YEAH?
LEMME SEE...
Hmmmmm...
FRECKLES.
BONY KNEES.
LUMPY HAIR.
WOW! I CAN HARDLY RECOGNIZE YOU!
OH, YES...
VERRRY WITTY!
LAUGH IF YOU WANT, BUT THIS IS THE YEAR EVERYTHING CHANGES FOR RHONDA BLEENIE!
OKAY! IF YOU SAY SO!
I SAY SO.
AND.
I.
HAVE.
CUTE.
KNEES.
the Runaways

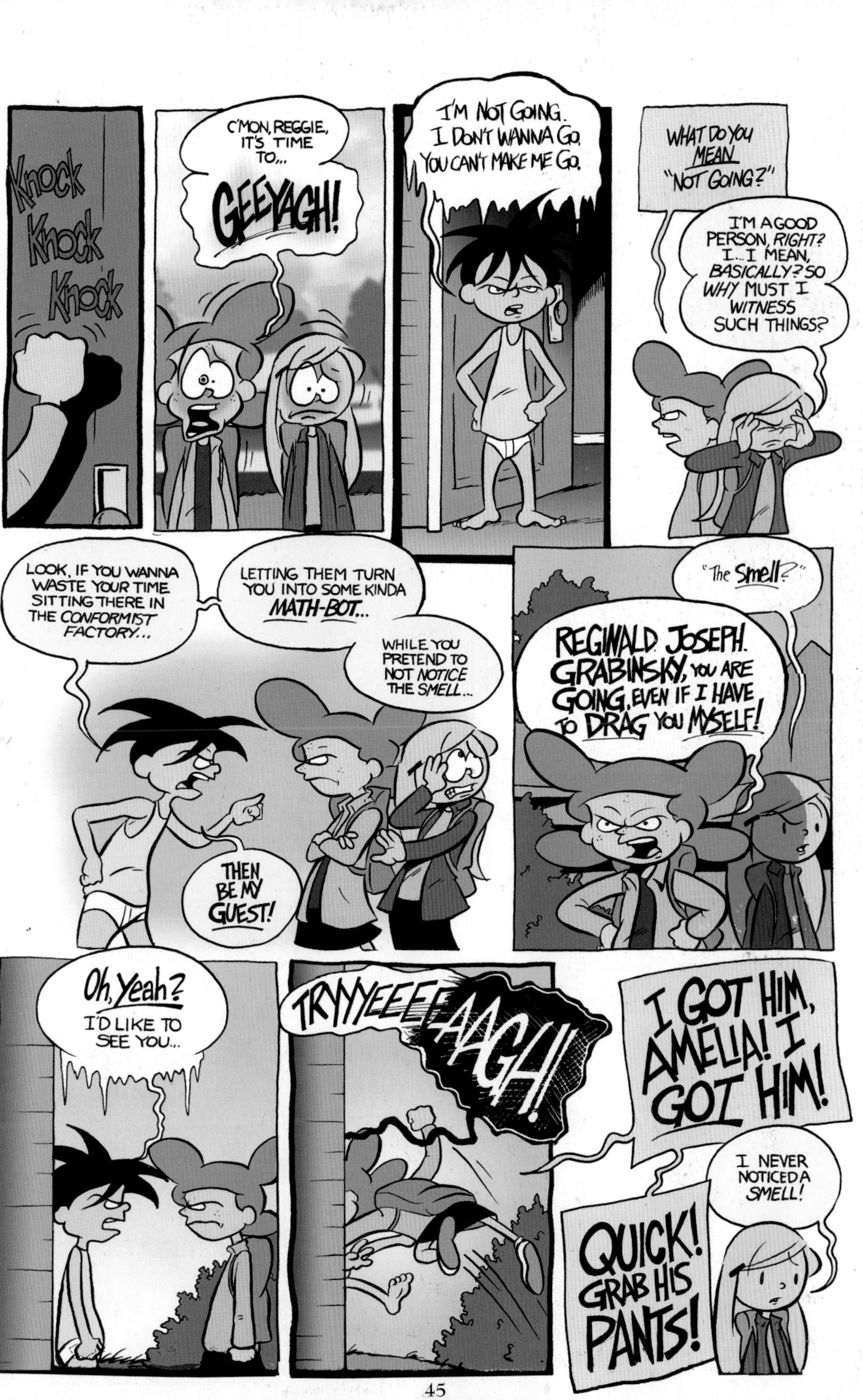
Knock Knock Knock
C'MON, REGGIE, IT'S TIME TO,..
GEEYAGH!
I'M NOT GOING. I DON'T WANNA GO. YOU CAN'T MAKE ME GO.
WHAT DO YOU MEAN "NOT GOING?"
I'M A GOOD PERSON, RIGHT? I...I MEAN, BASICALLY? SO WHY MUST I WITNESS SUCH THINGS?
LOOK, IF YOU WANNA WASTE YOUR TIME SITTING THERE IN THE CONFORMIST FACTORY...
LETTING THEM TURN YOU INTO SOME KINDA MATH-BOT...
WHILE YOU PRETEND TO NOT NOTICE THE SMELL...
THEN BE MY GUEST!
"The Smell?"
REGINALD. JOSEPH. GRABINSKY, YOU ARE GOING, EVEN IF I HAVE TO DRAG YOU MYSELF!
Oh, Yeah? I'D LIKE TO SEE YOU...
TRYYYEEEEAAGH!
I GOT HIM, AMELIA! I GOT HIM!
I NEVER NOTICED A SMELL!
QUICK! GRAB HIS PANTS!

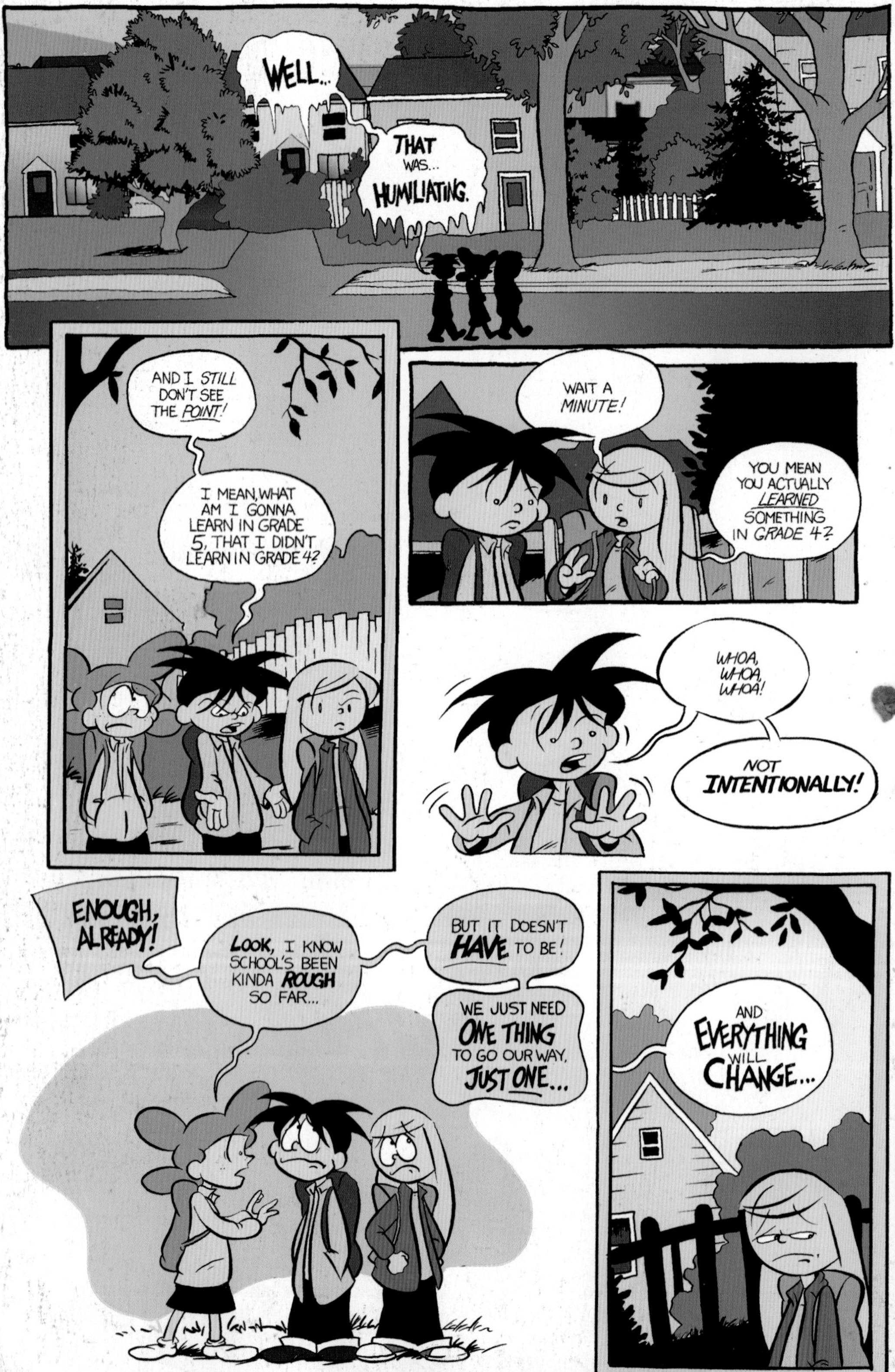
WELL...
THAT WAS... HUMILIATING.
AND I STILL DON'T SEE THE POINT!
I MEAN, WHAT AM I GONNA LEARN IN GRADE 5, THAT I DIDN'T LEARN IN GRADE 4?
WAIT A MINUTE!
YOU MEAN YOU ACTUALLY LEARNED SOMETHING IN GRADE 4?
WHOA, WHOA, WHOA!
NOT INTENTIONALLY!
ENOUGH, ALREADY!
LOOK, I KNOW SCHOOL'S BEEN KINDA ROUGH SO FAR...
BUT IT DOESN'T HAVE TO BE!
WE JUST NEED ONE THING TO GO OUR WAY, JUST ONE...
AND EVERYTHING WILL CHANGE...

"...EVERYTHING"

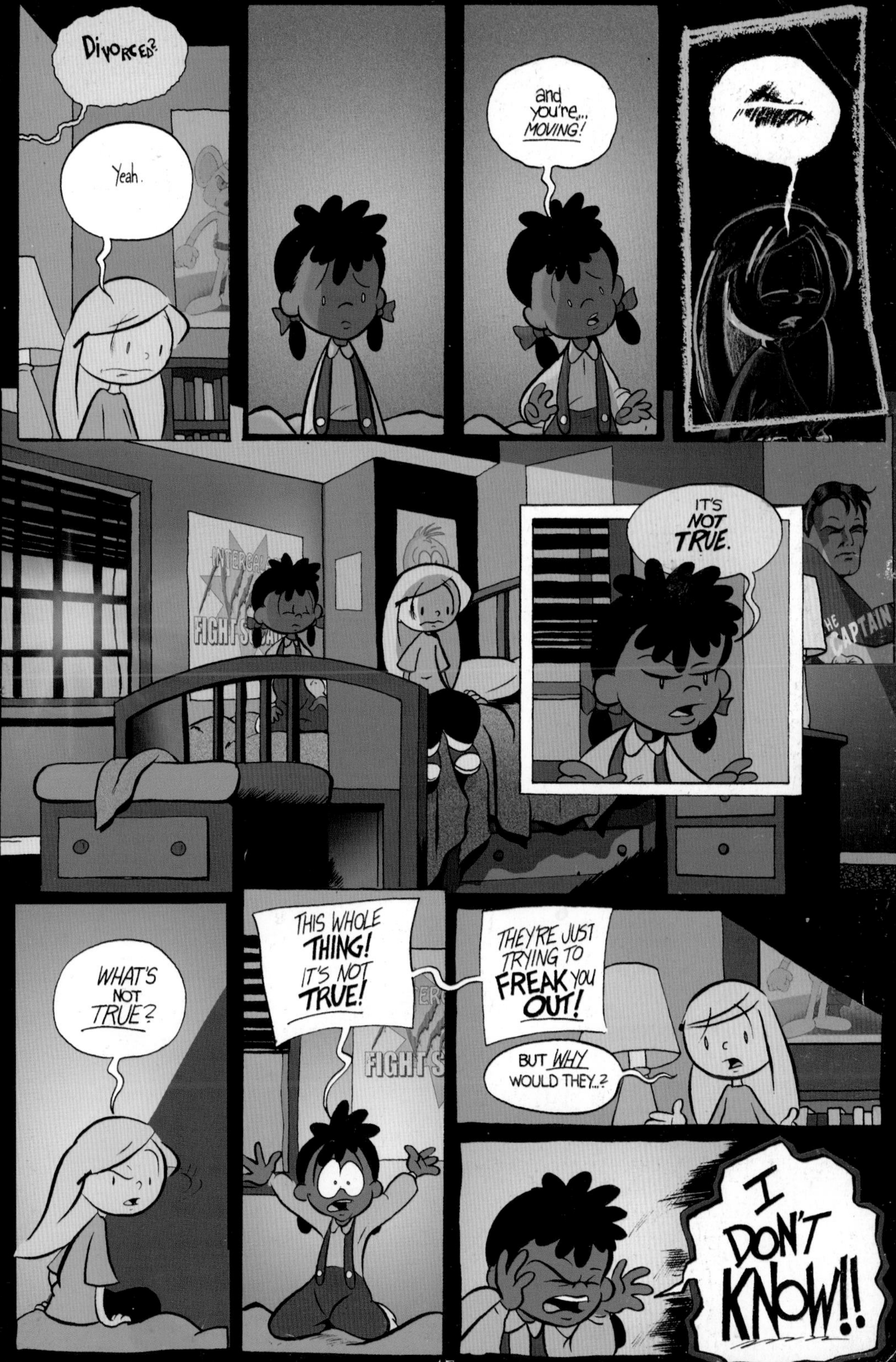
DIVORCED?
Yeah.
and you're... MOVING!
IT'S NOT TRUE.
INTERGA
FIGHT S
THE CAPTAIN
WHAT'S NOT TRUE?
THIS WHOLE THING! IT'S NOT TRUE!
THEY'RE JUST TRYING TO FREAK YOU OUT!
BUT WHY WOULD THEY...?
I DON'T KNOW!!

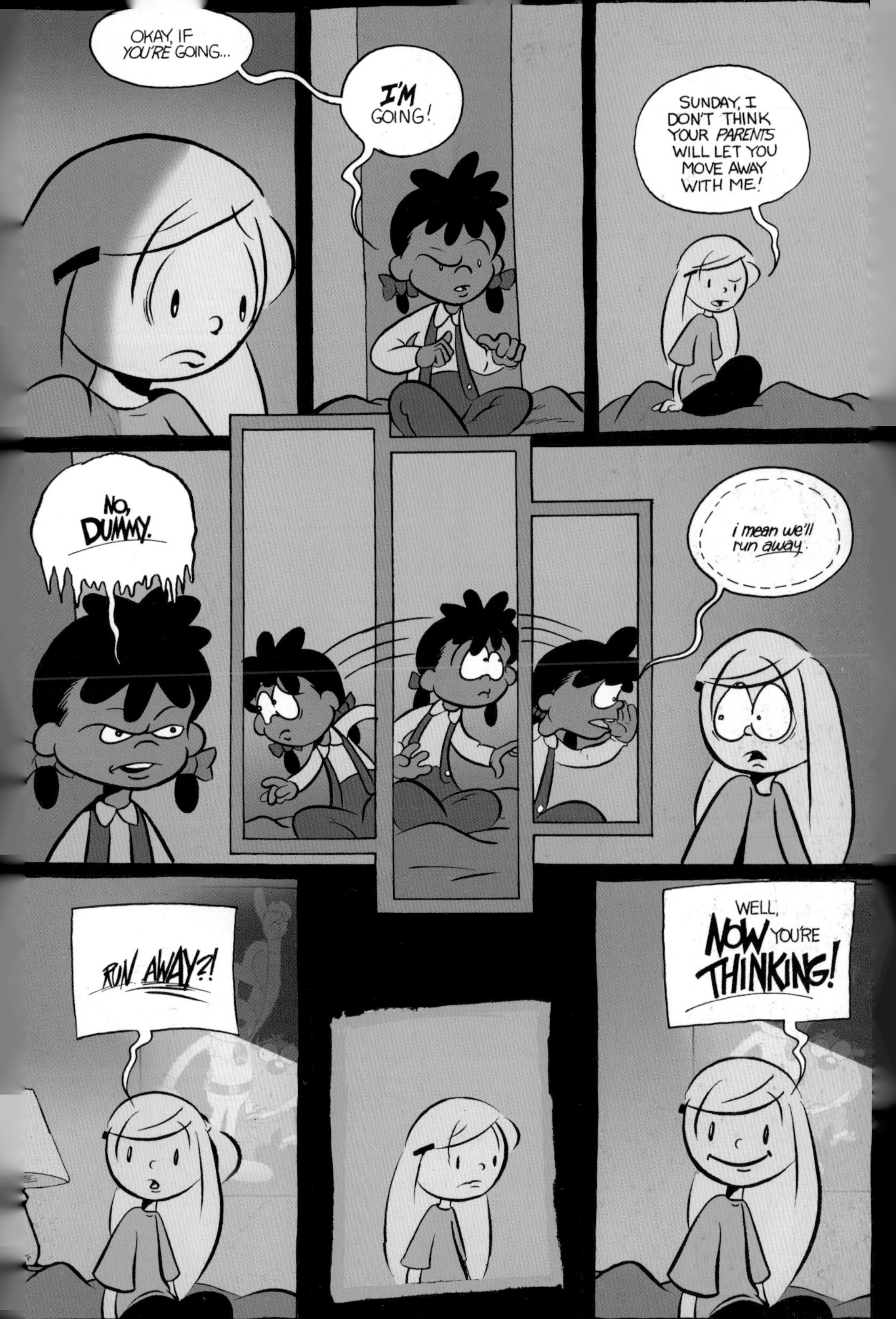
OKAY, IF *YOU'RE* GOING...
I'M GOING!
SUNDAY, I DON'T THINK YOUR *PARENTS* WILL LET YOU MOVE AWAY WITH ME!
NO, DUMMY.
i mean we'll run away.
RUN AWAY?!
WELL, NOW YOU'RE THINKING!

RRY's 5 A

HEY, GUYS, WAIT UP...

I NEED TO STOP IN HARRY'S FOR A MINUTE,

HEY, WAIT A SECOND...

I'VE BEEN HERE *BEFORE*! TANNER BROUGHT ME JUST AFTER WE MOVED IN.

WOW... WHAT A *THRILL* THAT MUST HAVE BEEN.

IT WAS PROBABLY LIKE, "WHAT *NEW YORK*?"

REGGIE, *SHUT UP*! THIS IS *IMPORTANT*!

EVERY YEAR, ON THE *FIRST DAY* OF SCHOOL, I STOP HERE, AND BUY A *NEW* *NOTEBOOK*!

>*SIGH*< THE CLEAN, *FRESH COVER*!

THE BLANK WHITE *PAGES*!

IT'S A *SYMBOL* OF *HOPE*!

OF THE *FUTURE*!

BUT LAST YEAR, I DIDN'T *GET ONE*! LAST YEAR, I *FORGOT*! AND SO, THE *FUTURE* WAS *DENIED* ME! BUT I WON'T LET THAT HAPPEN AGAIN, DO YOU HEAR ME? I *WON'T*!

BUT DON'T YOU *THINK*...

I SAID I WON'T!

Shake Shake Shake

OOooKKKKAAAY! OOKKAAAyy! OOOKKKKAAAy!

TO THE *FUTURE*!

>Koff Koff< You go ahead to the future without me, Amelia...

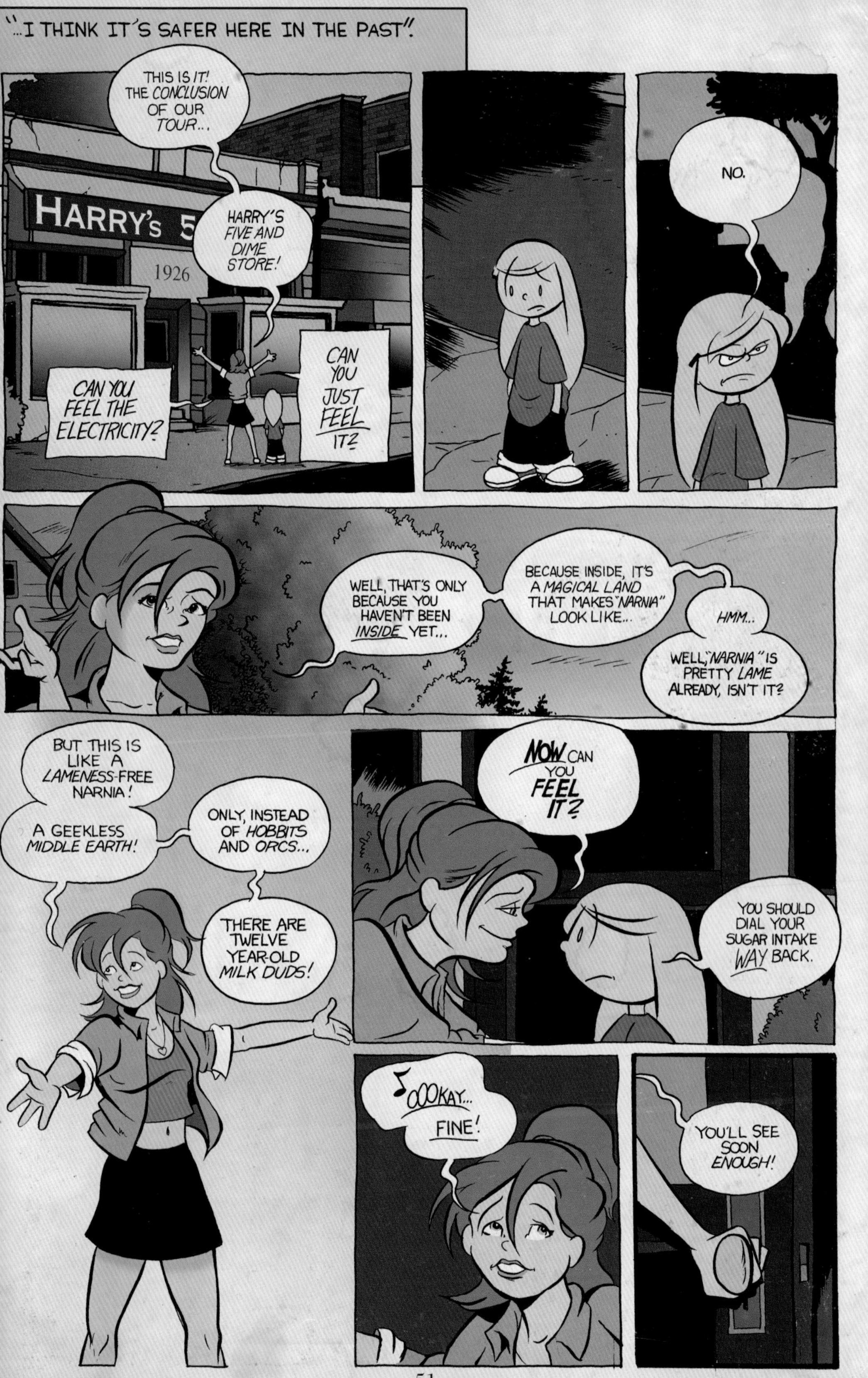
"...I THINK IT'S SAFER HERE IN THE PAST".
THIS IS IT! THE CONCLUSION OF OUR TOUR...
HARRY'S FIVE AND DIME STORE!
HARRY'S 5
1926
CAN YOU FEEL THE ELECTRICITY?
CAN YOU JUST FEEL IT?
NO.
WELL, THAT'S ONLY BECAUSE YOU HAVEN'T BEEN INSIDE YET...
BECAUSE INSIDE, IT'S A MAGICAL LAND THAT MAKES "NARNIA" LOOK LIKE...
HMM...
WELL, "NARNIA" IS PRETTY LAME ALREADY, ISN'T IT?
BUT THIS IS LIKE A LAMENESS-FREE NARNIA!
A GEEKLESS MIDDLE EARTH!
ONLY, INSTEAD OF HOBBITS AND ORCS...
THERE ARE TWELVE YEAR-OLD MILK DUDS!
NOW CAN YOU FEEL IT?
YOU SHOULD DIAL YOUR SUGAR INTAKE WAY BACK.
OOOKAY... FINE!
YOU'LL SEE SOON ENOUGH!

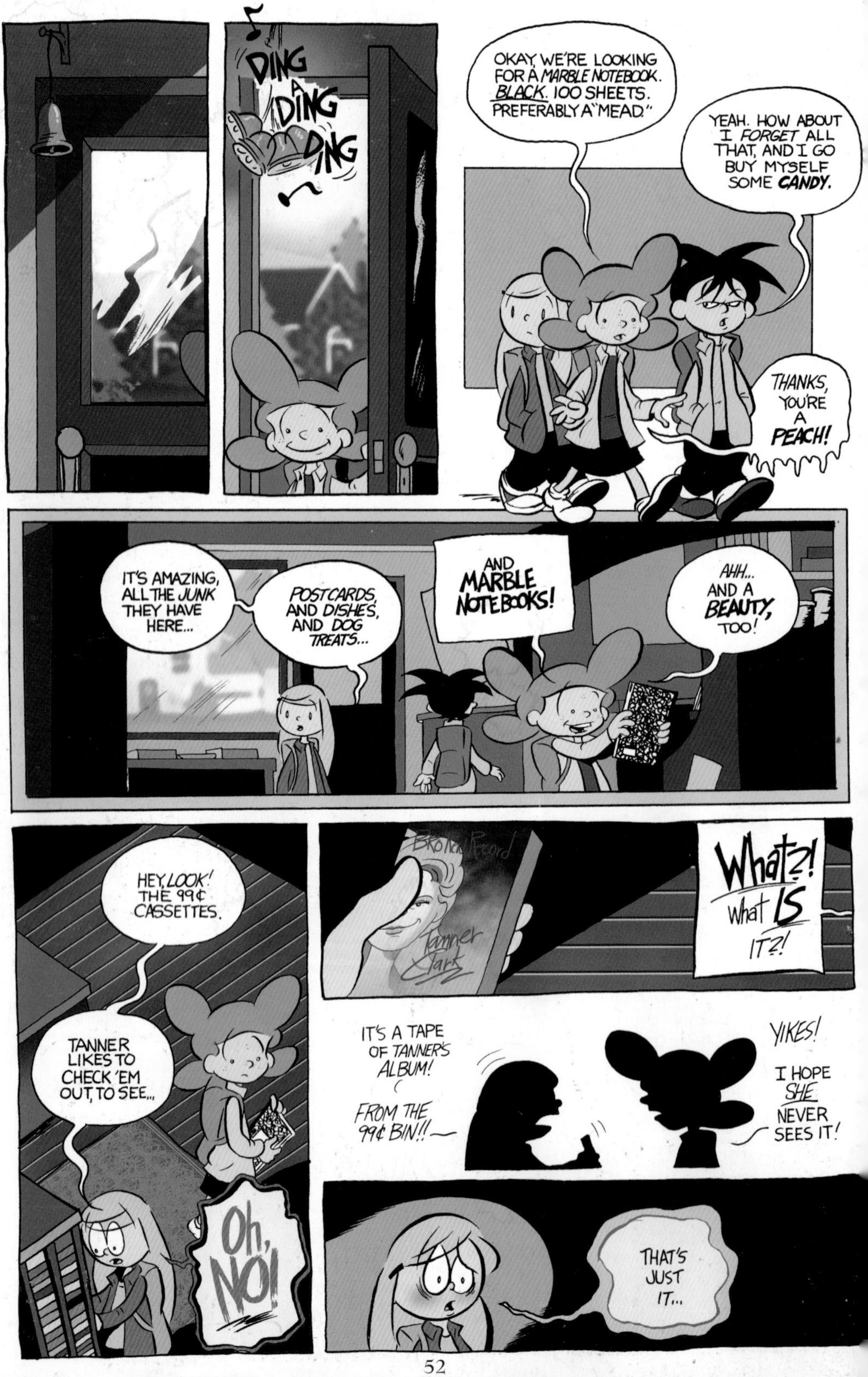
DING A DING DING
OKAY, WE'RE LOOKING FOR A MARBLE NOTEBOOK. BLACK. 100 SHEETS. PREFERABLY A "MEAD."
YEAH. HOW ABOUT I FORGET ALL THAT, AND I GO BUY MYSELF SOME CANDY.
THANKS, YOU'RE A PEACH!
IT'S AMAZING, ALL THE JUNK THEY HAVE HERE...
POSTCARDS, AND DISHES, AND DOG TREATS...
AND MARBLE NOTEBOOKS!
AHH... AND A BEAUTY, TOO!
HEY, LOOK! THE 99¢ CASSETTES.
TANNER LIKES TO CHECK 'EM OUT, TO SEE...
Oh, NO!
Tanner Clark
What?! What IS IT?!
IT'S A TAPE OF TANNER'S ALBUM!
FROM THE 99¢ BIN!!
YIKES!
I HOPE SHE NEVER SEES IT!
THAT'S JUST IT...

"...I THINK SHE ALREADY HAS."

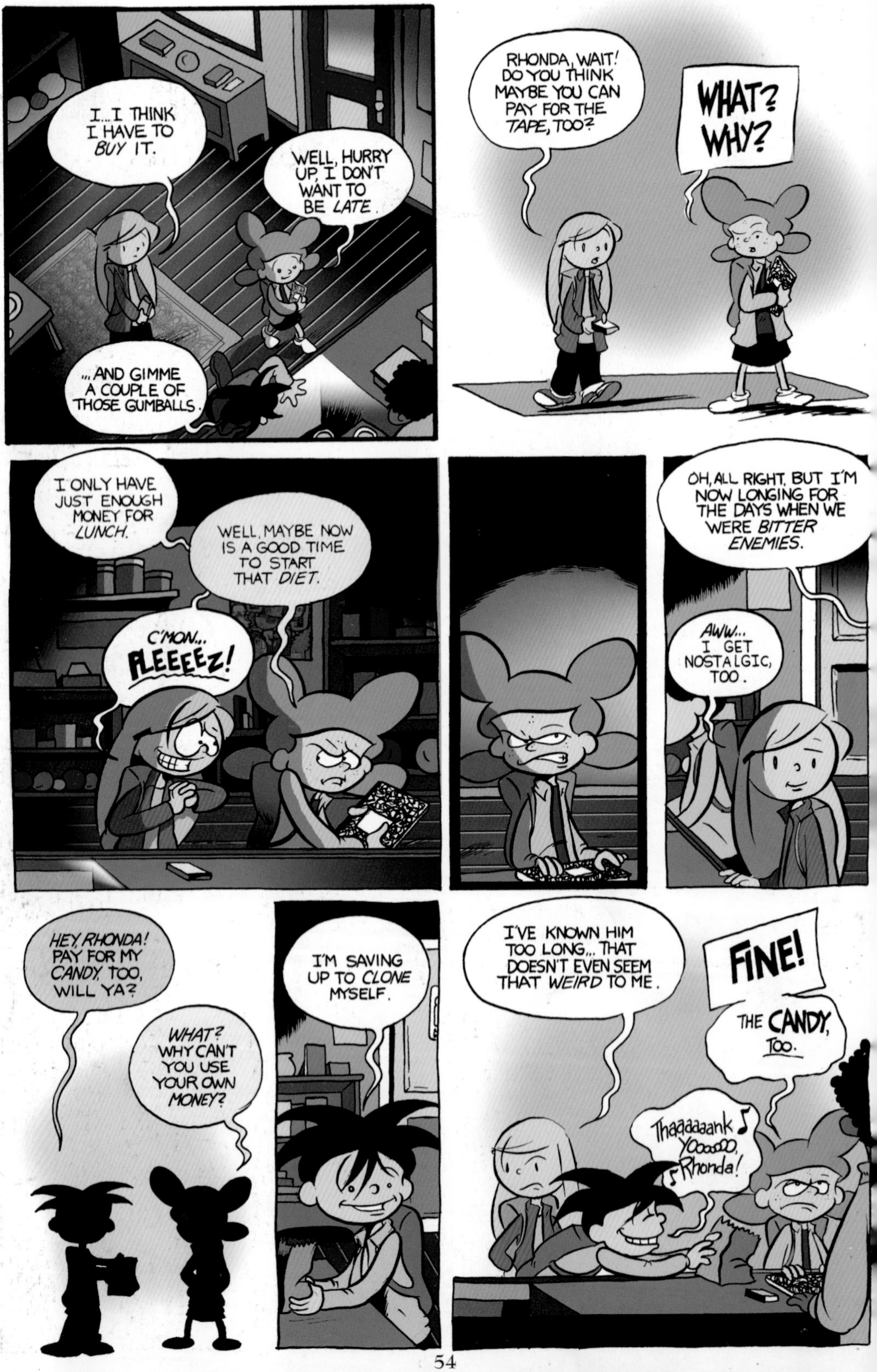
I... I THINK I HAVE TO *BUY* IT.
WELL, HURRY UP, I DON'T WANT TO BE *LATE*.
...AND GIMME A COUPLE OF THOSE GUMBALLS.
RHONDA, WAIT! DO YOU THINK MAYBE YOU CAN PAY FOR THE *TAPE*, TOO?
WHAT? WHY?
I ONLY HAVE JUST ENOUGH MONEY FOR *LUNCH*.
WELL, MAYBE NOW IS A GOOD TIME TO START THAT *DIET*.
C'MON... PLEEEEZ!
OH, ALL RIGHT, BUT I'M NOW LONGING FOR THE DAYS WHEN WE WERE *BITTER ENEMIES*.
AWW... I GET NOSTALGIC, TOO.
HEY, RHONDA! PAY FOR MY CANDY, TOO, WILL YA?
WHAT? WHY CAN'T YOU USE YOUR OWN MONEY?
I'M SAVING UP TO *CLONE* MYSELF.
I'VE KNOWN HIM TOO LONG... THAT DOESN'T EVEN SEEM THAT *WEIRD* TO ME.
FINE!
THE CANDY, TOO.
Thaaaaaank Yooooo, Rhonda!

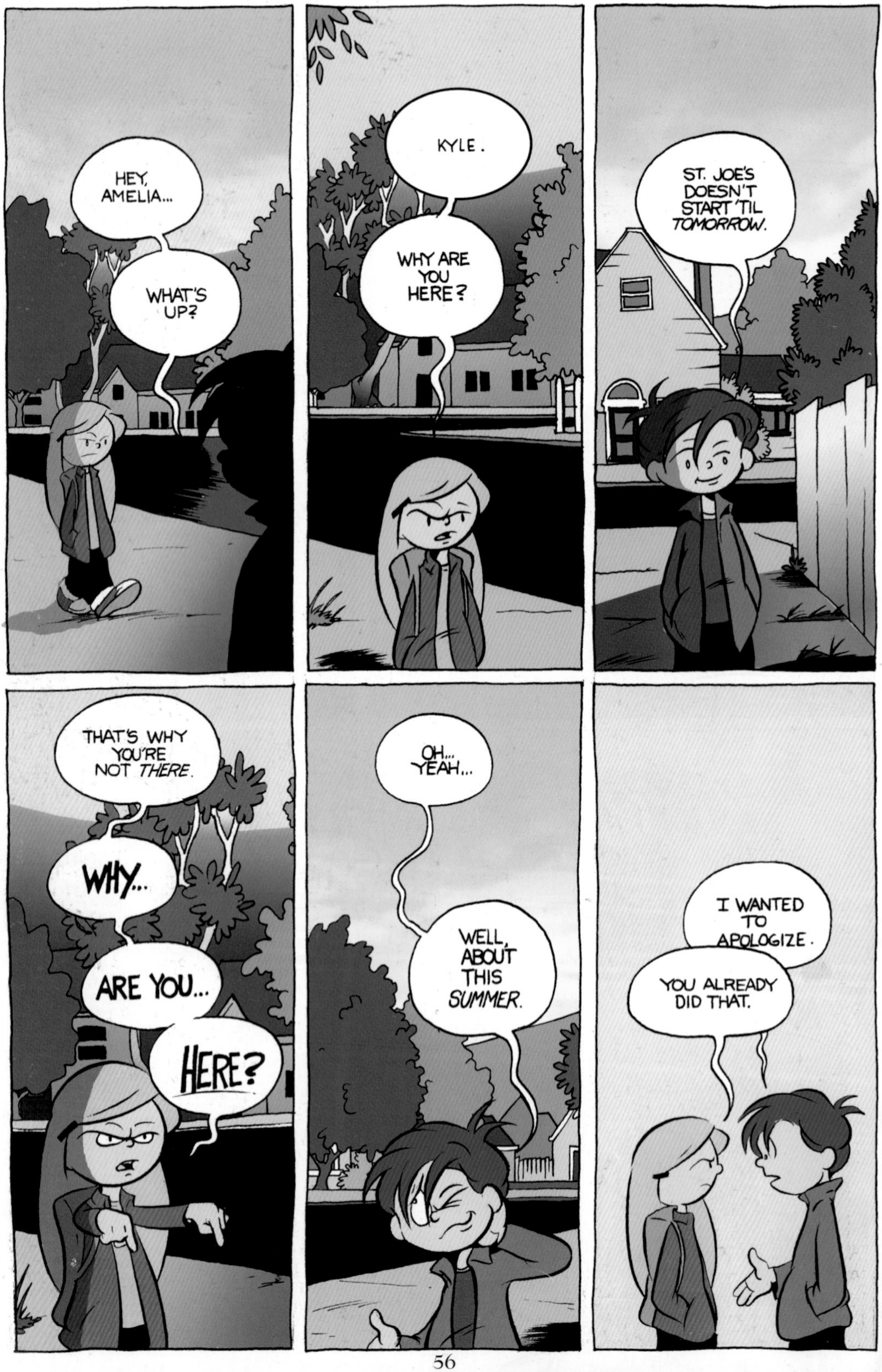
HEY, AMELIA...
WHAT'S UP?
KYLE.
WHY ARE YOU HERE?
ST. JOE'S DOESN'T START 'TIL *TOMORROW*.
THAT'S WHY YOU'RE NOT *THERE*.
WHY...
ARE YOU...
HERE?
OH... YEAH...
WELL, ABOUT THIS *SUMMER*.
I WANTED TO APOLOGIZE.
YOU ALREADY DID THAT.

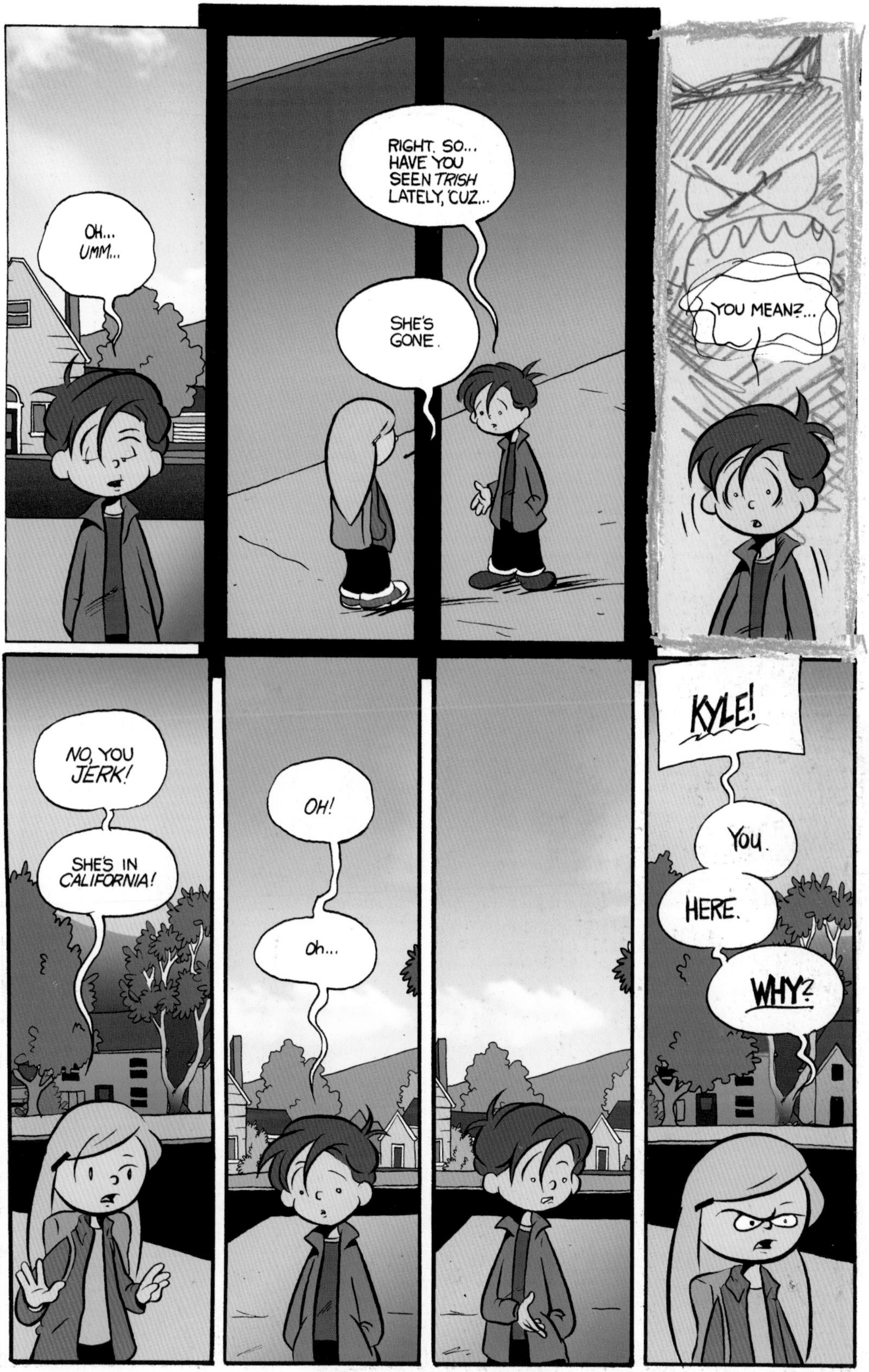
OH...
UMM...
RIGHT. SO... HAVE YOU SEEN TRISH LATELY, 'CUZ...
SHE'S GONE.
YOU MEAN?...
NO, YOU JERK!
SHE'S IN CALIFORNIA!
OH!
Oh...
KYLE!
YOU.
HERE.
WHY?

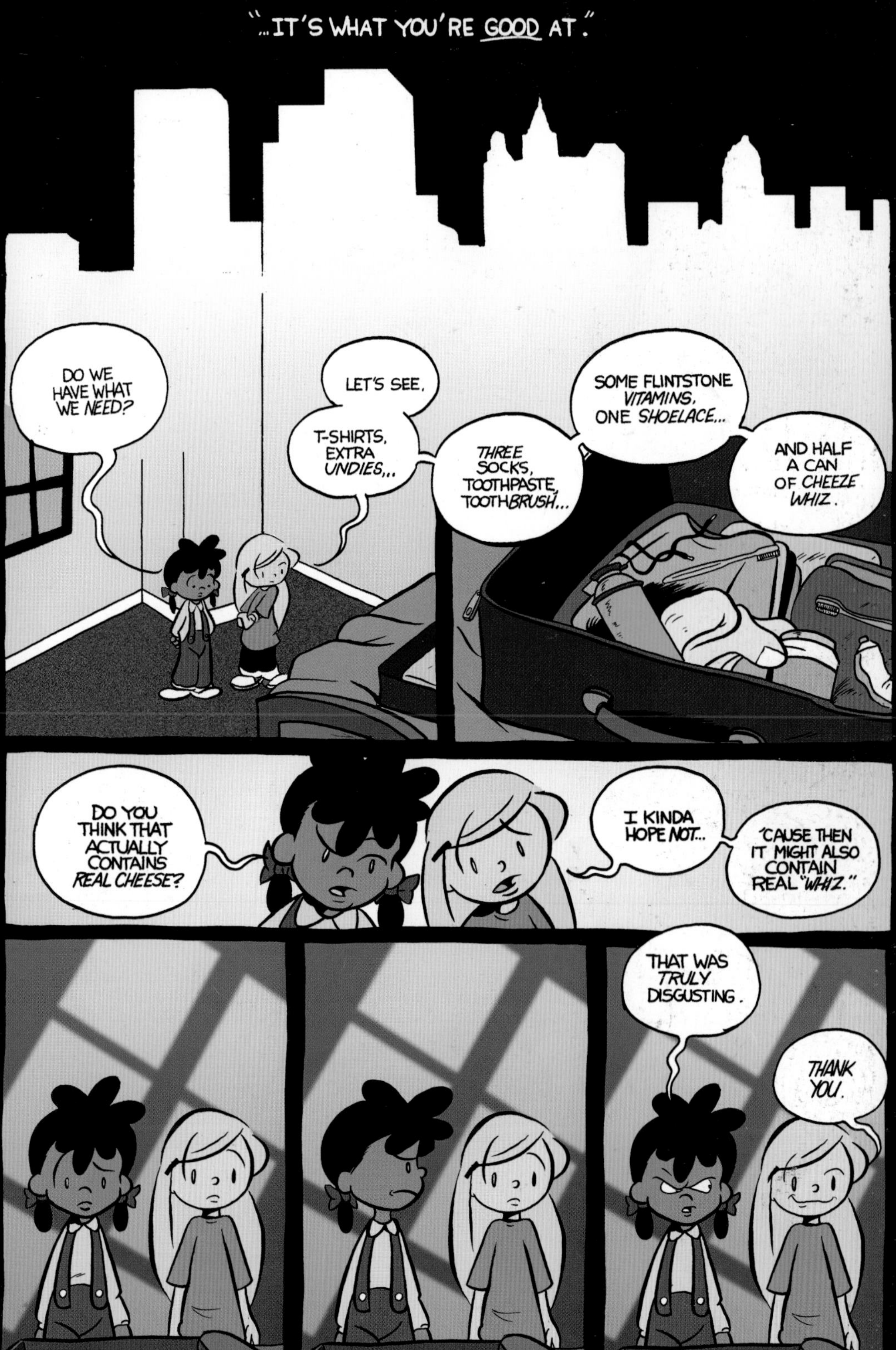
"...IT'S WHAT YOU'RE GOOD AT."
DO WE HAVE WHAT WE NEED?
LET'S SEE.
T-SHIRTS, EXTRA UNDIES,..
THREE SOCKS, TOOTHPASTE, TOOTHBRUSH...
SOME FLINTSTONE VITAMINS, ONE SHOELACE...
AND HALF A CAN OF CHEEZE WHIZ.
DO YOU THINK THAT ACTUALLY CONTAINS REAL CHEESE?
I KINDA HOPE NOT...
'CAUSE THEN IT MIGHT ALSO CONTAIN REAL "WHIZ."
THAT WAS TRULY DISGUSTING.
THANK YOU.

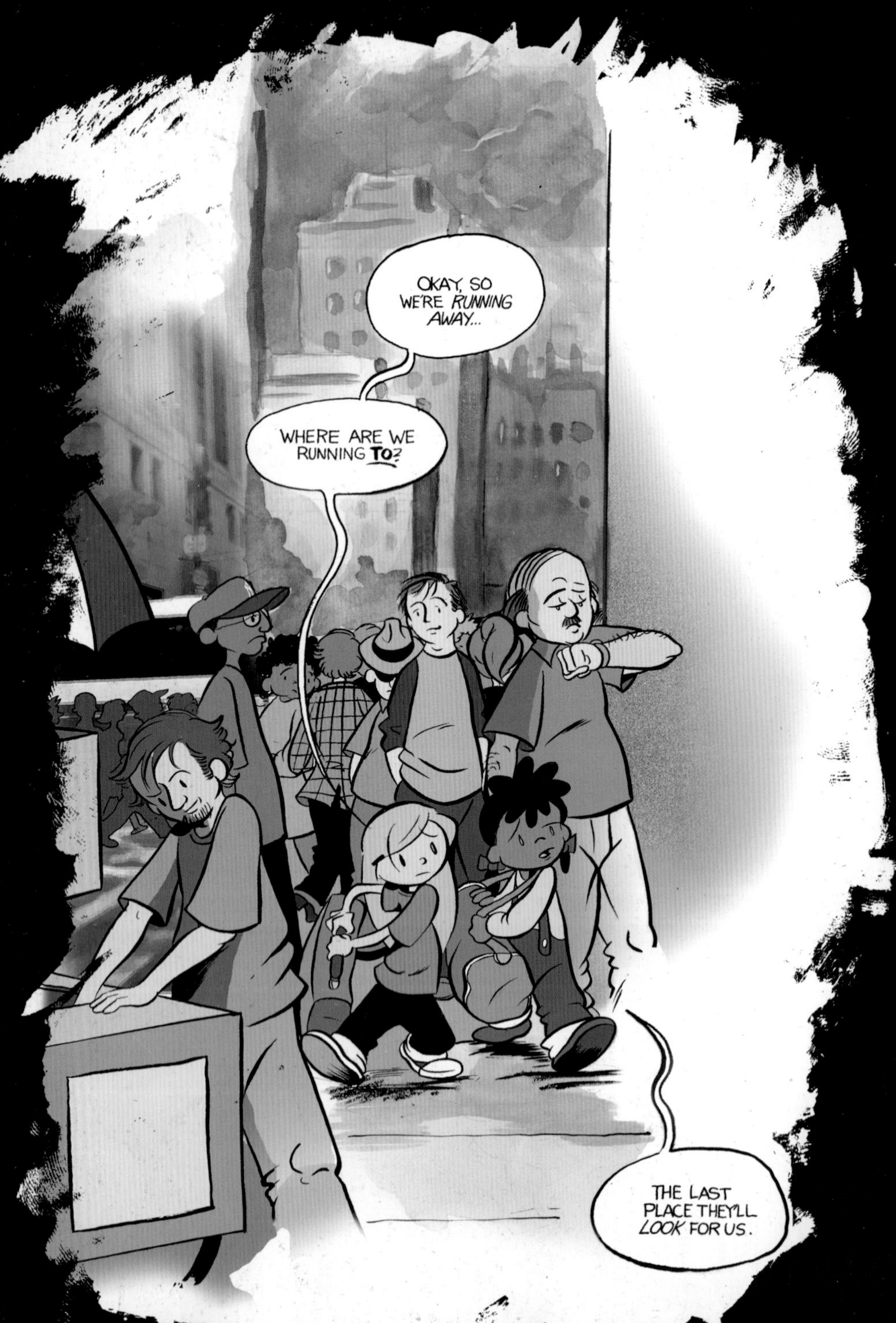
OKAY, SO WE'RE *RUNNING* AWAY...
WHERE ARE WE RUNNING **TO**?
THE LAST PLACE THEY'LL *LOOK* FOR US.

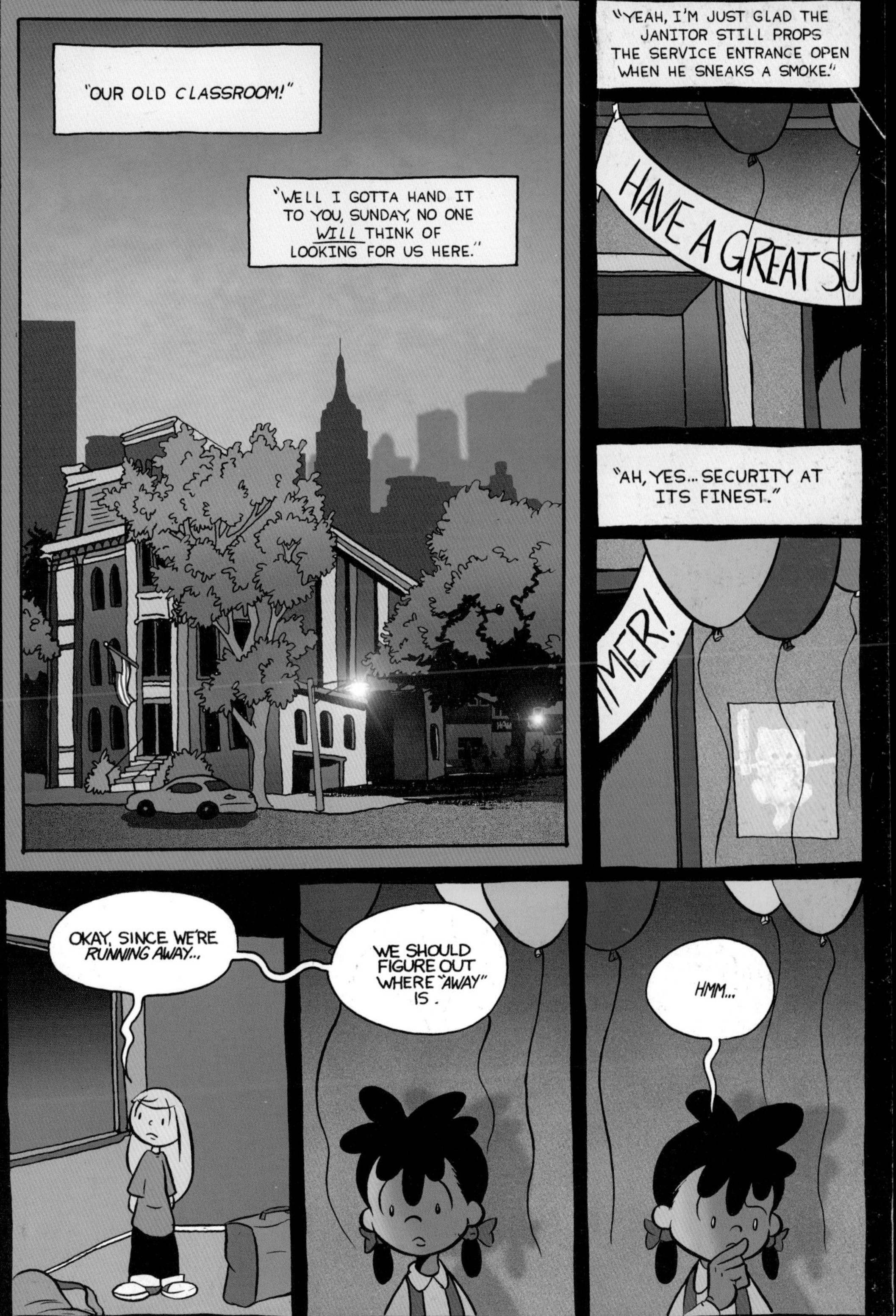
"OUR OLD CLASSROOM!"
"WELL I GOTTA HAND IT TO YOU, SUNDAY, NO ONE WILL THINK OF LOOKING FOR US HERE."
"YEAH, I'M JUST GLAD THE JANITOR STILL PROPS THE SERVICE ENTRANCE OPEN WHEN HE SNEAKS A SMOKE."
HAVE A GREAT SU
"AH, YES... SECURITY AT ITS FINEST."
MER!
OKAY, SINCE WE'RE RUNNING AWAY...
WE SHOULD FIGURE OUT WHERE "AWAY" IS.
HMM...

64

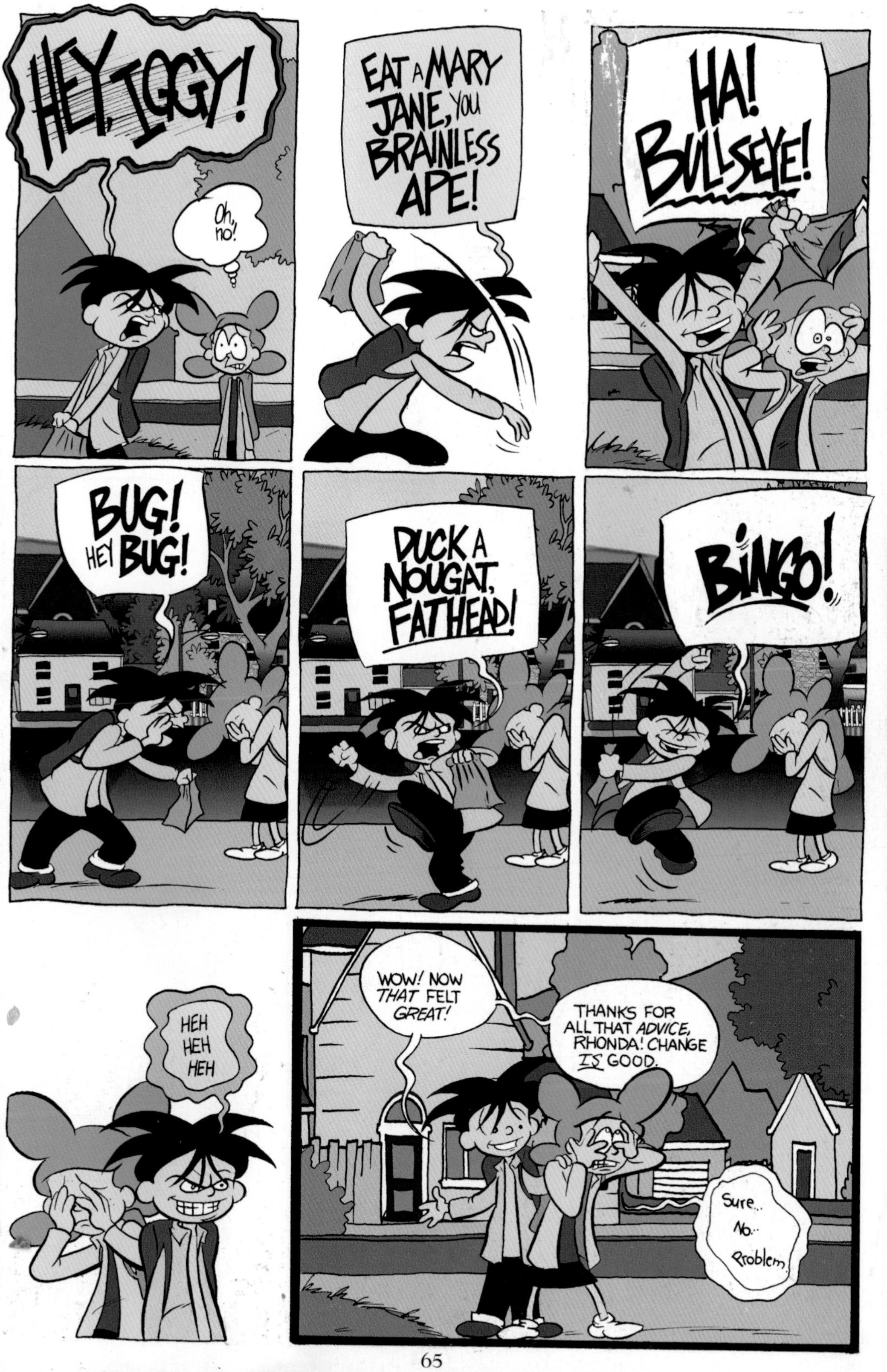
HEY, IGGY!
Oh, no!
EAT A MARY JANE, YOU BRAINLESS APE!
HA! BULLSEYE!
BUG! HEY BUG!
DUCK A NOUGAT, FATHEAD!
BINGO!
HEH HEH HEH
WOW! NOW THAT FELT GREAT!
THANKS FOR ALL THAT ADVICE, RHONDA! CHANGE IS GOOD.
Sure... No... Problem.

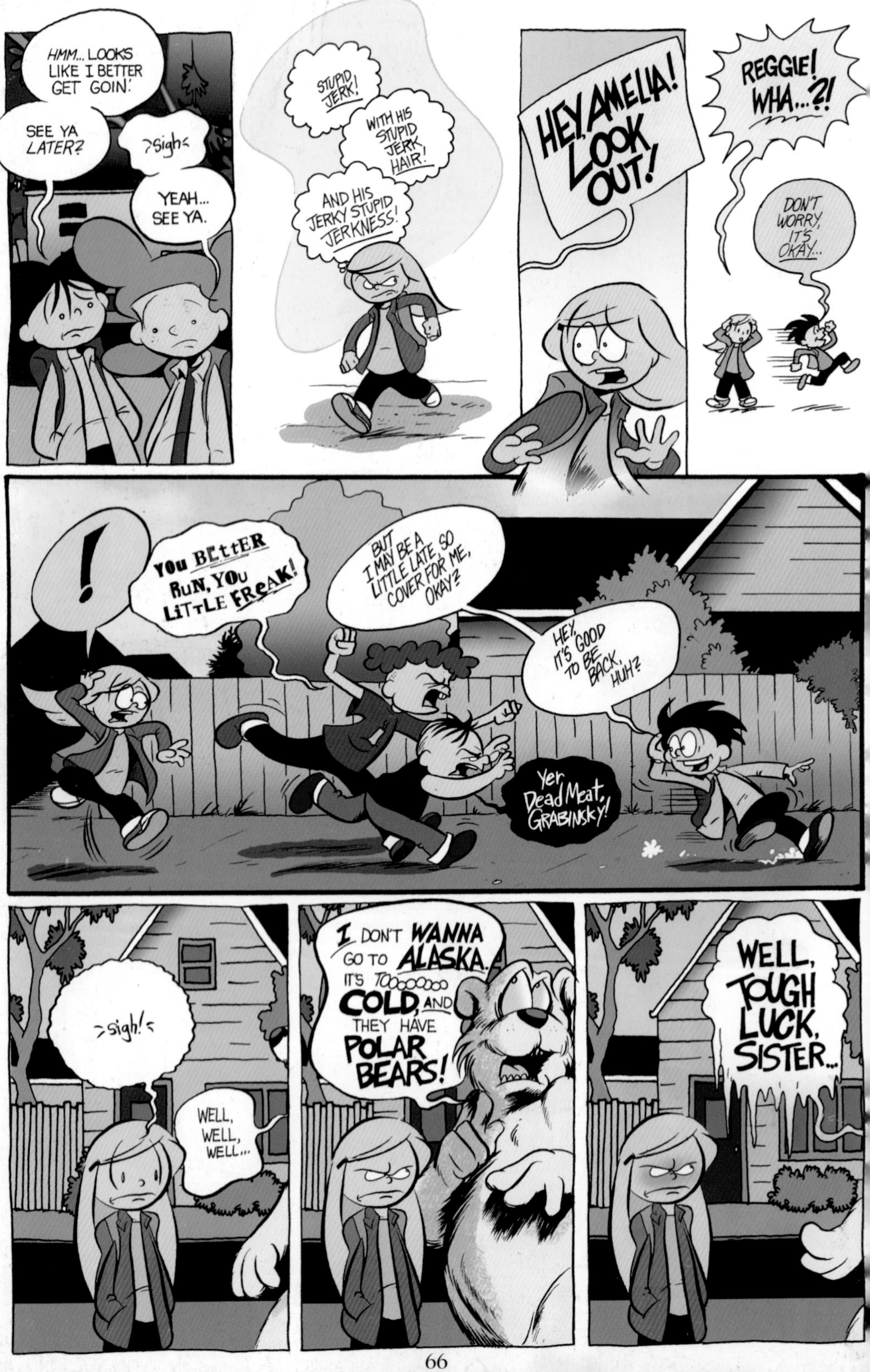
HMM... LOOKS LIKE I BETTER GET GOIN'.
SEE YA LATER?
>sigh<
YEAH... SEE YA.
STUPID JERK!
WITH HIS STUPID JERK HAIR!
AND HIS JERKY STUPID JERKNESS!
HEY, AMELIA! LOOK OUT!
REGGIE! WHA...?!
DON'T WORRY, IT'S OKAY...
!
YOU BETTER RUN, YOU LITTLE FREAK!
BUT I MAY BE A LITTLE LATE, SO COVER FOR ME, OKAY?
HEY, IT'S GOOD TO BE BACK, HUH?
Yer Dead Meat, GRABINSKY!
>sigh!<
WELL, WELL, WELL...
I DON'T WANNA GO TO ALASKA. IT'S TOOOOOOOO COLD, AND THEY HAVE POLAR BEARS!
WELL, TOUGH LUCK, SISTER...

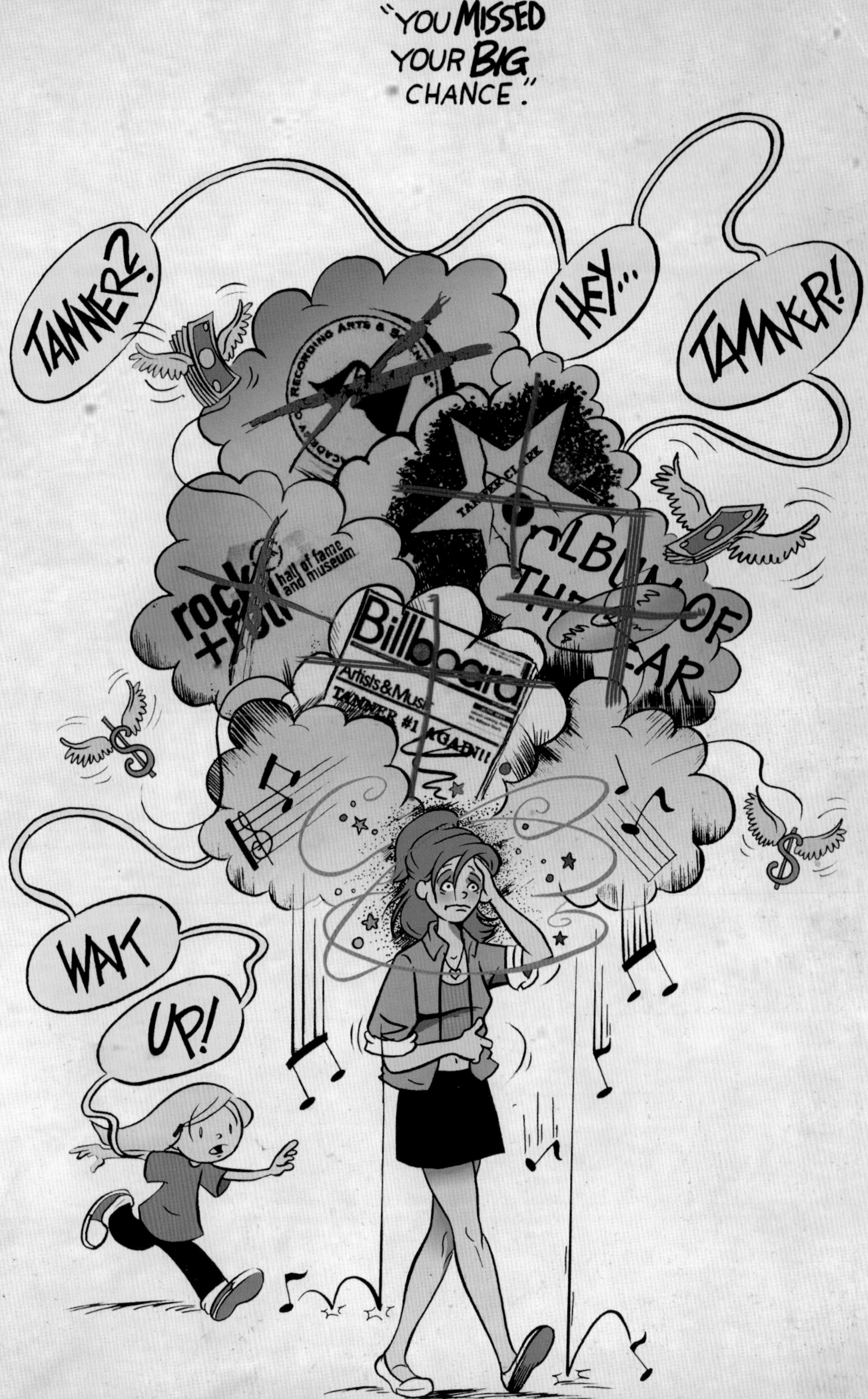
"YOU MISSED YOUR BIG CHANCE."
TANNER?
HEY...
TANNER!
hall of fame and museum
Billboard
WAIT UP!

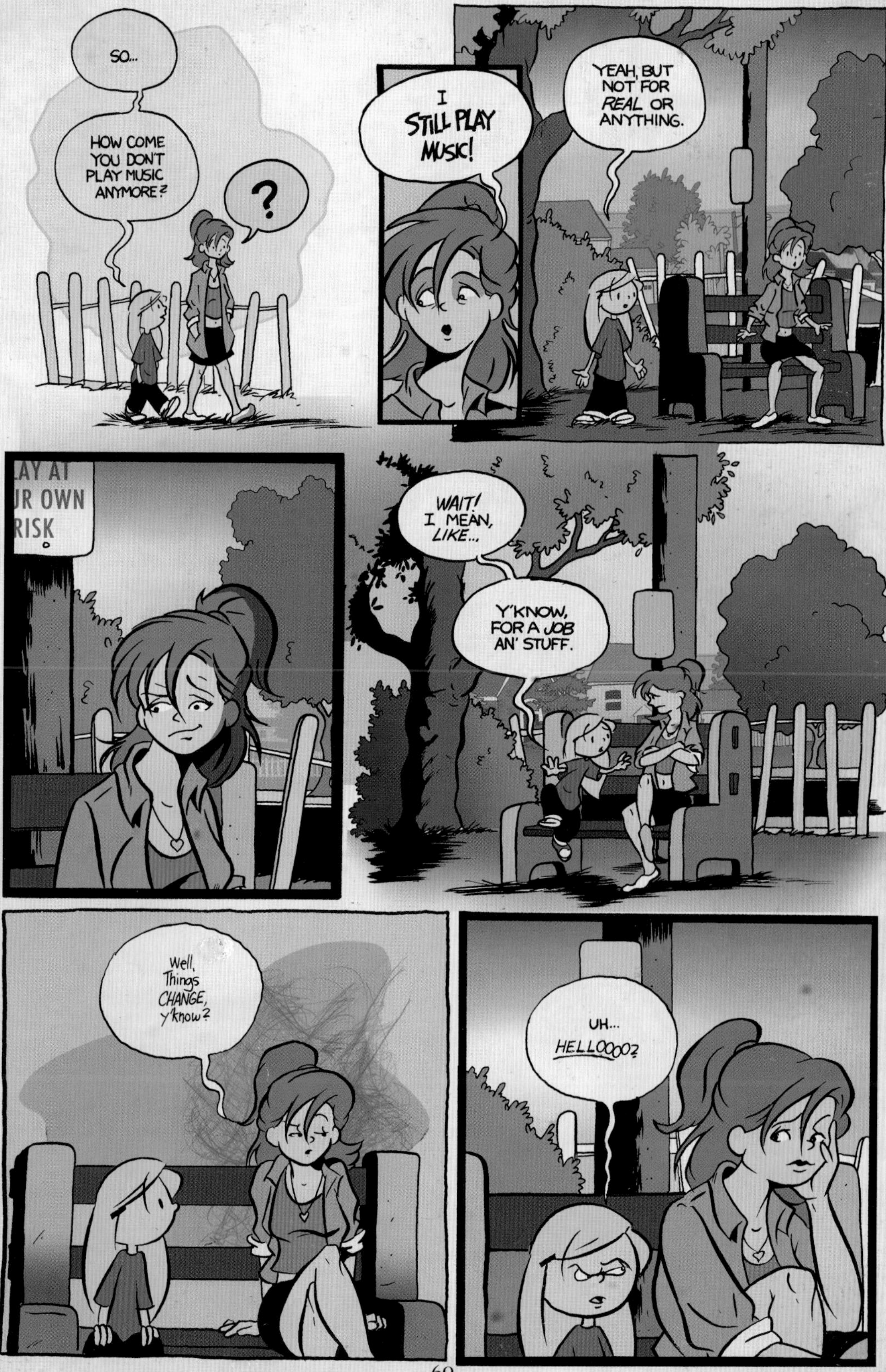
SO...
HOW COME YOU DON'T PLAY MUSIC ANYMORE?
?
I STILL PLAY MUSIC!
YEAH, BUT NOT FOR REAL OR ANYTHING.
LAY AT UR OWN RISK
WAIT! I MEAN, LIKE...
Y'KNOW, FOR A JOB AN' STUFF.
Well, Things CHANGE, y'know?
UH... HELLOOOO?

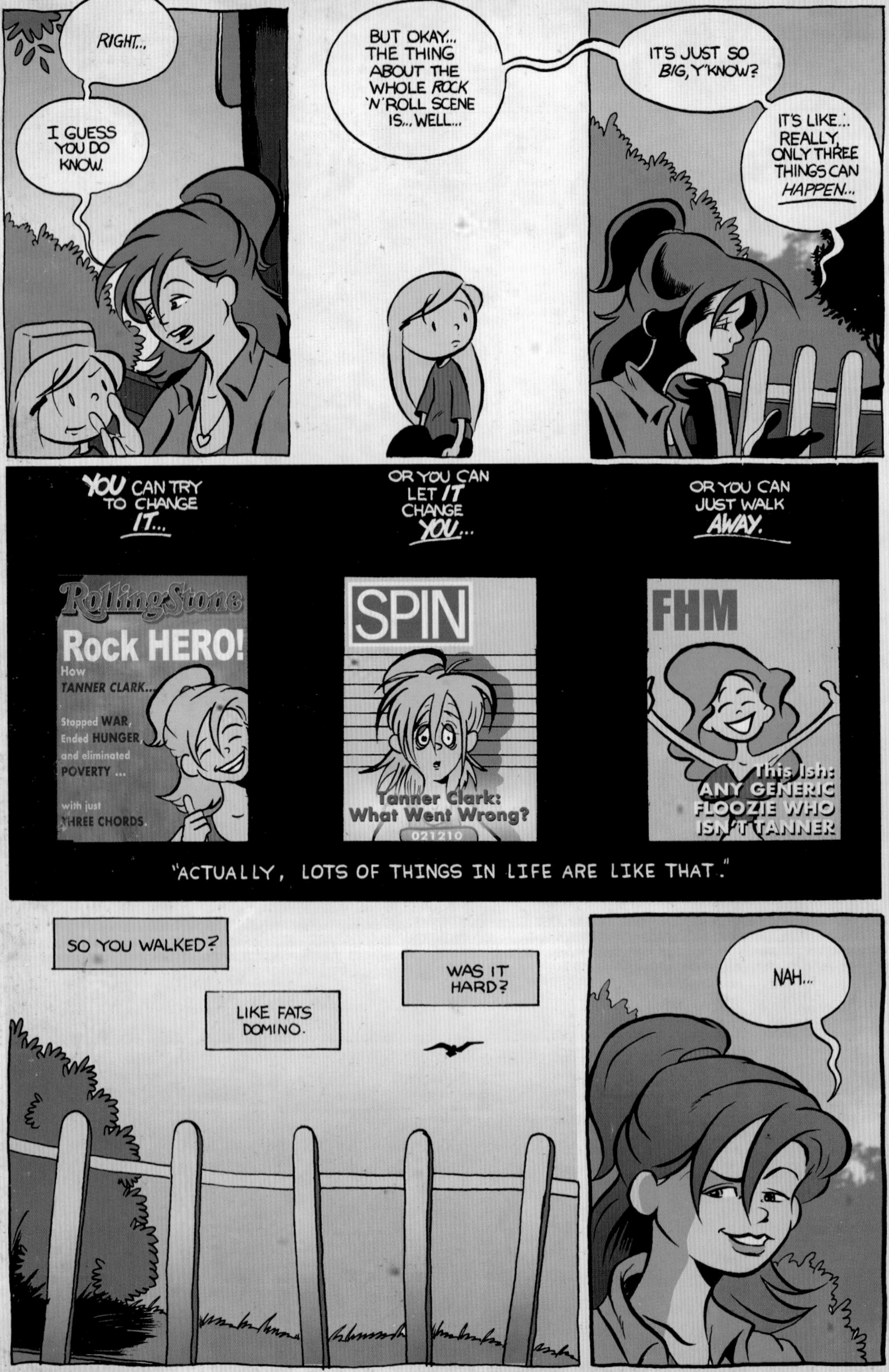
RIGHT...
I GUESS YOU DO KNOW.
BUT OKAY... THE THING ABOUT THE WHOLE ROCK 'N' ROLL SCENE IS... WELL...
IT'S JUST SO BIG, Y'KNOW?
IT'S LIKE... REALLY, ONLY THREE THINGS CAN HAPPEN...
YOU CAN TRY TO CHANGE IT...
OR YOU CAN LET IT CHANGE YOU...
OR YOU CAN JUST WALK AWAY.
RollingStone
Rock HERO!
How TANNER CLARK...
Stopped WAR, Ended HUNGER, and eliminated POVERTY ...
with just THREE CHORDS.
SPIN
Tanner Clark: What Went Wrong?
021210
FHM
This Ish: ANY GENERIC FLOOZIE WHO ISN'T TANNER
"ACTUALLY, LOTS OF THINGS IN LIFE ARE LIKE THAT."
SO YOU WALKED?
LIKE FATS DOMINO.
WAS IT HARD?
NAH...

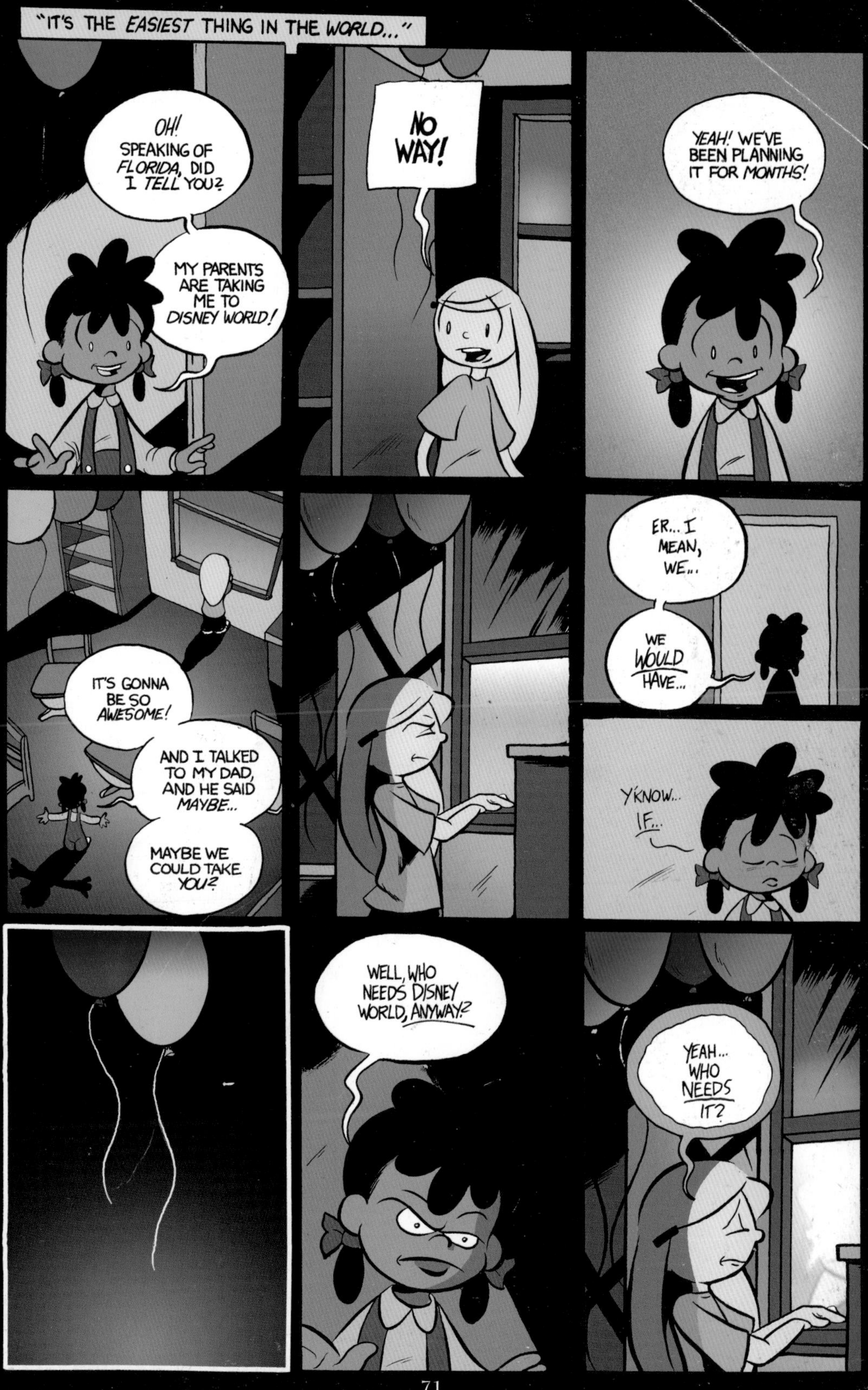
"IT'S THE EASIEST THING IN THE WORLD..."
OH! SPEAKING OF FLORIDA, DID I TELL YOU?
MY PARENTS ARE TAKING ME TO DISNEY WORLD!
NO WAY!
YEAH! WE'VE BEEN PLANNING IT FOR MONTHS!
IT'S GONNA BE SO AWESOME!
AND I TALKED TO MY DAD, AND HE SAID MAYBE...
MAYBE WE COULD TAKE YOU?
ER... I MEAN, WE...
WE WOULD HAVE...
Y'KNOW... IF...
WELL, WHO NEEDS DISNEY WORLD, ANYWAY?
YEAH... WHO NEEDS IT?

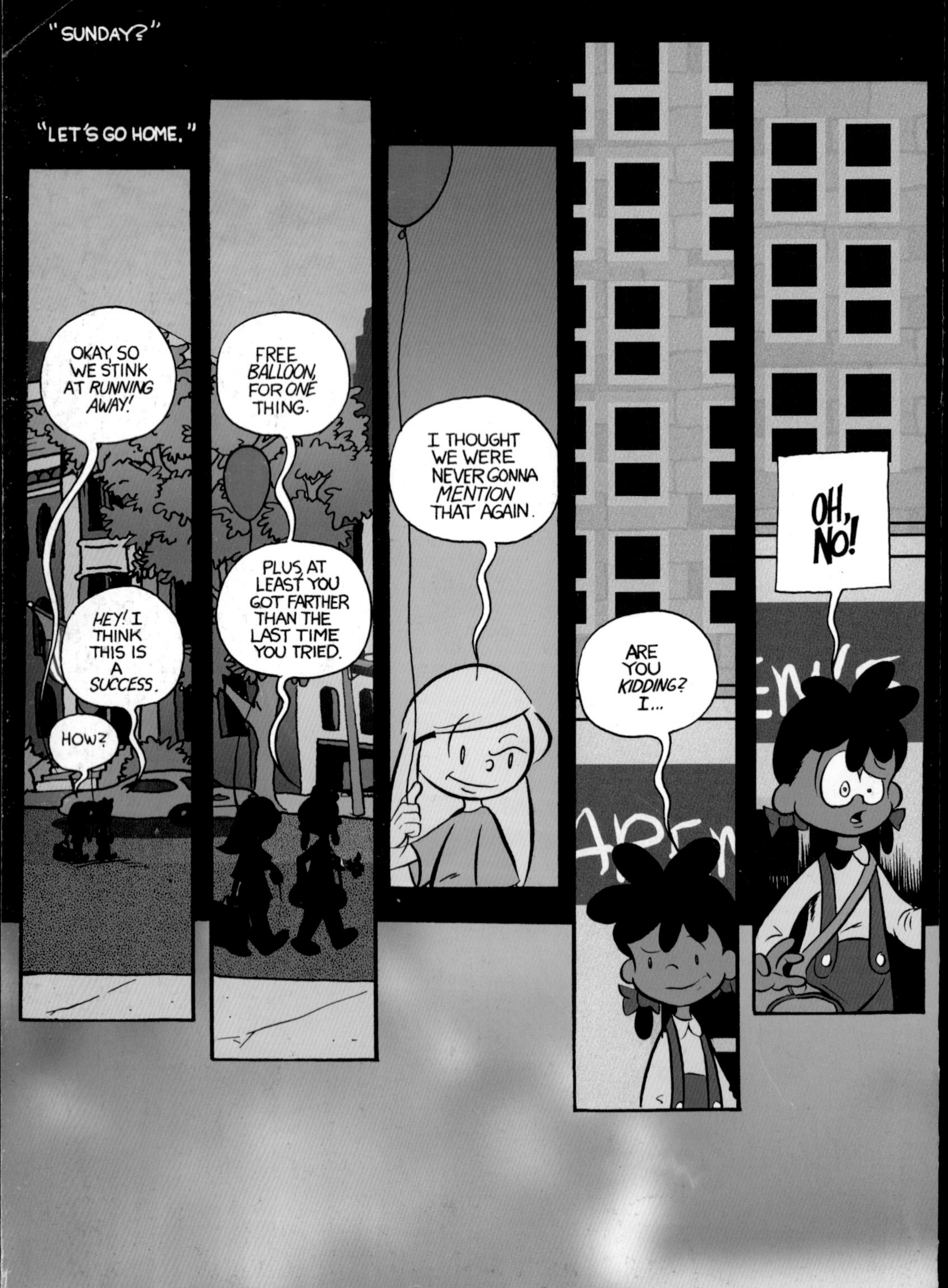

"SUNDAY?"
"LET'S GO HOME."
OKAY, SO WE STINK AT RUNNING AWAY!
HEY! I THINK THIS IS A SUCCESS.
HOW?
FREE BALLOON, FOR ONE THING.
PLUS, AT LEAST YOU GOT FARTHER THAN THE LAST TIME YOU TRIED.
I THOUGHT WE WERE NEVER GONNA MENTION THAT AGAIN.
ARE YOU KIDDING? I...
OH, NO!

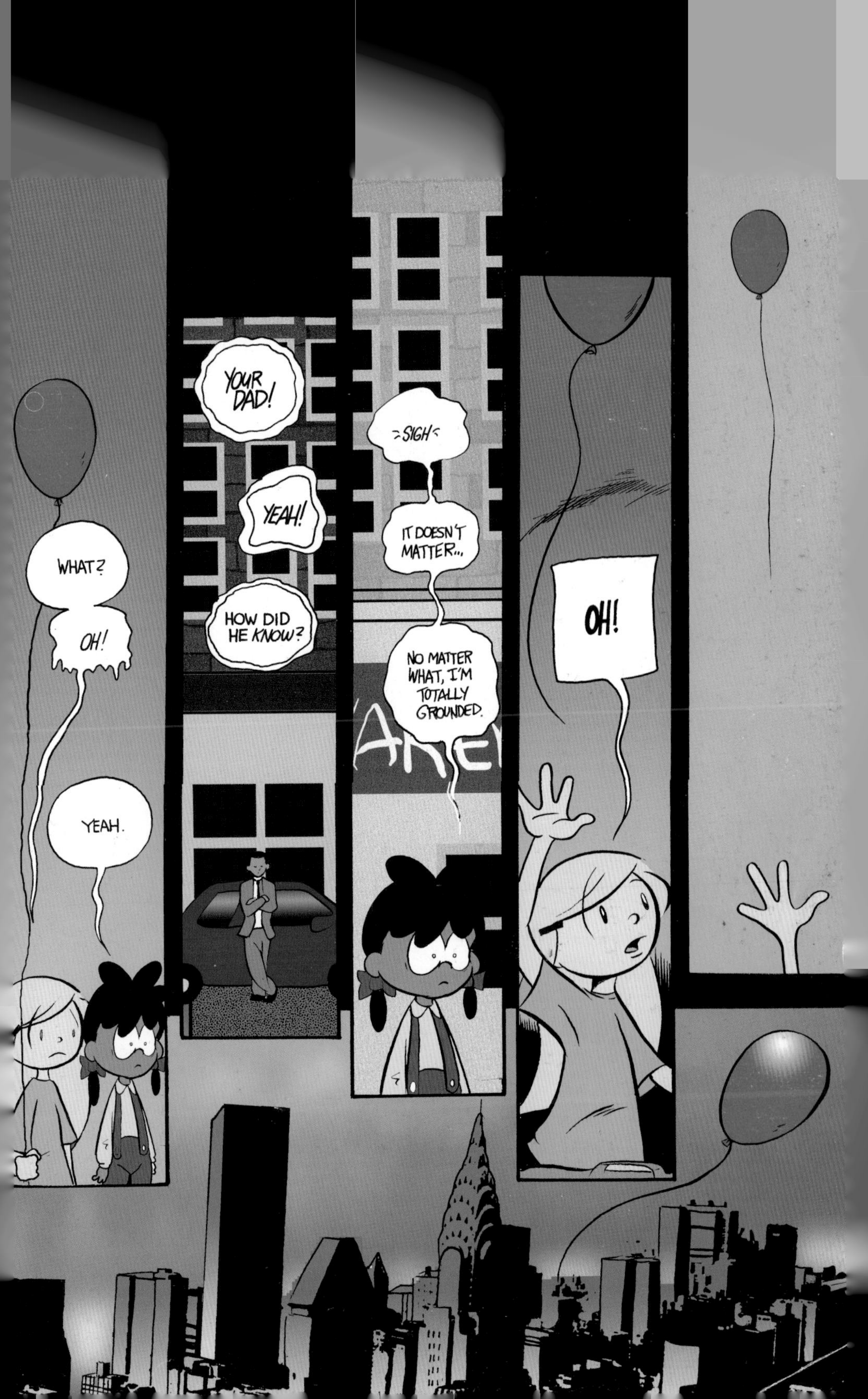
WHAT?
OH!
YEAH.
YOUR DAD!
YEAH!
HOW DID HE KNOW?
SIGH
IT DOESN'T MATTER...
NO MATTER WHAT, I'M TOTALLY GROUNDED.
OH!

HEY, RHONDA! WHAT *HAPPENED?*

WELL, WE WERE TALKING... YKNOW? JUST... *TALKING...*

AND THEN, BUG AND IGGY STARTED TO *ANNOY* REGGIE.

BY DOING *WHAT?*

EXISTING.

YEAH, THAT *IS* ANNOYING.

SO REGGIE CREASED THEIR BEANS WITH A *JUJYFRUIT.*

AND THEN... THERE WAS... THE *CHAOS...*

ALWAYS...

ALWAYS THE *CHAOS.*

BUT RHONDA, IT DOESN'T *HAVE* TO BE... SEE, YOU WERE *RIGHT...*

I'VE BEEN THINKING... AND, YKNOW, MAYBE THINGS CAN BE *BETTER.*

AND BESIDES, IT'S NOT LIKE THIS IS SOMETHING WE CAN RUN AWAY FROM.

SO WHADAYA SAY, *HUH?* LET'S GO *GET* 'EM!

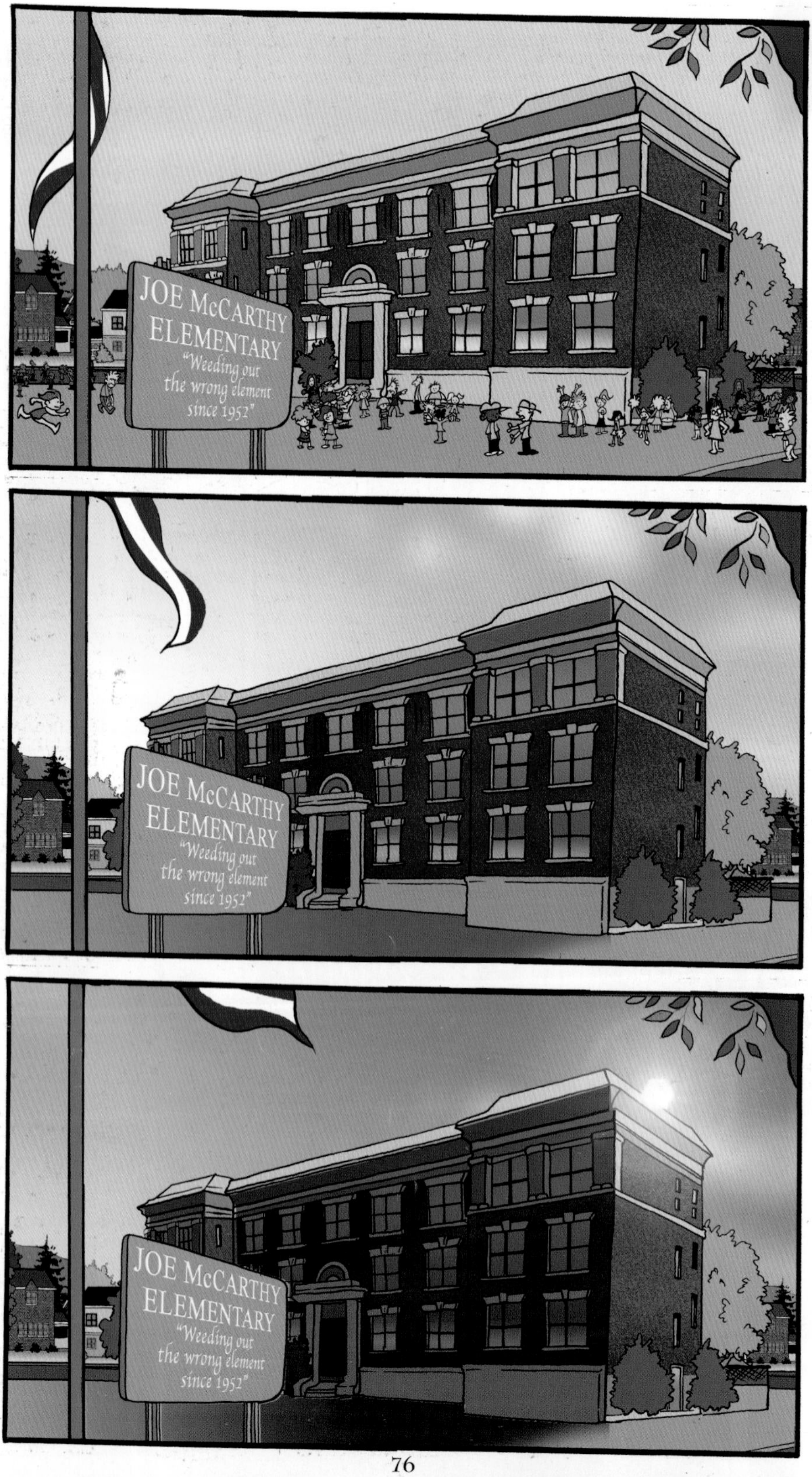
JOE McCARTHY ELEMENTARY
"Weeding out the wrong element since 1952"
JOE McCARTHY ELEMENTARY
"Weeding out the wrong element since 1952"
JOE McCARTHY ELEMENTARY
"Weeding out the wrong element since 1952"

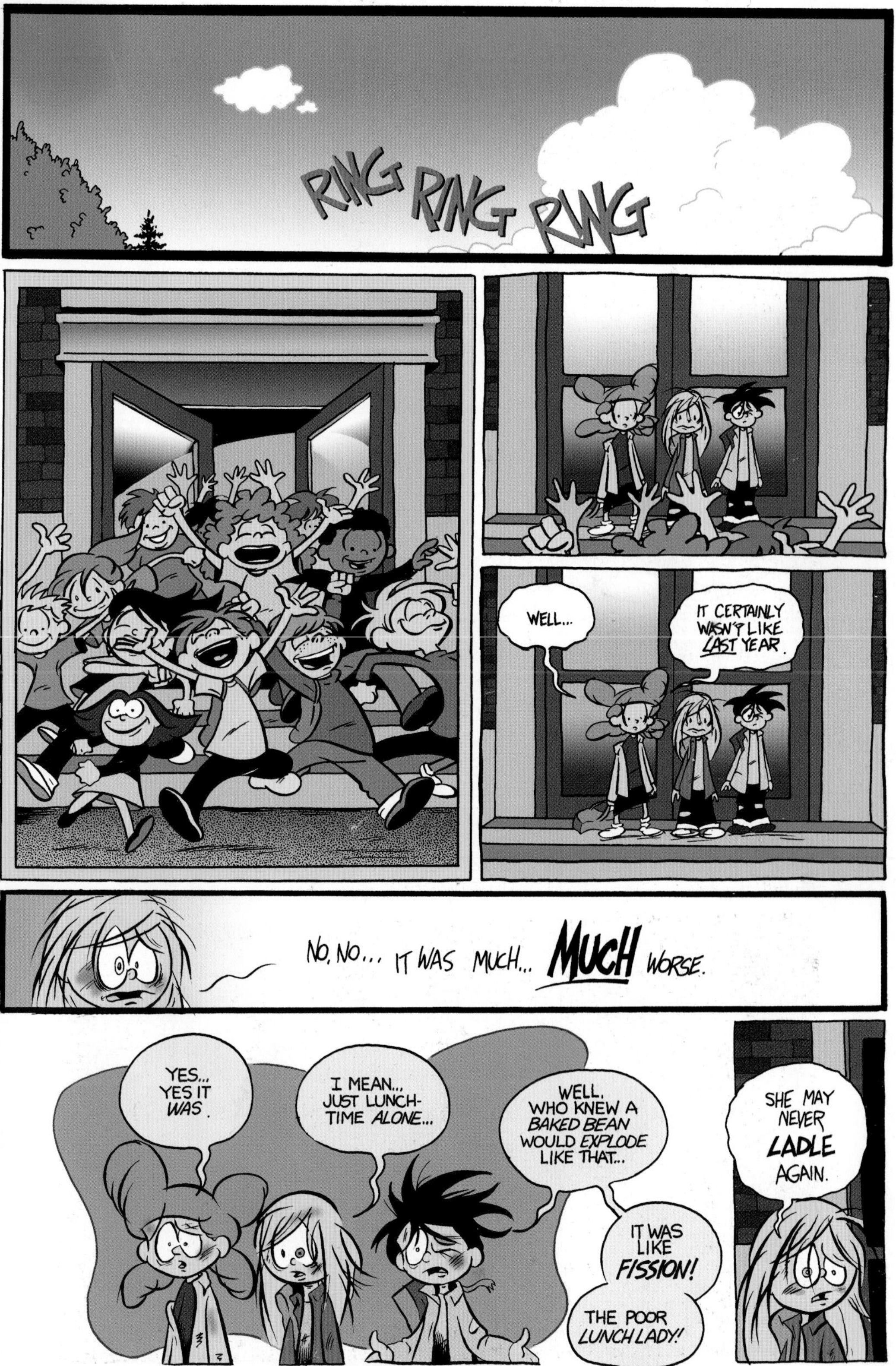
RING RING RING
WELL...
IT CERTAINLY WASN'T LIKE LAST YEAR.
NO, NO... IT WAS MUCH... MUCH WORSE.
YES... YES IT WAS.
I MEAN... JUST LUNCH-TIME ALONE...
WELL, WHO KNEW A BAKED BEAN WOULD EXPLODE LIKE THAT...
IT WAS LIKE FISSION!
THE POOR LUNCH LADY!
SHE MAY NEVER LADLE AGAIN.

78

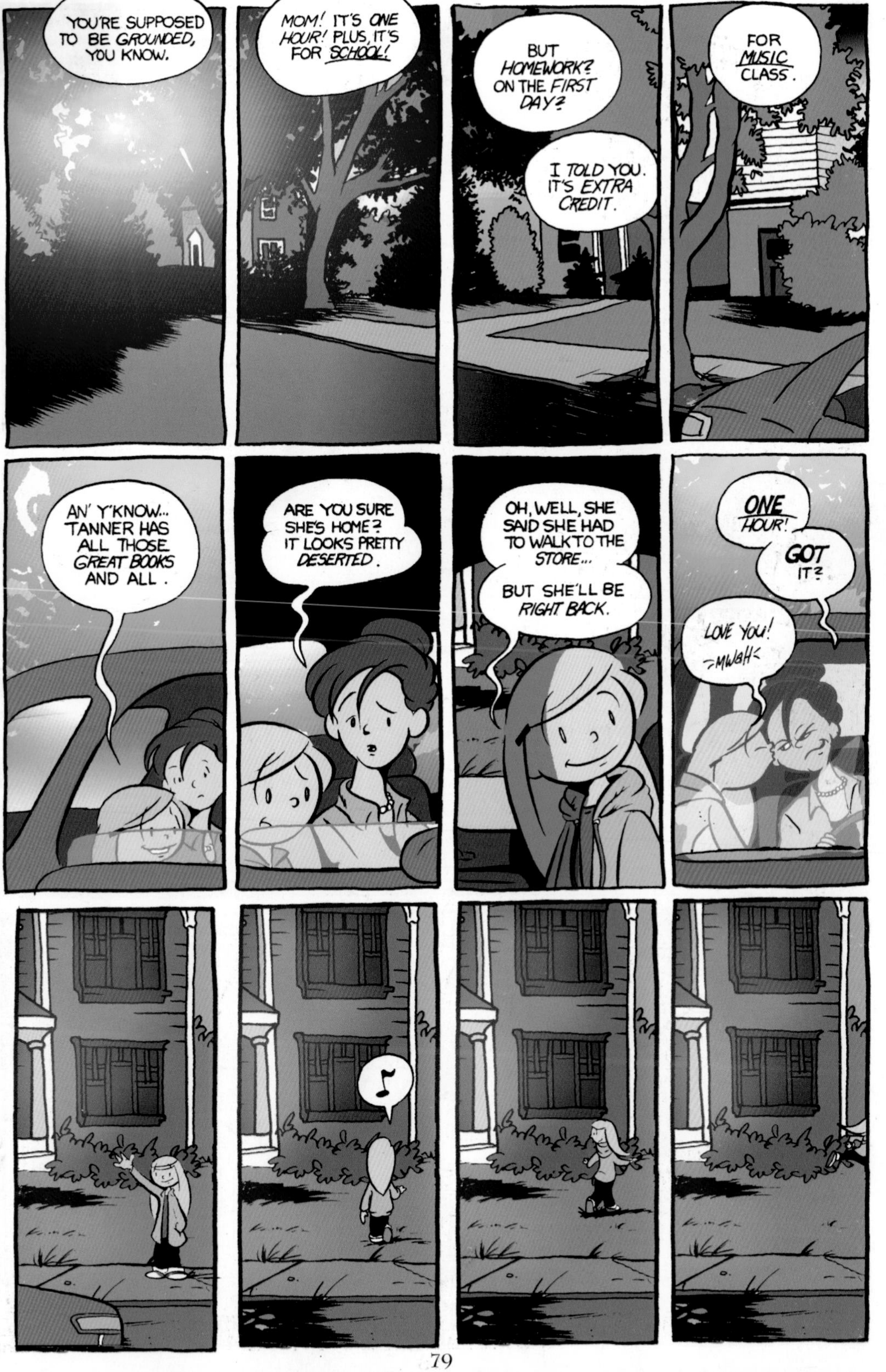
YOU'RE SUPPOSED TO BE GROUNDED, YOU KNOW.
MOM! IT'S ONE HOUR! PLUS, IT'S FOR SCHOOL!
BUT HOMEWORK? ON THE FIRST DAY?
I TOLD YOU. IT'S EXTRA CREDIT.
FOR MUSIC CLASS.
AN' Y'KNOW... TANNER HAS ALL THOSE GREAT BOOKS AND ALL.
ARE YOU SURE SHE'S HOME? IT LOOKS PRETTY DESERTED.
OH, WELL, SHE SAID SHE HAD TO WALK TO THE STORE...
BUT SHE'LL BE RIGHT BACK.
ONE HOUR!
GOT IT?
LOVE YOU!
=MWAH=

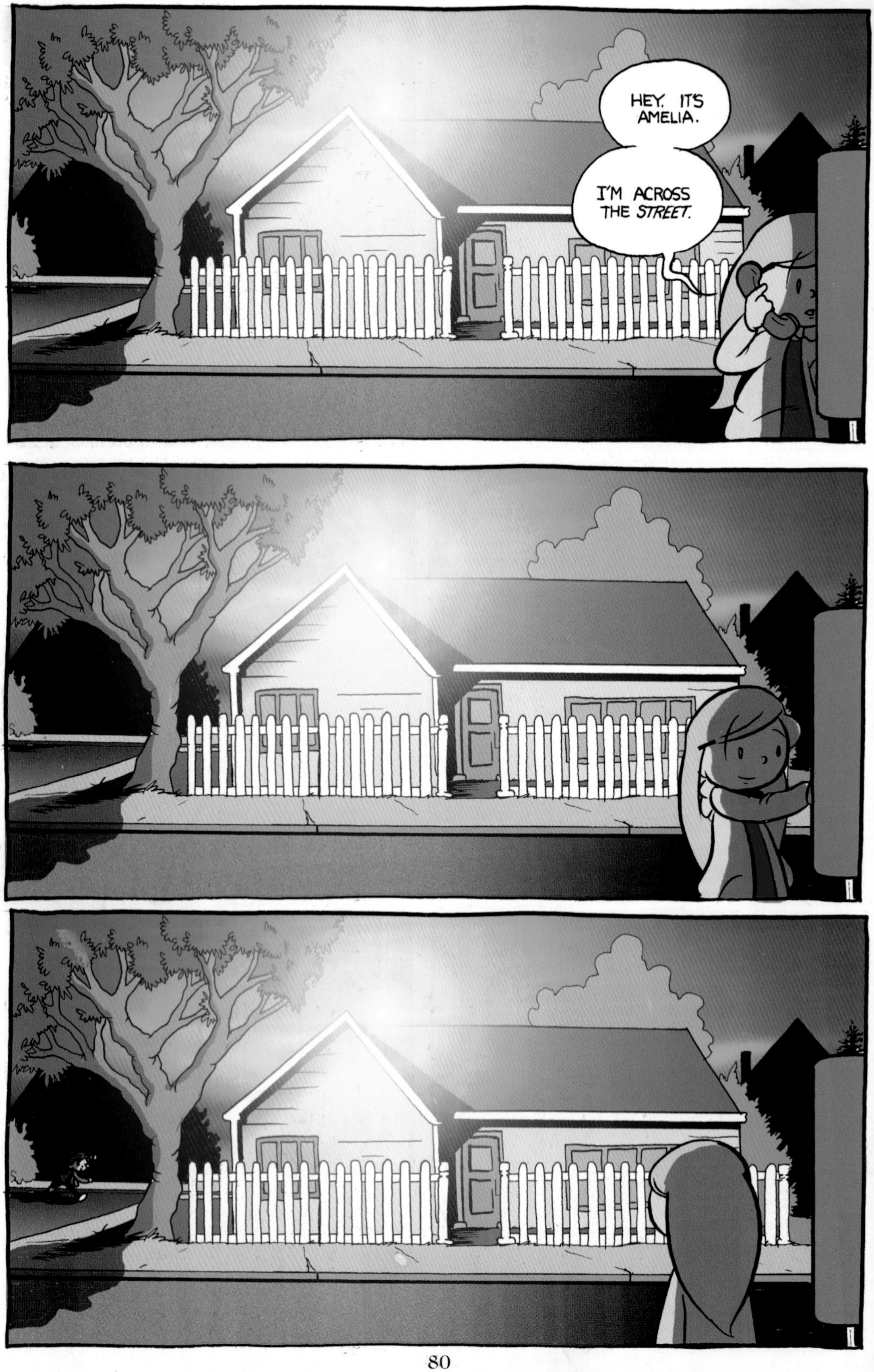
HEY. IT'S AMELIA.
I'M ACROSS THE *STREET*.

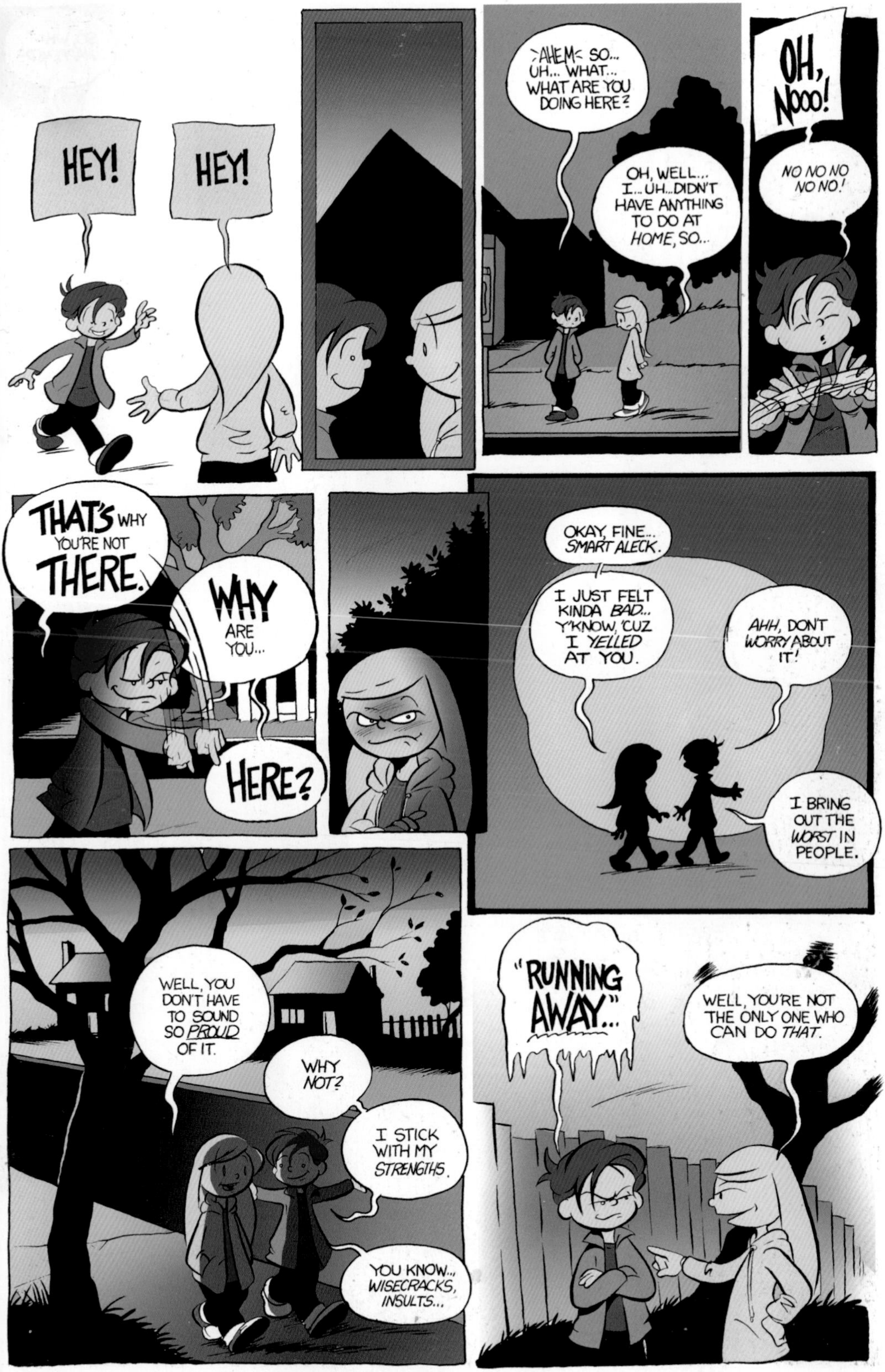
HEY!
HEY!
>AHEM< SO... UH... WHAT... WHAT ARE YOU DOING HERE?
OH, WELL... I... UH... DIDN'T HAVE ANYTHING TO DO AT HOME, SO...
OH, NOOO!
NO NO NO NO NO!
THAT'S WHY YOU'RE NOT THERE.
WHY ARE YOU...
HERE?
OKAY, FINE... SMART ALECK.
I JUST FELT KINDA BAD... Y'KNOW, 'CUZ I YELLED AT YOU.
AHH, DON'T WORRY ABOUT IT!
I BRING OUT THE WORST IN PEOPLE.
WELL, YOU DON'T HAVE TO SOUND SO PROUD OF IT.
WHY NOT?
I STICK WITH MY STRENGTHS.
YOU KNOW... WISECRACKS, INSULTS...
"RUNNING AWAY"...
WELL, YOU'RE NOT THE ONLY ONE WHO CAN DO THAT.

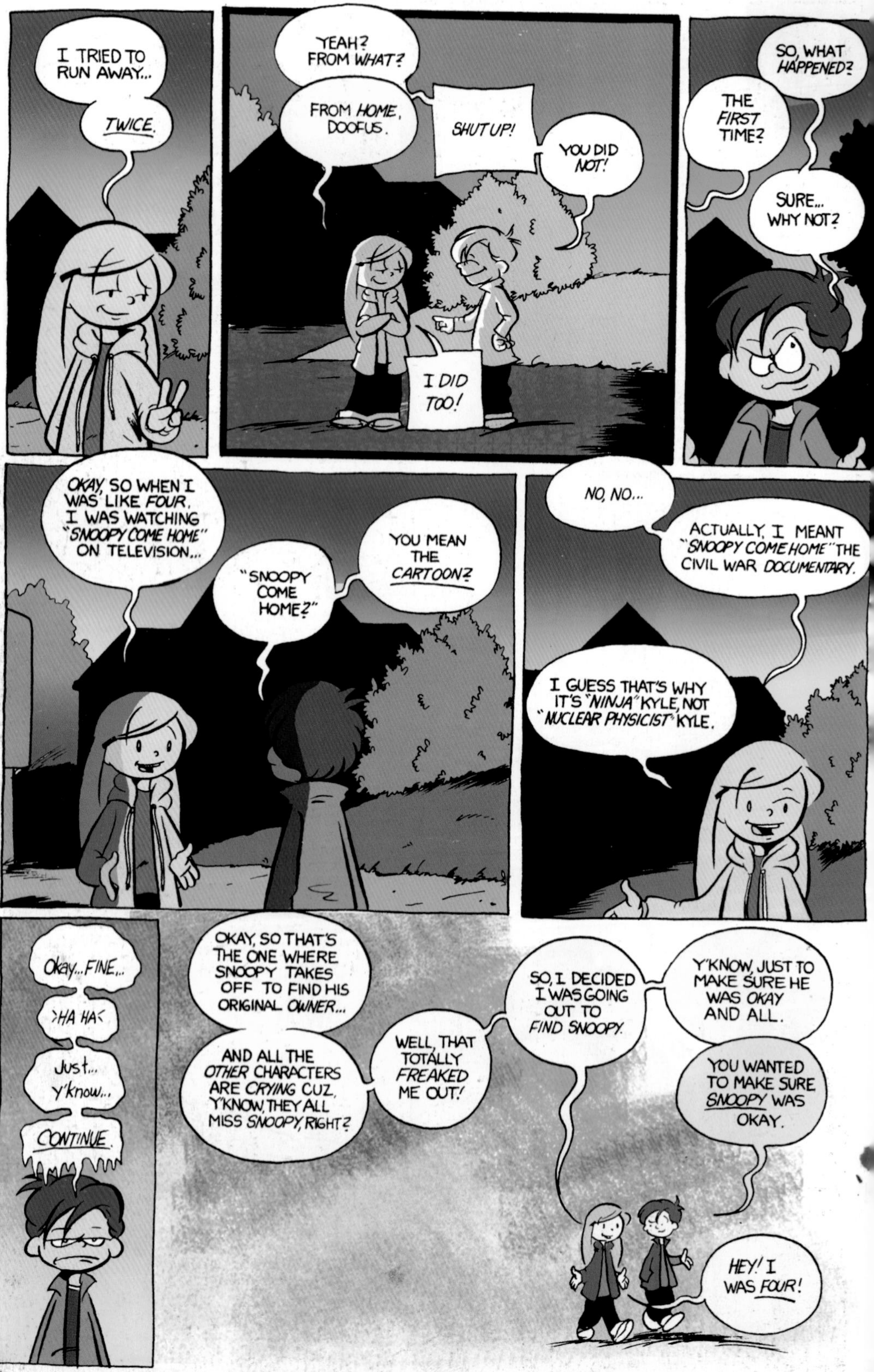
I TRIED TO RUN AWAY...
TWICE.
YEAH? FROM WHAT?
FROM HOME, DOOFUS.
SHUT UP!
YOU DID NOT!
I DID TOO!
SO, WHAT HAPPENED?
THE FIRST TIME?
SURE... WHY NOT?
OKAY, SO WHEN I WAS LIKE FOUR, I WAS WATCHING "SNOOPY COME HOME" ON TELEVISION...
"SNOOPY COME HOME?"
YOU MEAN THE CARTOON?
NO, NO...
ACTUALLY, I MEANT "SNOOPY COME HOME" THE CIVIL WAR DOCUMENTARY.
I GUESS THAT'S WHY IT'S "NINJA" KYLE, NOT "NUCLEAR PHYSICIST" KYLE.
Okay... FINE...
>HA HA<
Just... y'know...
CONTINUE.
OKAY, SO THAT'S THE ONE WHERE SNOOPY TAKES OFF TO FIND HIS ORIGINAL OWNER...
AND ALL THE OTHER CHARACTERS ARE CRYING CUZ, Y'KNOW, THEY ALL MISS SNOOPY, RIGHT?
WELL, THAT TOTALLY FREAKED ME OUT!
SO, I DECIDED I WAS GOING OUT TO FIND SNOOPY.
Y'KNOW, JUST TO MAKE SURE HE WAS OKAY AND ALL.
YOU WANTED TO MAKE SURE SNOOPY WAS OKAY.
HEY! I WAS FOUR!

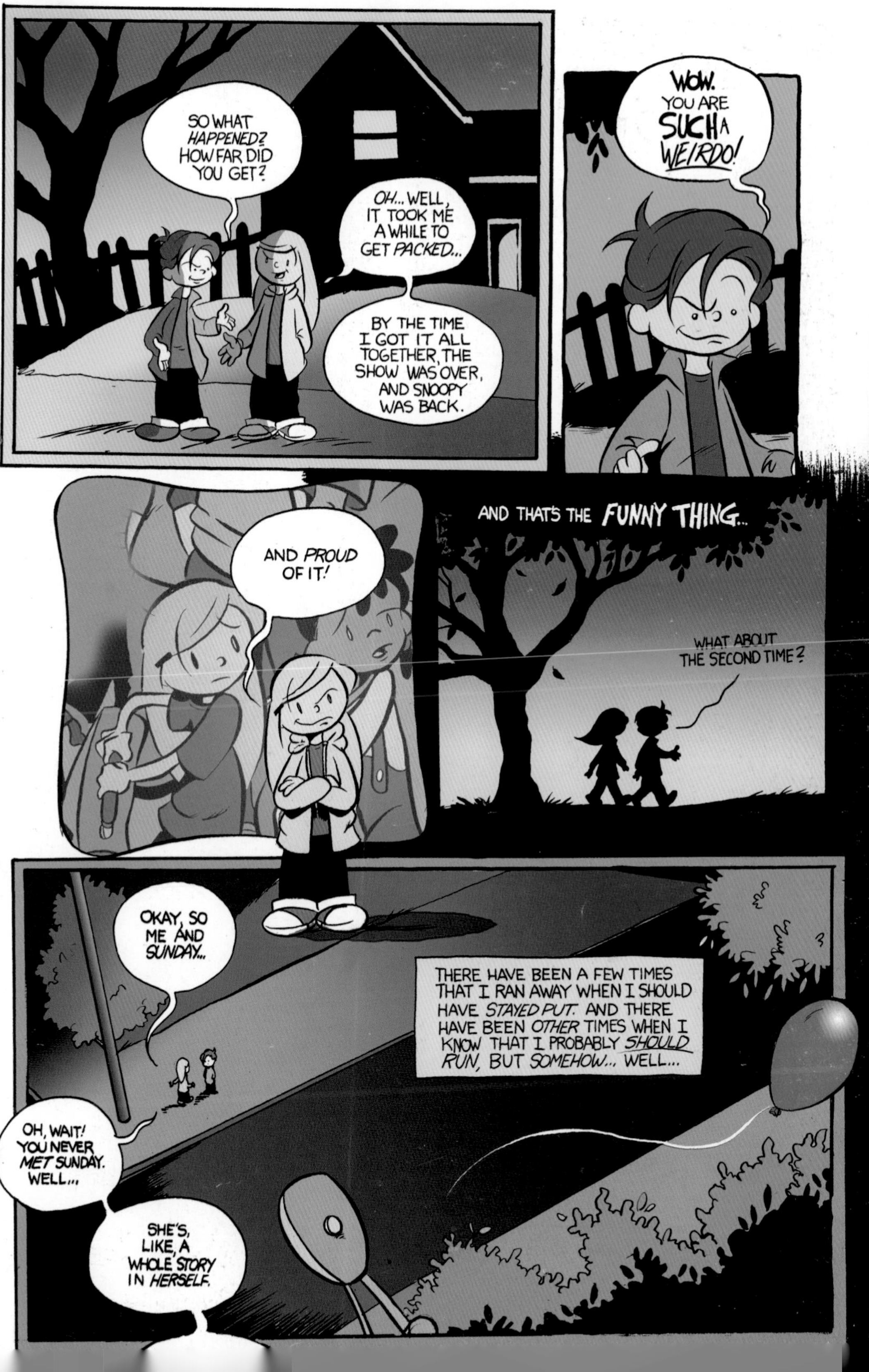
SO WHAT HAPPENED? HOW FAR DID YOU GET?
OH... WELL, IT TOOK ME A WHILE TO GET PACKED...
BY THE TIME I GOT IT ALL TOGETHER, THE SHOW WAS OVER, AND SNOOPY WAS BACK.
WOW. YOU ARE SUCH A WEIRDO!
AND PROUD OF IT!
AND THAT'S THE FUNNY THING...
WHAT ABOUT THE SECOND TIME?
OKAY, SO ME AND SUNDAY...
THERE HAVE BEEN A FEW TIMES THAT I RAN AWAY WHEN I SHOULD HAVE STAYED PUT. AND THERE HAVE BEEN OTHER TIMES WHEN I KNOW THAT I PROBABLY SHOULD RUN, BUT SOMEHOW... WELL...
OH, WAIT! YOU NEVER MET SUNDAY. WELL...
SHE'S, LIKE, A WHOLE STORY IN HERSELF.

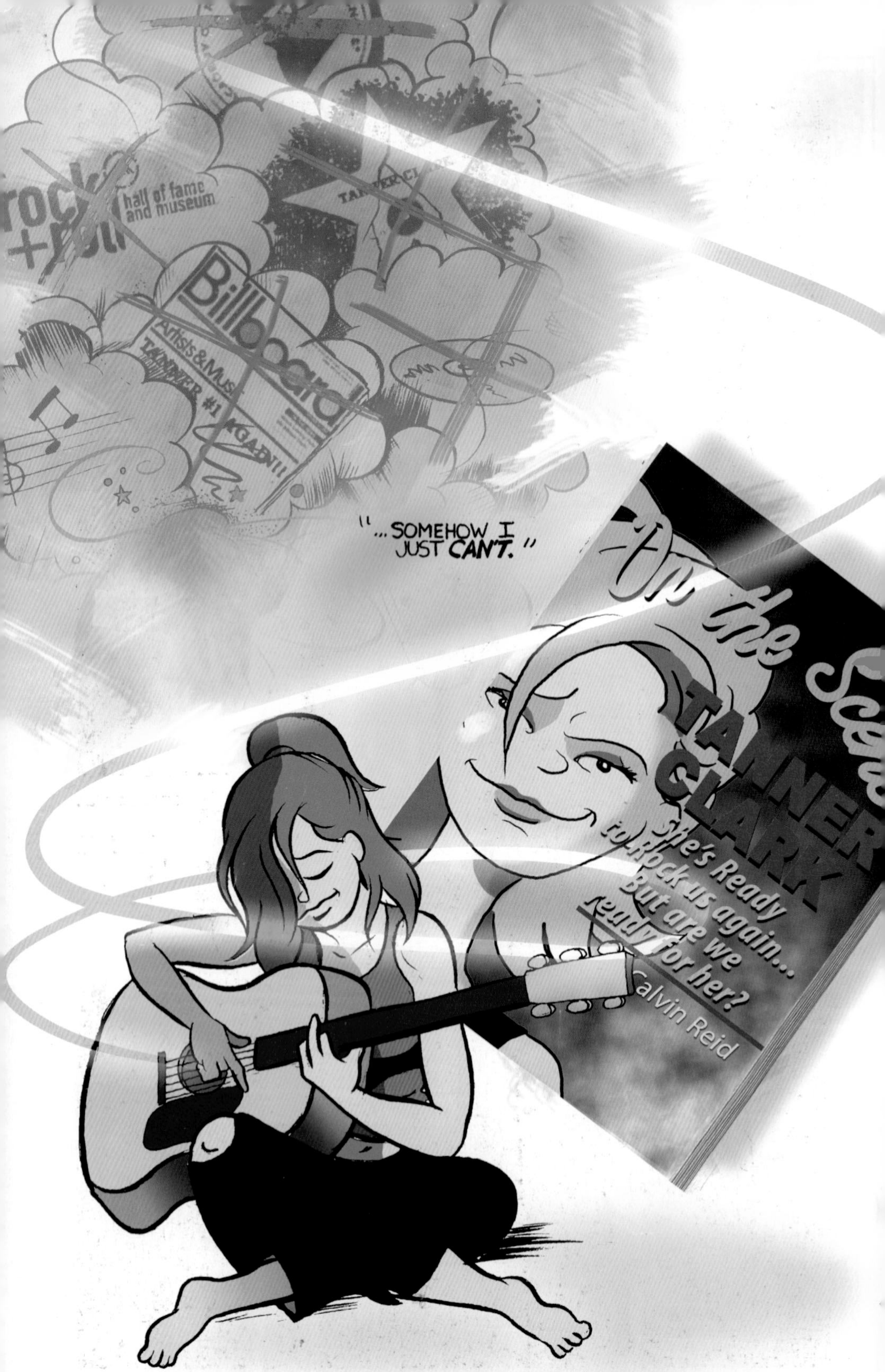
rock + roll hall of fame and museum
Billboard
Artists & Music
TANNER #1 AGAIN!!
"...SOMEHOW I JUST CAN'T."
On the Scene
TANNER CLARK
She's Ready to Rock us again... But are we ready for her?
Calvin Reid

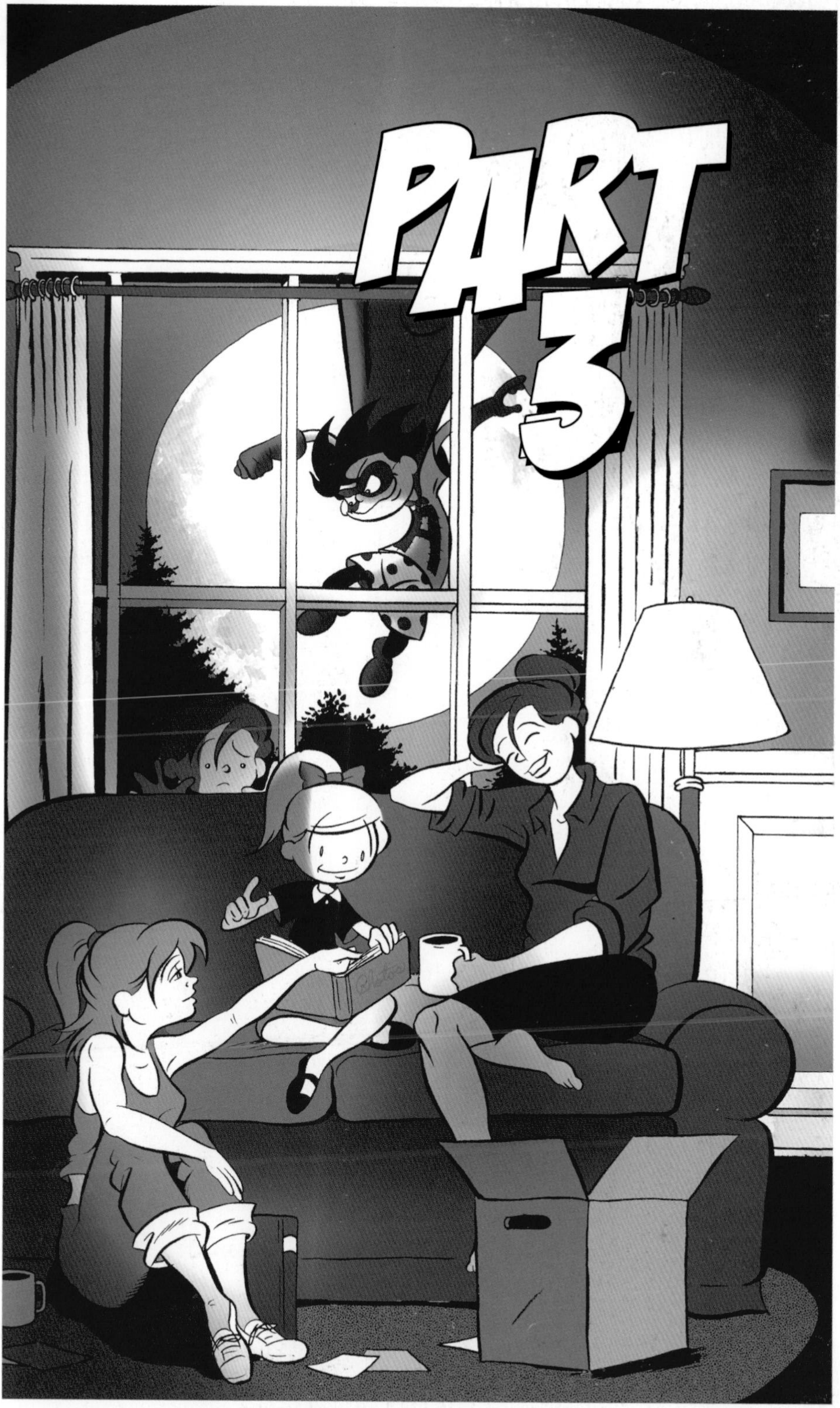
PART 3

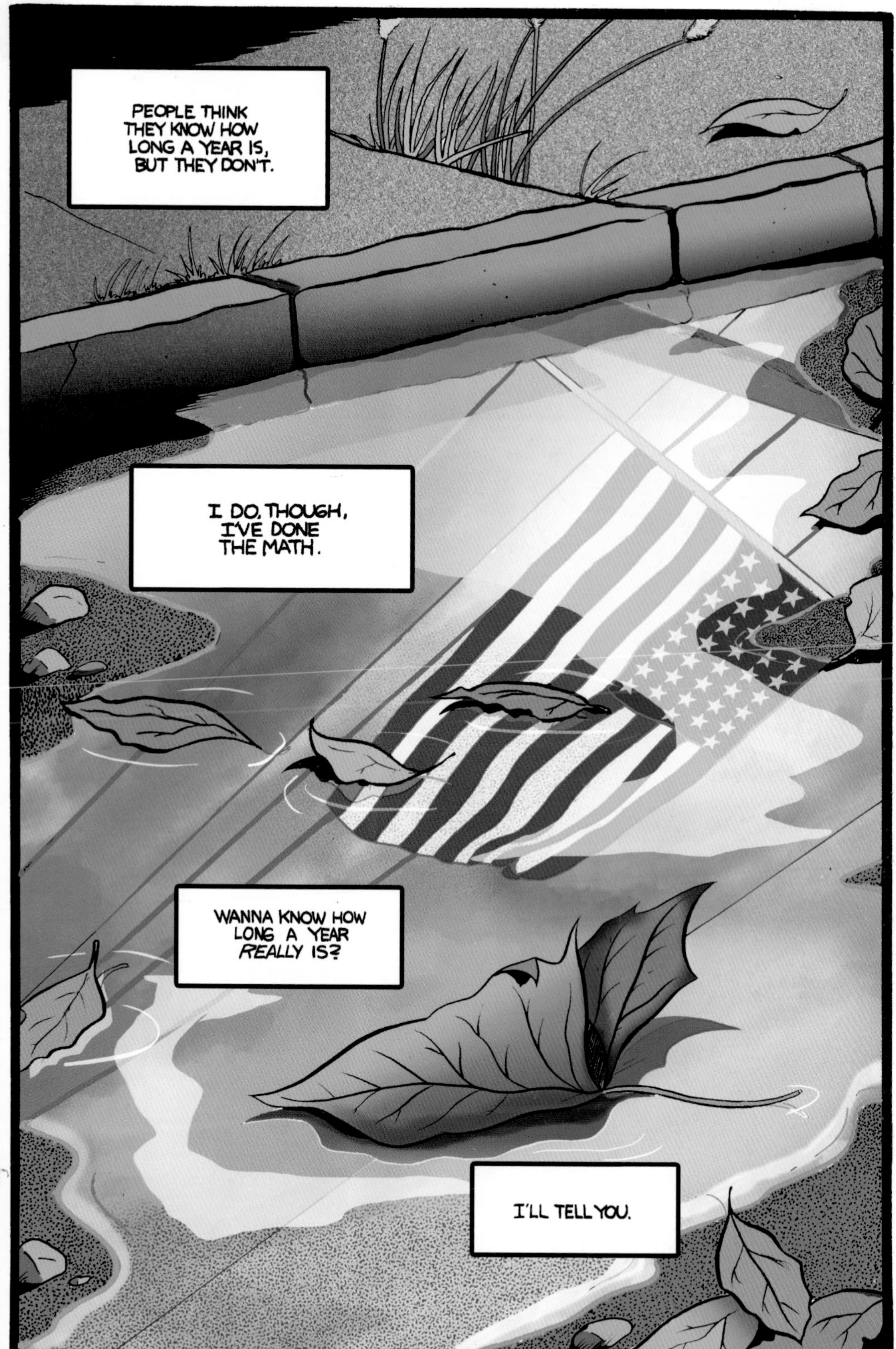
PEOPLE THINK THEY KNOW HOW LONG A YEAR IS, BUT THEY DON'T.
I DO, THOUGH. I'VE DONE THE MATH.
WANNA KNOW HOW LONG A YEAR *REALLY* IS?
I'LL TELL YOU.

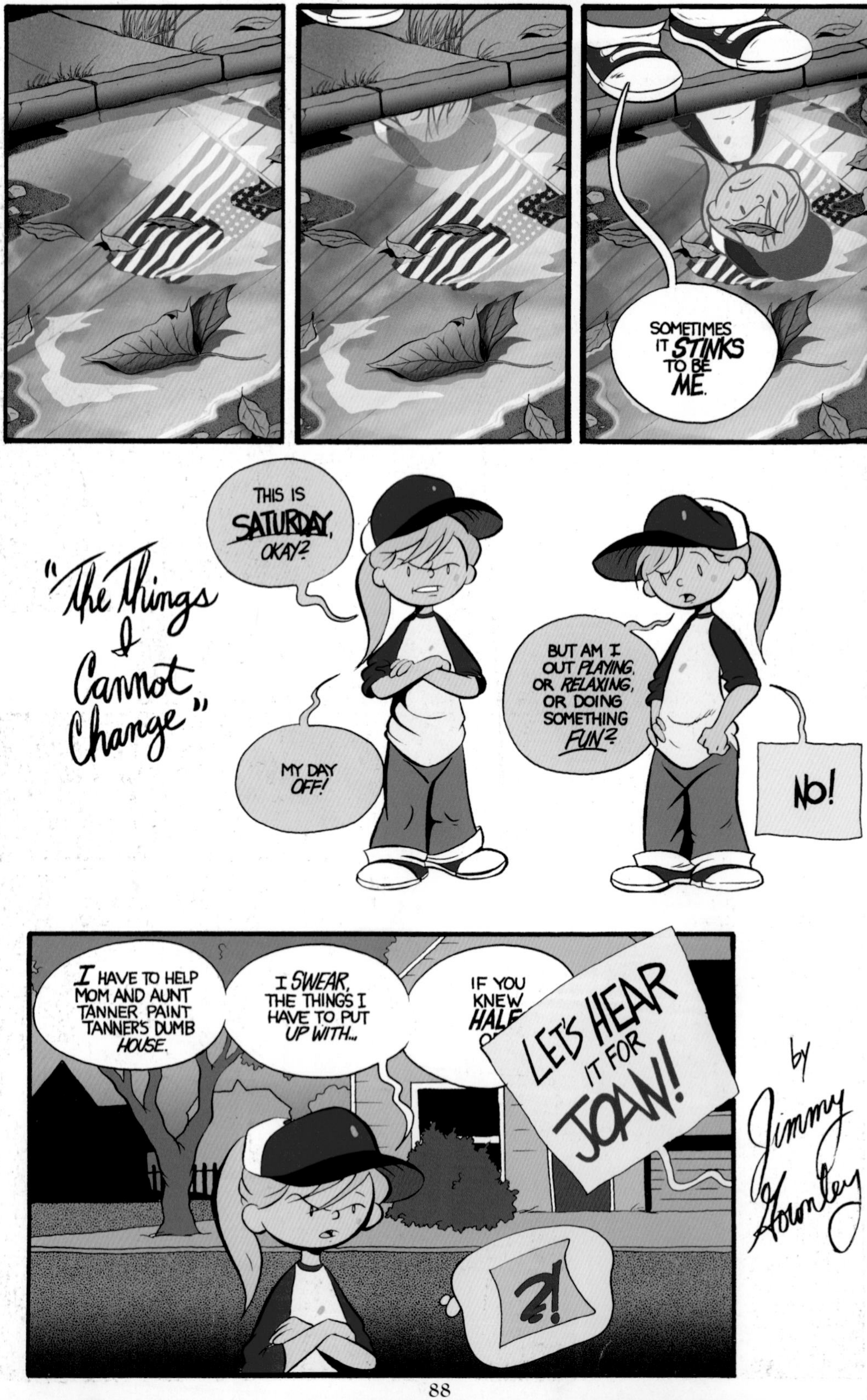
SOMETIMES IT STINKS TO BE ME.
"The Things I Cannot Change"
THIS IS SATURDAY, OKAY?
MY DAY OFF!
BUT AM I OUT PLAYING, OR RELAXING, OR DOING SOMETHING FUN?
NO!
I HAVE TO HELP MOM AND AUNT TANNER PAINT TANNER'S DUMB HOUSE.
I SWEAR, THE THINGS I HAVE TO PUT UP WITH...
IF YOU KNEW HALF
LET'S HEAR IT FOR JOAN!
?!
by Jimmy Gownley

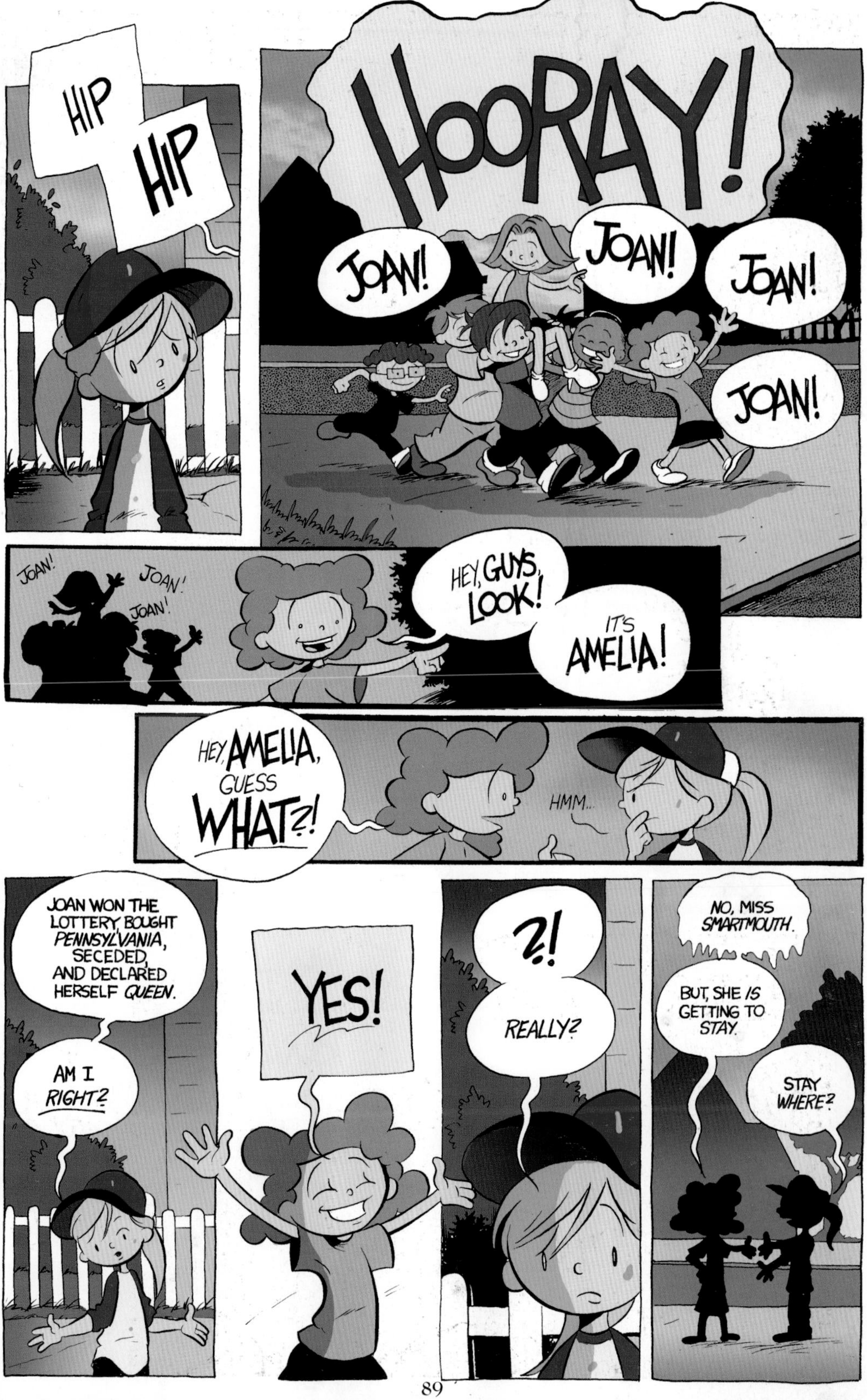
HIP
HIP
HOORAY!
JOAN!
JOAN!
JOAN!
JOAN!
JOAN!
JOAN!
JOAN!
HEY, GUYS, LOOK!
IT'S AMELIA!
HEY, AMELIA, GUESS WHAT?!
HMM...
JOAN WON THE LOTTERY, BOUGHT PENNSYLVANIA, SECEDED, AND DECLARED HERSELF QUEEN.
AM I RIGHT?
YES!
?!
REALLY?
NO, MISS SMARTMOUTH.
BUT, SHE IS GETTING TO STAY.
STAY WHERE?

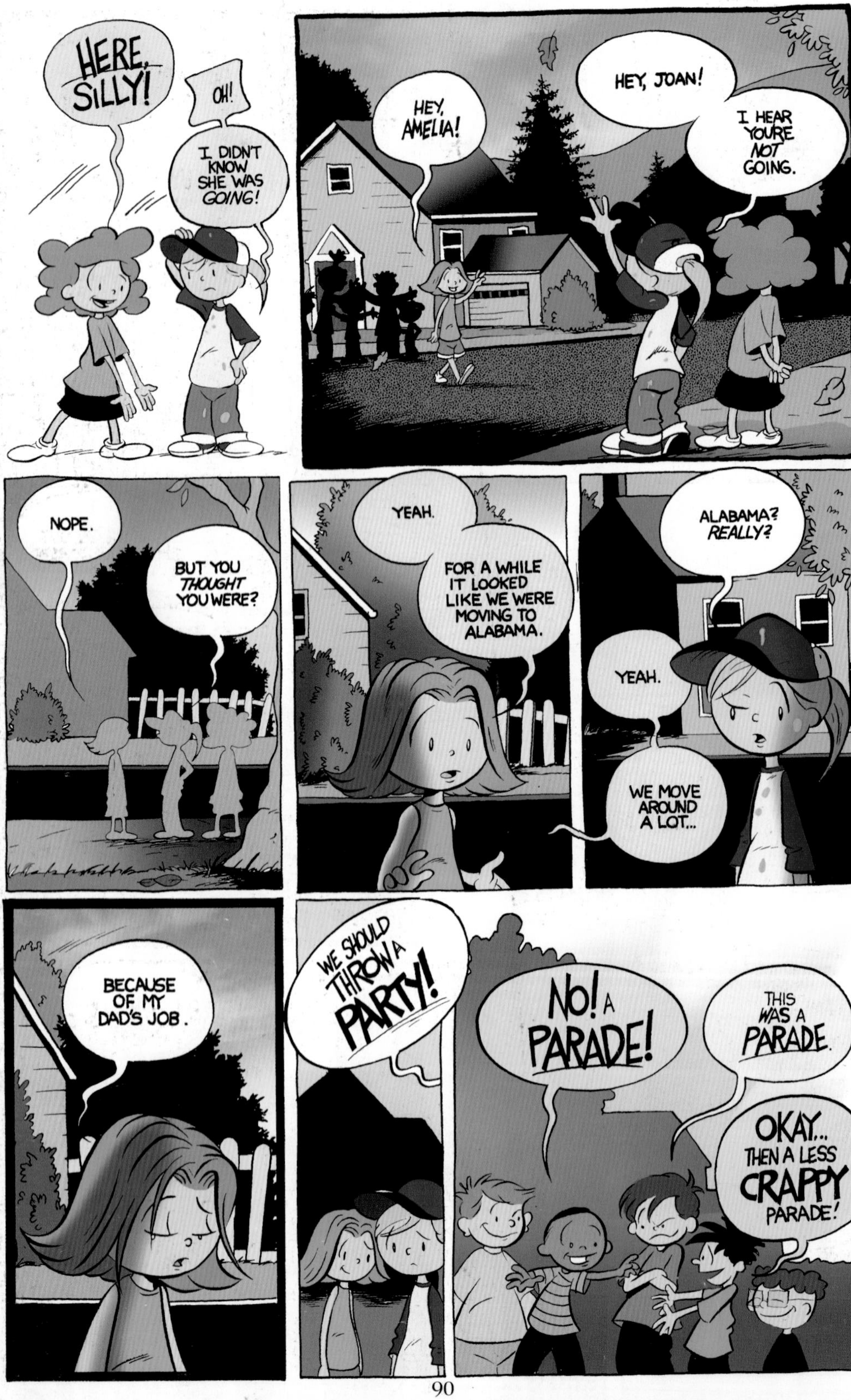
HERE, SILLY!
OH!
I DIDN'T KNOW SHE WAS GOING!
HEY, AMELIA!
HEY, JOAN!
I HEAR YOU'RE NOT GOING.
NOPE.
BUT YOU THOUGHT YOU WERE?
YEAH.
FOR A WHILE IT LOOKED LIKE WE WERE MOVING TO ALABAMA.
ALABAMA? REALLY?
YEAH.
WE MOVE AROUND A LOT...
BECAUSE OF MY DAD'S JOB.
WE SHOULD THROW A PARTY!
NO! A PARADE!
THIS WAS A PARADE.
OKAY... THEN A LESS CRAPPY PARADE!

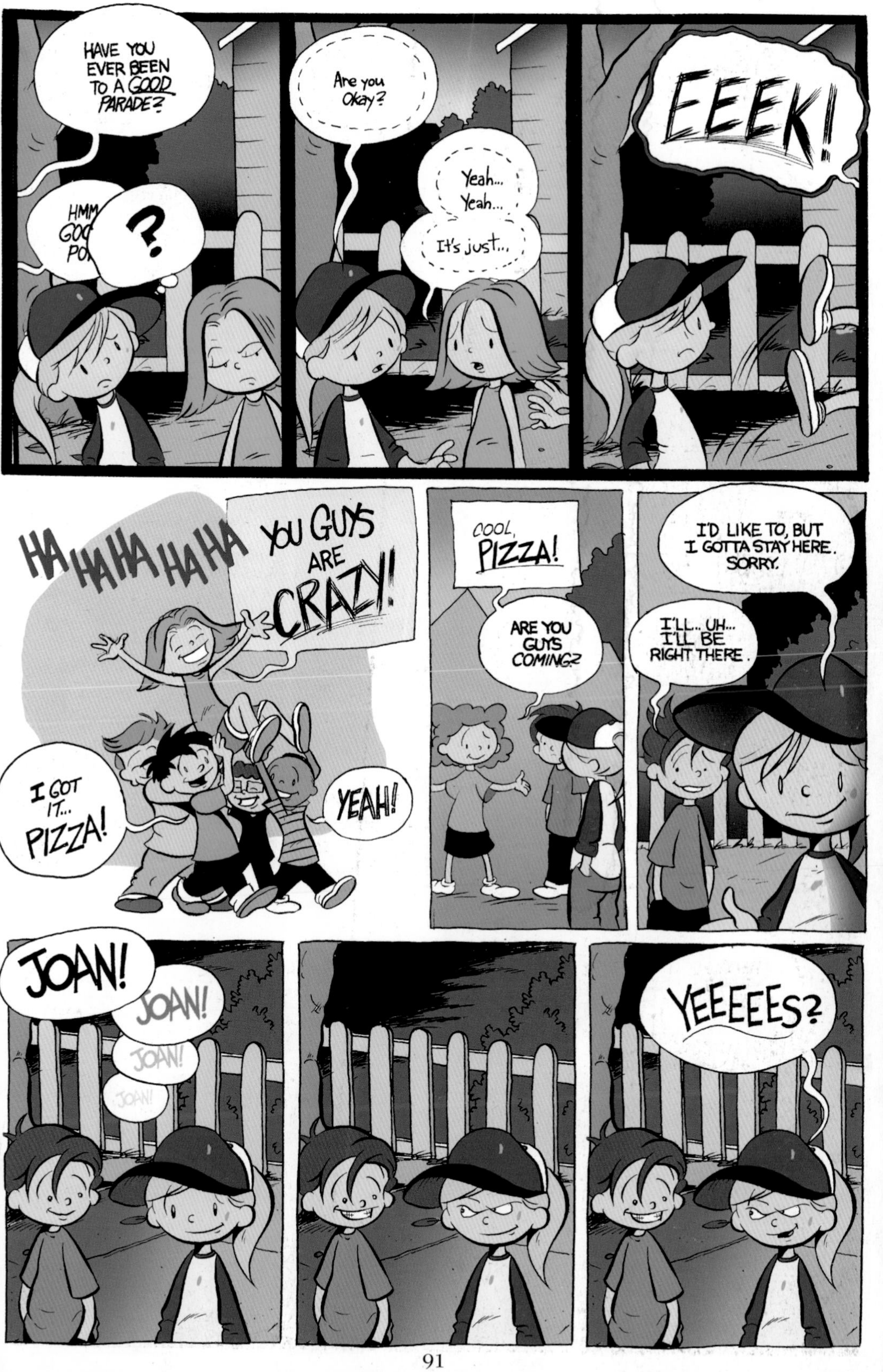
HAVE YOU EVER BEEN TO A GOOD PARADE?
?
Are you Okay?
Yeah... Yeah...
It's just...
EEEK!
HA HAHA HAHA
YOU GUYS ARE CRAZY!
I GOT IT... PIZZA!
YEAH!
COOL, PIZZA!
ARE YOU GUYS COMING?
I'D LIKE TO, BUT I GOTTA STAY HERE. SORRY.
I'LL... UH... I'LL BE RIGHT THERE.
JOAN!
JOAN!
JOAN!
JOAN!
YEEEEES?

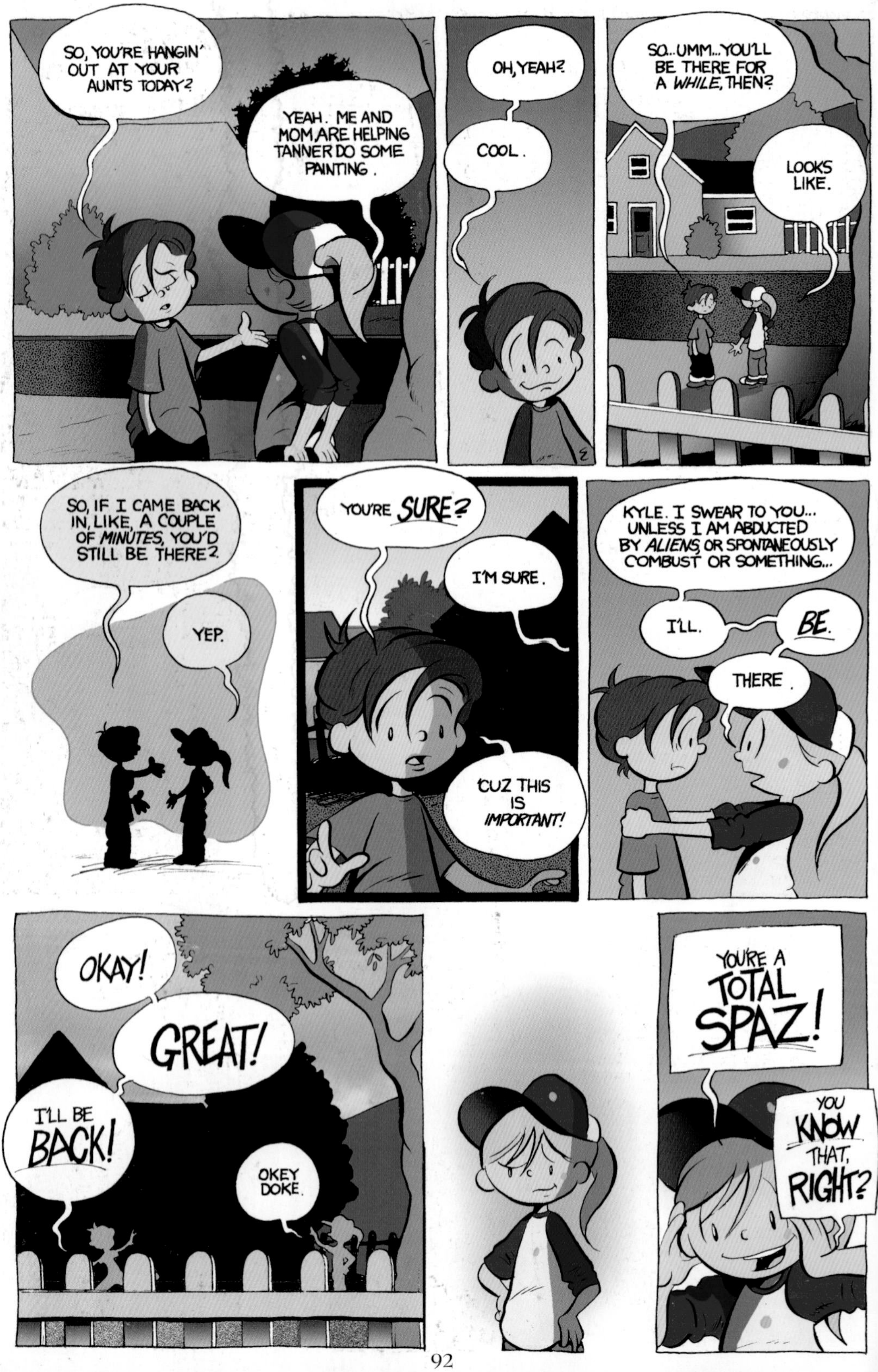
SO, YOU'RE HANGIN' OUT AT YOUR AUNT'S TODAY?
YEAH. ME AND MOM ARE HELPING TANNER DO SOME PAINTING.
OH, YEAH?
COOL.
SO...UMM...YOU'LL BE THERE FOR A WHILE, THEN?
LOOKS LIKE.
SO, IF I CAME BACK IN, LIKE, A COUPLE OF MINUTES, YOU'D STILL BE THERE?
YEP.
YOU'RE SURE?
I'M SURE.
'CUZ THIS IS IMPORTANT!
KYLE. I SWEAR TO YOU... UNLESS I AM ABDUCTED BY ALIENS, OR SPONTANEOUSLY COMBUST OR SOMETHING...
I'LL.
BE.
THERE.
OKAY!
GREAT!
I'LL BE BACK!
OKEY DOKE.
YOU'RE A TOTAL SPAZ!
YOU KNOW THAT, RIGHT?

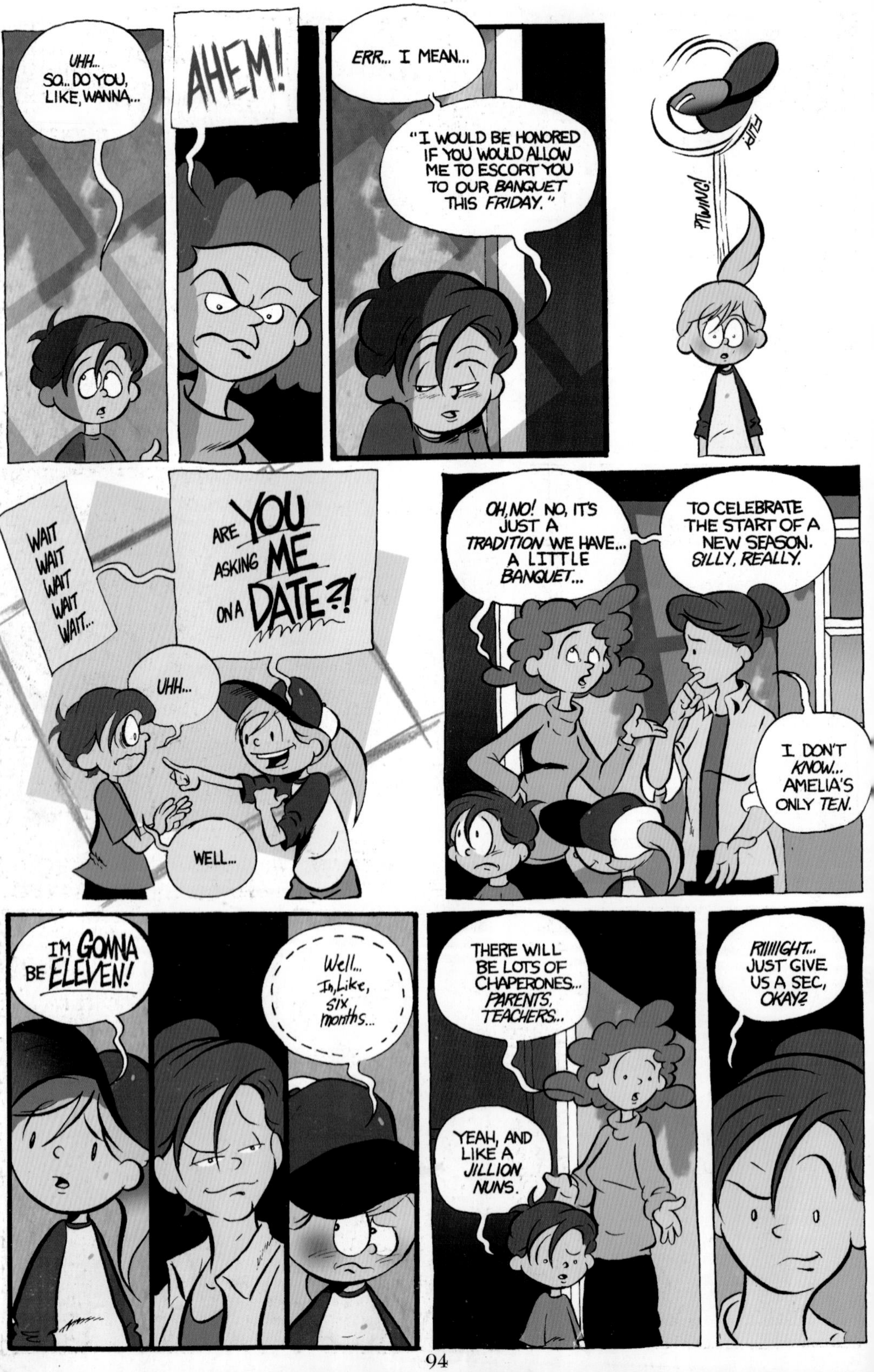
UHH... SO... DO YOU, LIKE, WANNA...
AHEM!
ERR... I MEAN...
"I WOULD BE HONORED IF YOU WOULD ALLOW ME TO ESCORT YOU TO OUR BANQUET THIS FRIDAY."
FLIP
PTWING!
WAIT WAIT WAIT WAIT WAIT...
ARE YOU ASKING ME ON A DATE?!
UHH...
WELL...
OH, NO! NO, IT'S JUST A TRADITION WE HAVE... A LITTLE BANQUET...
TO CELEBRATE THE START OF A NEW SEASON. SILLY, REALLY.
I DON'T KNOW... AMELIA'S ONLY TEN.
I'M GONNA BE ELEVEN!
Well... In, Like, six months...
THERE WILL BE LOTS OF CHAPERONES... PARENTS, TEACHERS...
YEAH, AND LIKE A JILLION NUNS.
RIIIIIGHT... JUST GIVE US A SEC, OKAY?

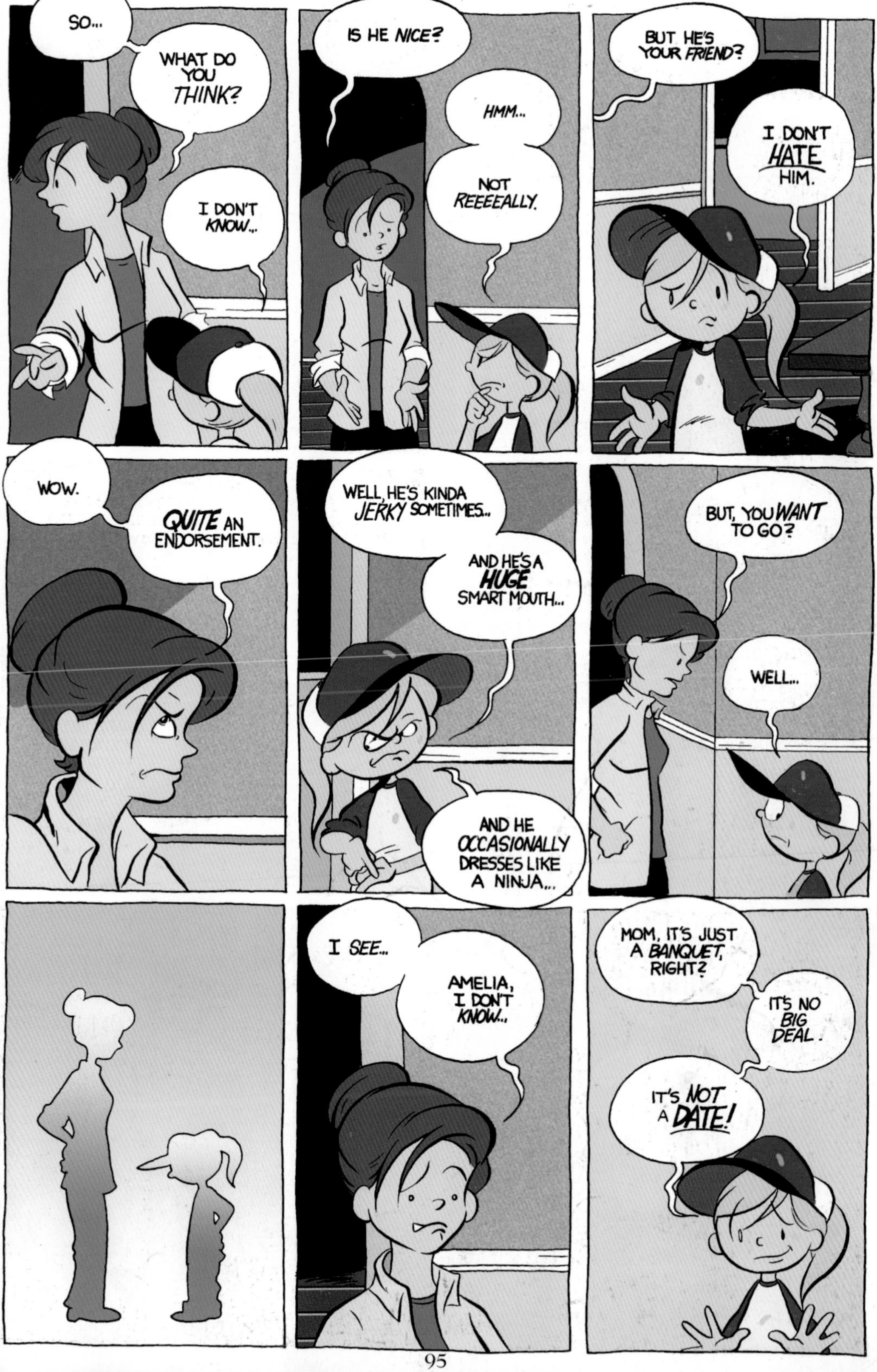
SO...
WHAT DO YOU *THINK*?
I DON'T *KNOW*...
IS HE *NICE*?
HMM...
NOT *REEEEALLY*.
BUT HE'S YOUR *FRIEND*?
I DON'T *HATE* HIM.
WOW.
QUITE AN ENDORSEMENT.
WELL, HE'S KINDA *JERKY* SOMETIMES...
AND HE'S A *HUGE* SMART MOUTH...
AND HE *OCCASIONALLY* DRESSES LIKE A NINJA...
BUT, YOU *WANT* TO GO?
WELL...
I *SEE*...
AMELIA, I DON'T *KNOW*...
MOM, IT'S JUST A *BANQUET*, RIGHT?
IT'S NO *BIG DEAL*.
IT'S *NOT* A *DATE*!

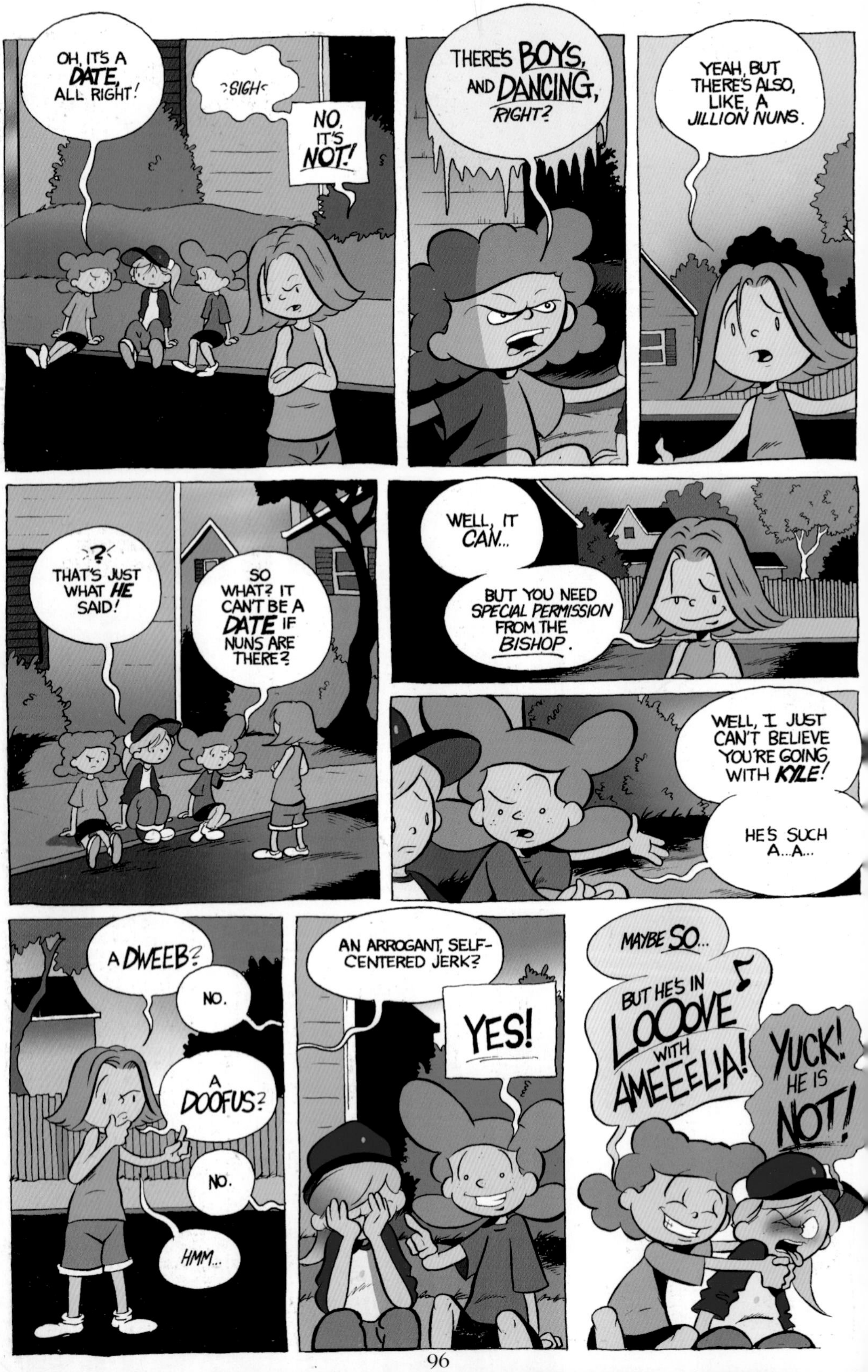
OH, IT'S A DATE, ALL RIGHT!
SIGH
NO, IT'S NOT!
THERE'S BOYS, AND DANCING, RIGHT?
YEAH, BUT THERE'S ALSO, LIKE, A JILLION NUNS.
? THAT'S JUST WHAT HE SAID!
SO WHAT? IT CAN'T BE A DATE IF NUNS ARE THERE?
WELL, IT CAN...
BUT YOU NEED SPECIAL PERMISSION FROM THE BISHOP.
WELL, I JUST CAN'T BELIEVE YOU'RE GOING WITH KYLE!
HE'S SUCH A...A...
A DWEEB?
NO.
A DOOFUS?
NO.
HMM...
AN ARROGANT, SELF-CENTERED JERK?
YES!
MAYBE SO...
BUT HE'S IN LOOOVE WITH AMEEELIA!
YUCK! HE IS NOT!

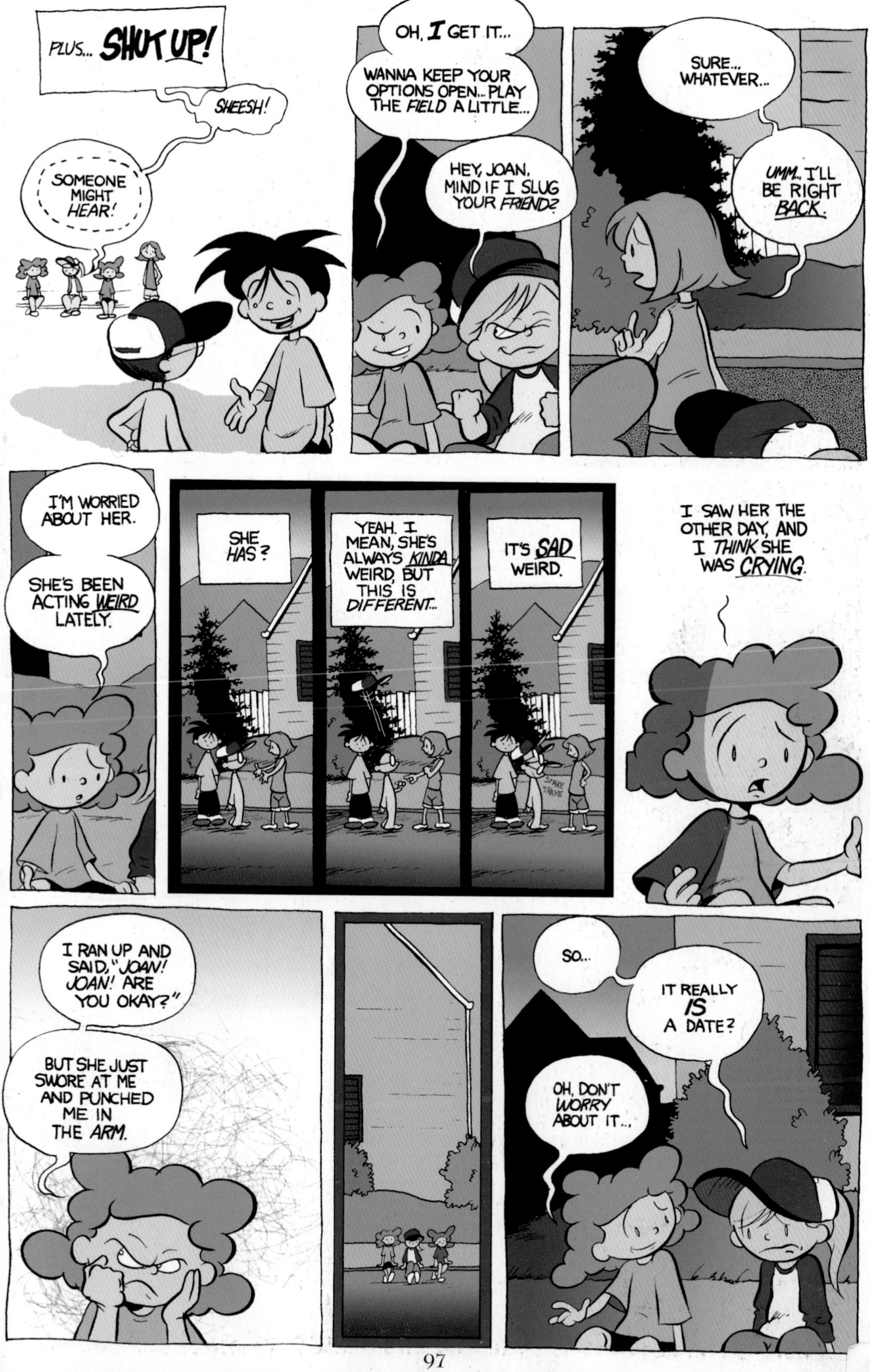
PLUS... SHUT UP!
SHEESH!
SOMEONE MIGHT HEAR!
OH, I GET IT...
WANNA KEEP YOUR OPTIONS OPEN... PLAY THE FIELD A LITTLE...
HEY, JOAN, MIND IF I SLUG YOUR FRIEND?
SURE... WHATEVER...
UMM.. I'LL BE RIGHT BACK.
I'M WORRIED ABOUT HER.
SHE'S BEEN ACTING WEIRD LATELY.
SHE HAS?
YEAH. I MEAN, SHE'S ALWAYS KINDA WEIRD, BUT THIS IS DIFFERENT...
IT'S SAD WEIRD.
I SAW HER THE OTHER DAY, AND I THINK SHE WAS CRYING.
I RAN UP AND SAID, "JOAN! JOAN! ARE YOU OKAY?"
BUT SHE JUST SWORE AT ME AND PUNCHED ME IN THE ARM.
SO...
IT REALLY IS A DATE?
OH, DON'T WORRY ABOUT IT...

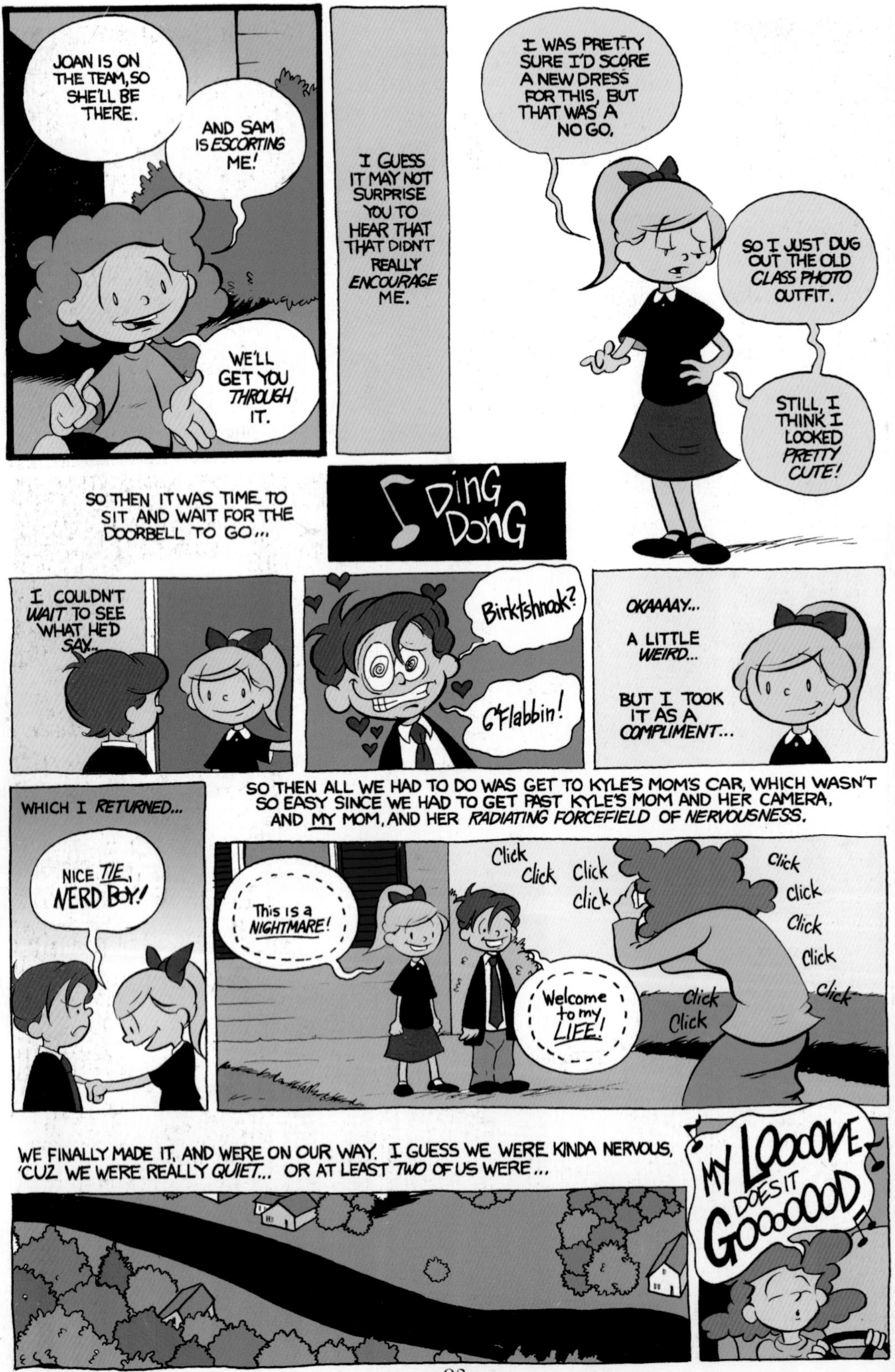

JOAN IS ON THE TEAM, SO SHE'LL BE THERE.
AND SAM IS ESCORTING ME!
WE'LL GET YOU THROUGH IT.
I GUESS IT MAY NOT SURPRISE YOU TO HEAR THAT THAT DIDN'T REALLY ENCOURAGE ME.
I WAS PRETTY SURE I'D SCORE A NEW DRESS FOR THIS, BUT THAT WAS A NO GO.
SO I JUST DUG OUT THE OLD CLASS PHOTO OUTFIT.
STILL, I THINK I LOOKED PRETTY CUTE!
SO THEN IT WAS TIME TO SIT AND WAIT FOR THE DOORBELL TO GO...
DinG DonG
I COULDN'T WAIT TO SEE WHAT HE'D SAY...
Birktshnook?
G'Flabbin!
OKAAAAY...
A LITTLE WEIRD...
BUT I TOOK IT AS A COMPLIMENT...
WHICH I RETURNED...
NICE TIE, NERD BOY!
SO THEN ALL WE HAD TO DO WAS GET TO KYLE'S MOM'S CAR, WHICH WASN'T SO EASY SINCE WE HAD TO GET PAST KYLE'S MOM AND HER CAMERA, AND MY MOM, AND HER RADIATING FORCEFIELD OF NERVOUSNESS.
This is a NIGHTMARE!
Welcome to my LIFE!
Click Click Click Click
Click Click Click Click Click
Click Click
WE FINALLY MADE IT, AND WERE ON OUR WAY. I GUESS WE WERE KINDA NERVOUS, 'CUZ WE WERE REALLY QUIET... OR AT LEAST TWO OF US WERE...
MY LOOOOVE DOES IT GOOOOOOD!

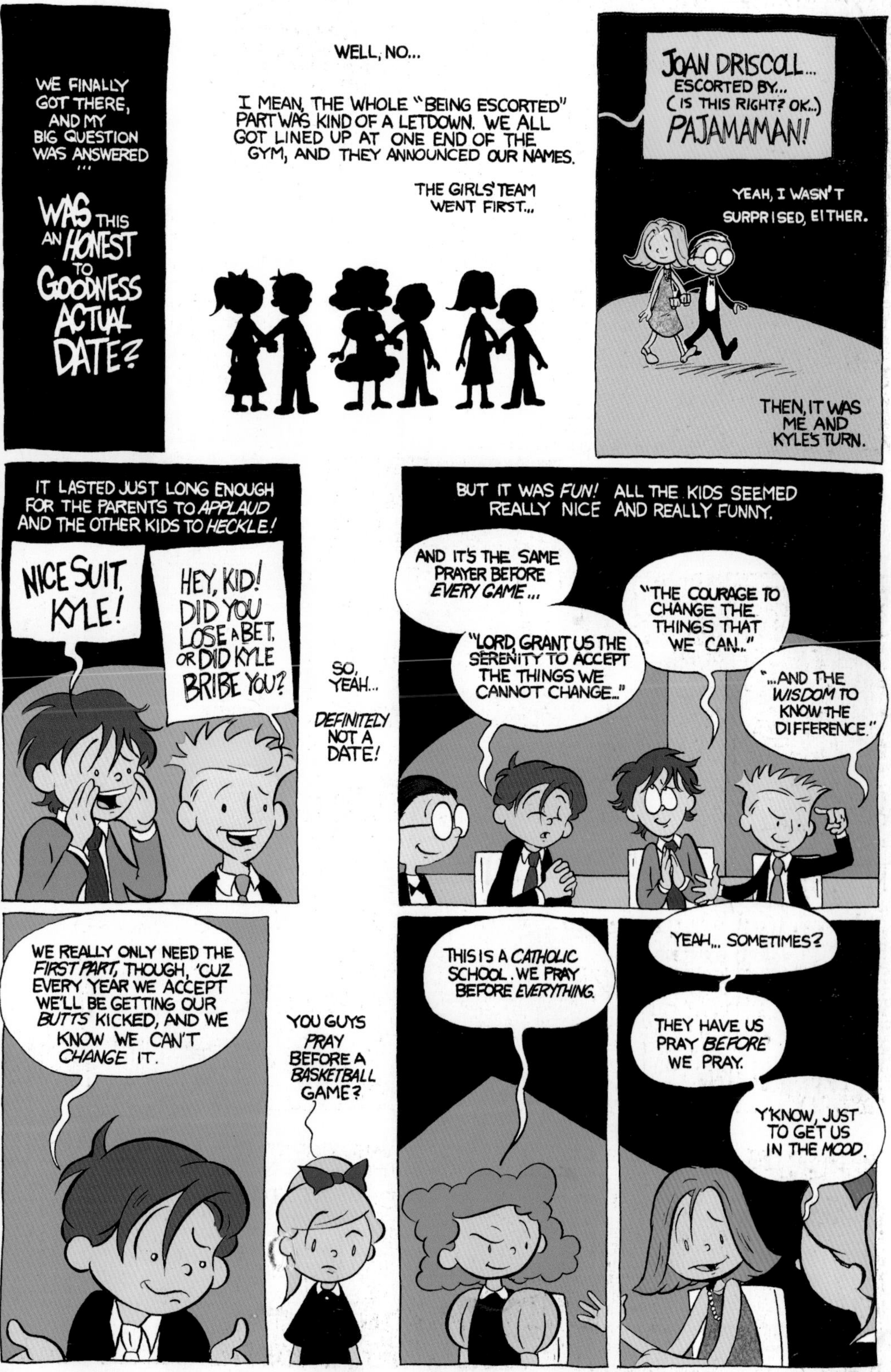
WE FINALLY GOT THERE, AND MY BIG QUESTION WAS ANSWERED ...
WAS THIS AN HONEST TO GOODNESS ACTUAL DATE?
WELL, NO...
I MEAN, THE WHOLE "BEING ESCORTED" PART WAS KIND OF A LETDOWN. WE ALL GOT LINED UP AT ONE END OF THE GYM, AND THEY ANNOUNCED OUR NAMES.
THE GIRLS' TEAM WENT FIRST...
JOAN DRISCOLL... ESCORTED BY... (IS THIS RIGHT? OK..) PAJAMAMAN!
YEAH, I WASN'T SURPRISED, EITHER.
THEN, IT WAS ME AND KYLE'S TURN.
IT LASTED JUST LONG ENOUGH FOR THE PARENTS TO APPLAUD AND THE OTHER KIDS TO HECKLE!
NICE SUIT, KYLE!
HEY, KID! DID YOU LOSE A BET, OR DID KYLE BRIBE YOU?
SO, YEAH...
DEFINITELY NOT A DATE!
BUT IT WAS FUN! ALL THE KIDS SEEMED REALLY NICE AND REALLY FUNNY.
AND IT'S THE SAME PRAYER BEFORE EVERY GAME...
"LORD, GRANT US THE SERENITY TO ACCEPT THE THINGS WE CANNOT CHANGE..."
"THE COURAGE TO CHANGE THE THINGS THAT WE CAN..."
"...AND THE WISDOM TO KNOW THE DIFFERENCE."
WE REALLY ONLY NEED THE FIRST PART, THOUGH, 'CUZ EVERY YEAR WE ACCEPT WE'LL BE GETTING OUR BUTTS KICKED, AND WE KNOW WE CAN'T CHANGE IT.
YOU GUYS PRAY BEFORE A BASKETBALL GAME?
THIS IS A CATHOLIC SCHOOL. WE PRAY BEFORE EVERYTHING.
YEAH... SOMETIMES?
THEY HAVE US PRAY BEFORE WE PRAY.
Y'KNOW, JUST TO GET US IN THE MOOD.

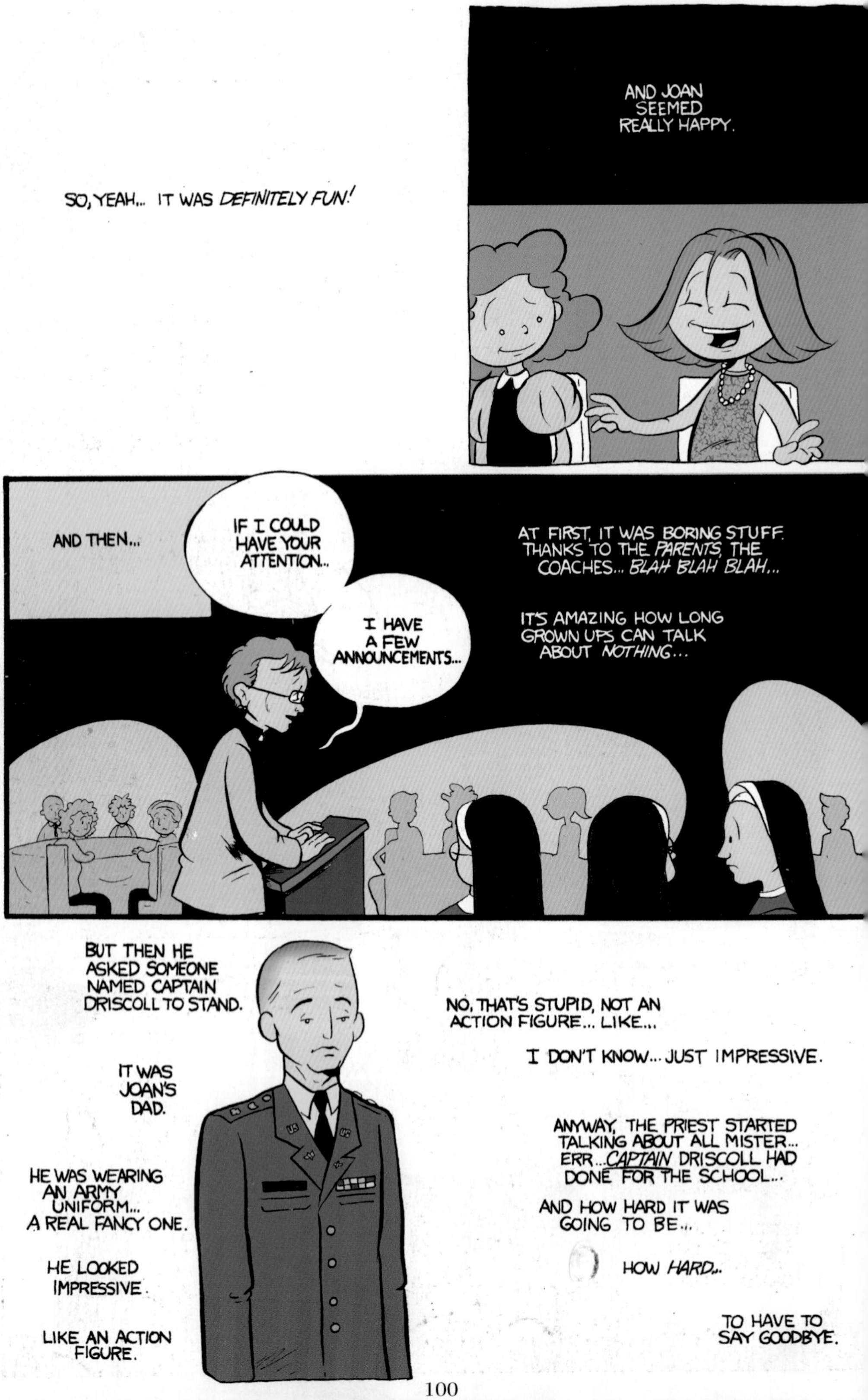
SO, YEAH... IT WAS DEFINITELY FUN!
AND JOAN SEEMED REALLY HAPPY.
AND THEN...
IF I COULD HAVE YOUR ATTENTION...
I HAVE A FEW ANNOUNCEMENTS...
AT FIRST, IT WAS BORING STUFF. THANKS TO THE PARENTS, THE COACHES... BLAH BLAH BLAH...
IT'S AMAZING HOW LONG GROWN UPS CAN TALK ABOUT NOTHING...
BUT THEN HE ASKED SOMEONE NAMED CAPTAIN DRISCOLL TO STAND.
IT WAS JOAN'S DAD.
HE WAS WEARING AN ARMY UNIFORM... A REAL FANCY ONE.
HE LOOKED IMPRESSIVE.
LIKE AN ACTION FIGURE.
NO, THAT'S STUPID, NOT AN ACTION FIGURE... LIKE...
I DON'T KNOW... JUST IMPRESSIVE.
ANYWAY, THE PRIEST STARTED TALKING ABOUT ALL MISTER... ERR...CAPTAIN DRISCOLL HAD DONE FOR THE SCHOOL...
AND HOW HARD IT WAS GOING TO BE...
HOW HARD...
TO HAVE TO SAY GOODBYE.

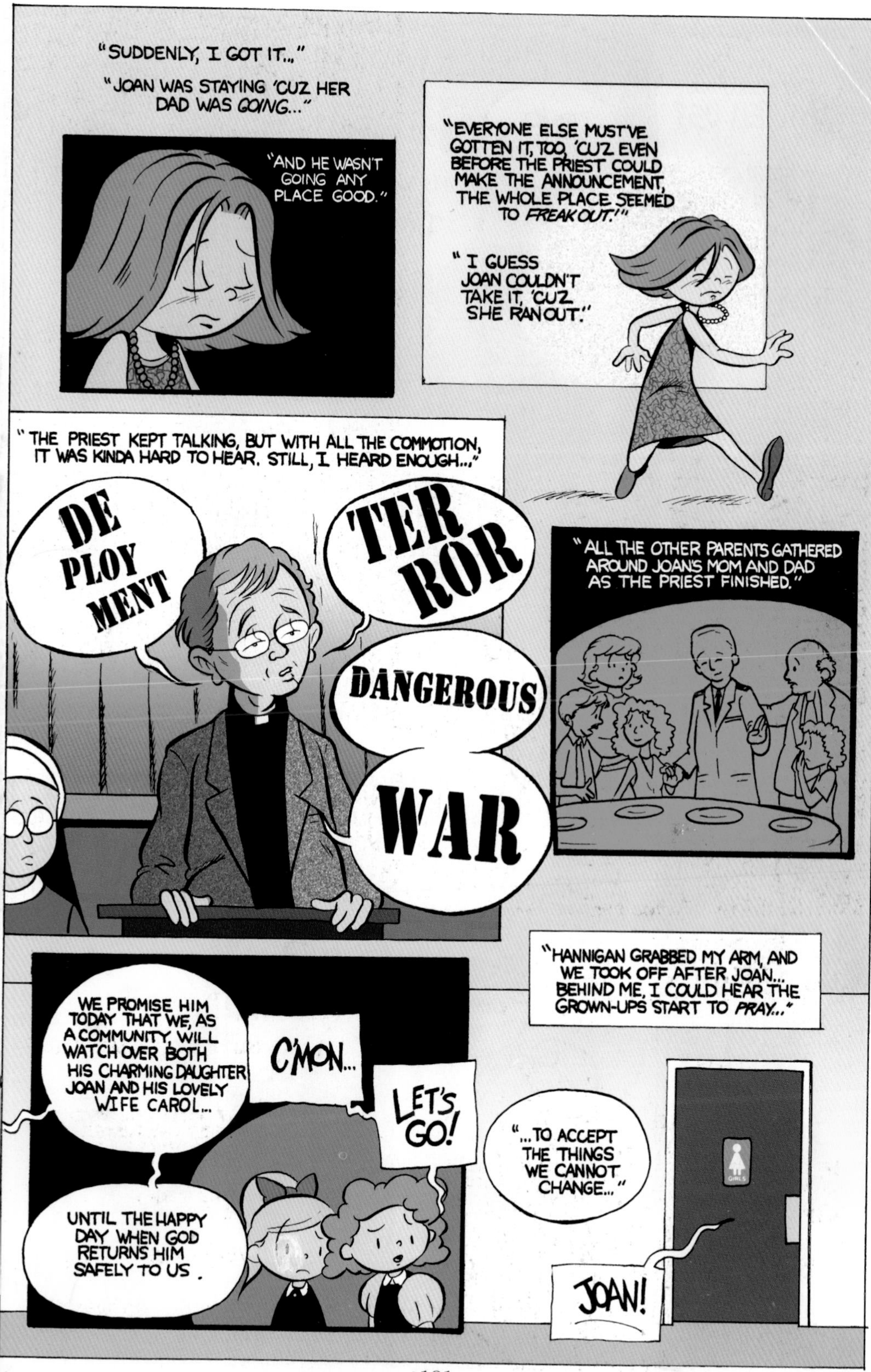
"SUDDENLY, I GOT IT..."
"JOAN WAS STAYING 'CUZ HER DAD WAS GOING..."
"AND HE WASN'T GOING ANY PLACE GOOD."
"EVERYONE ELSE MUST'VE GOTTEN IT, TOO, 'CUZ EVEN BEFORE THE PRIEST COULD MAKE THE ANNOUNCEMENT, THE WHOLE PLACE SEEMED TO FREAK OUT!"
"I GUESS JOAN COULDN'T TAKE IT, 'CUZ SHE RAN OUT."
"THE PRIEST KEPT TALKING, BUT WITH ALL THE COMMOTION, IT WAS KINDA HARD TO HEAR. STILL, I HEARD ENOUGH..."
DE PLOY MENT
TER ROR
DANGEROUS
WAR
"ALL THE OTHER PARENTS GATHERED AROUND JOAN'S MOM AND DAD AS THE PRIEST FINISHED."
WE PROMISE HIM TODAY THAT WE, AS A COMMUNITY, WILL WATCH OVER BOTH HIS CHARMING DAUGHTER JOAN AND HIS LOVELY WIFE CAROL...
UNTIL THE HAPPY DAY WHEN GOD RETURNS HIM SAFELY TO US.
C'MON...
LET'S GO!
"HANNIGAN GRABBED MY ARM, AND WE TOOK OFF AFTER JOAN... BEHIND ME, I COULD HEAR THE GROWN-UPS START TO PRAY..."
"...TO ACCEPT THE THINGS WE CANNOT CHANGE..."
JOAN!

103

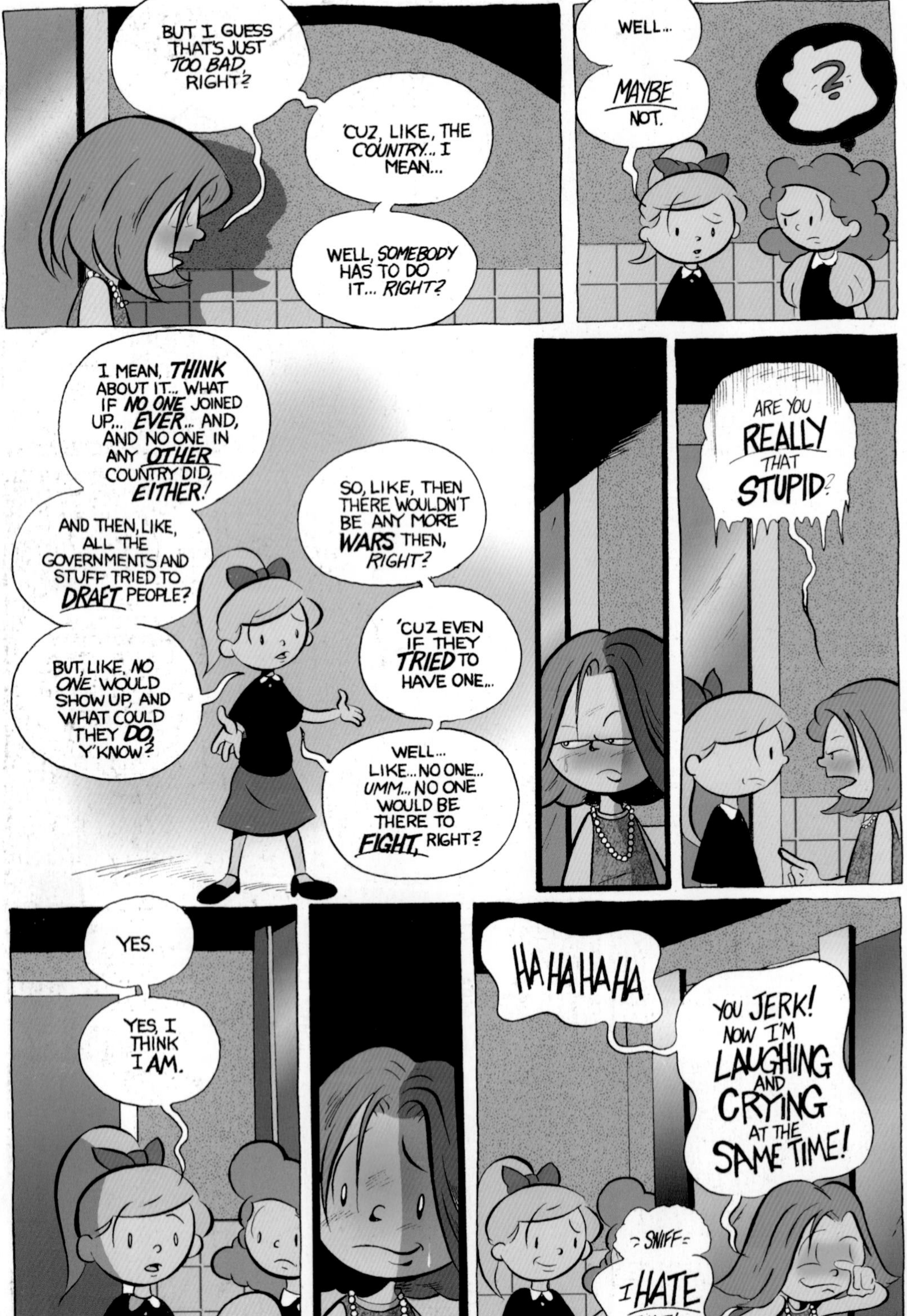
BUT I GUESS THAT'S JUST TOO BAD, RIGHT?
'CUZ, LIKE, THE COUNTRY... I MEAN...
WELL, SOMEBODY HAS TO DO IT... RIGHT?
WELL...
MAYBE NOT.
?
I MEAN, THINK ABOUT IT... WHAT IF NO ONE JOINED UP... EVER... AND, AND NO ONE IN ANY OTHER COUNTRY DID, EITHER!
AND THEN, LIKE, ALL THE GOVERNMENTS AND STUFF TRIED TO DRAFT PEOPLE?
BUT, LIKE, NO ONE WOULD SHOW UP, AND WHAT COULD THEY DO, Y'KNOW?
SO, LIKE, THEN THERE WOULDN'T BE ANY MORE WARS THEN, RIGHT?
'CUZ EVEN IF THEY TRIED TO HAVE ONE...
WELL... LIKE... NO ONE... UMM... NO ONE WOULD BE THERE TO FIGHT, RIGHT?
ARE YOU REALLY THAT STUPID?
YES.
YES, I THINK I AM.
HA HA HA HA
YOU JERK! NOW I'M LAUGHING AND CRYING AT THE SAME TIME!
SNIFF
I HATE THAT!

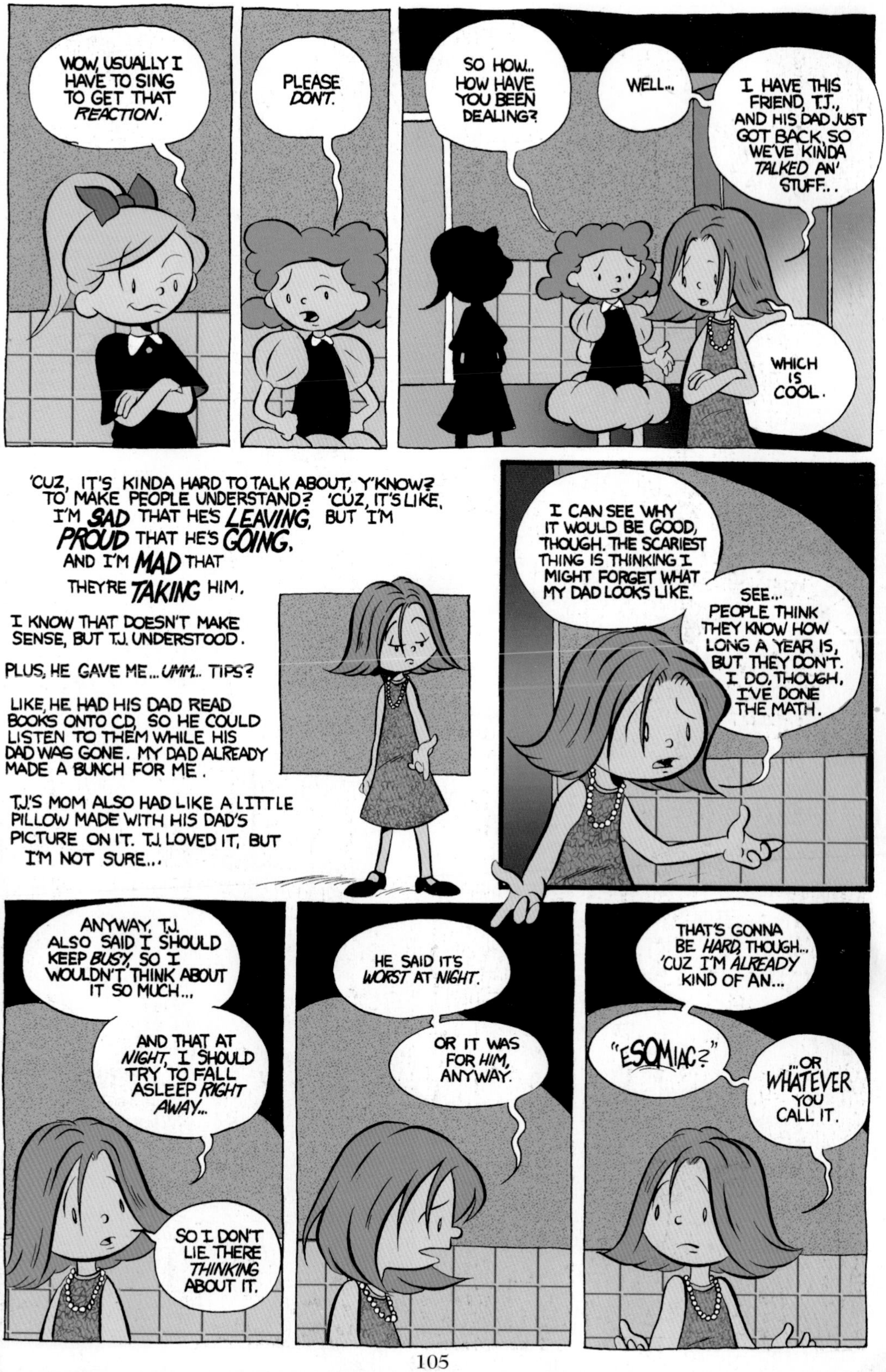
WOW, USUALLY I HAVE TO SING TO GET THAT REACTION.
PLEASE DON'T.
SO HOW... HOW HAVE YOU BEEN DEALING?
WELL...
I HAVE THIS FRIEND, T.J., AND HIS DAD JUST GOT BACK, SO WE'VE KINDA TALKED AN' STUFF...
WHICH IS COOL.
'CUZ, IT'S KINDA HARD TO TALK ABOUT, Y'KNOW? TO MAKE PEOPLE UNDERSTAND? 'CUZ, IT'S LIKE, I'M SAD THAT HE'S LEAVING, BUT I'M PROUD THAT HE'S GOING. AND I'M MAD THAT THEY'RE TAKING HIM.
I KNOW THAT DOESN'T MAKE SENSE, BUT T.J. UNDERSTOOD.
PLUS, HE GAVE ME... UMM... TIPS?
LIKE, HE HAD HIS DAD READ BOOKS ONTO CD, SO HE COULD LISTEN TO THEM WHILE HIS DAD WAS GONE. MY DAD ALREADY MADE A BUNCH FOR ME.
T.J.'S MOM ALSO HAD LIKE A LITTLE PILLOW MADE WITH HIS DAD'S PICTURE ON IT. T.J. LOVED IT, BUT I'M NOT SURE...
I CAN SEE WHY IT WOULD BE GOOD, THOUGH. THE SCARIEST THING IS THINKING I MIGHT FORGET WHAT MY DAD LOOKS LIKE.
SEE... PEOPLE THINK THEY KNOW HOW LONG A YEAR IS, BUT THEY DON'T. I DO, THOUGH, I'VE DONE THE MATH.
ANYWAY, T.J. ALSO SAID I SHOULD KEEP BUSY, SO I WOULDN'T THINK ABOUT IT SO MUCH...
AND THAT AT NIGHT, I SHOULD TRY TO FALL ASLEEP RIGHT AWAY...
SO I DON'T LIE THERE THINKING ABOUT IT.
HE SAID IT'S WORST AT NIGHT.
OR IT WAS FOR HIM, ANYWAY.
THAT'S GONNA BE HARD, THOUGH... 'CUZ I'M ALREADY KIND OF AN...
"ESOMIAC?"
...OR WHATEVER YOU CALL IT.

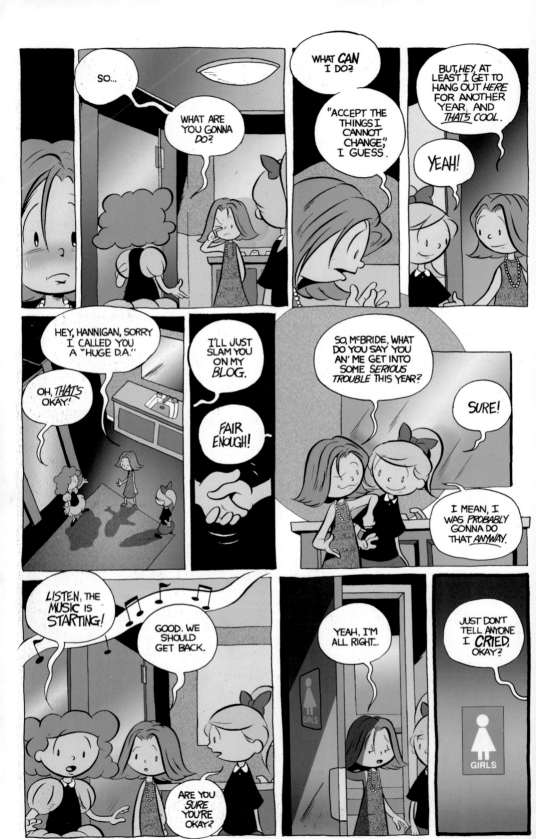

106

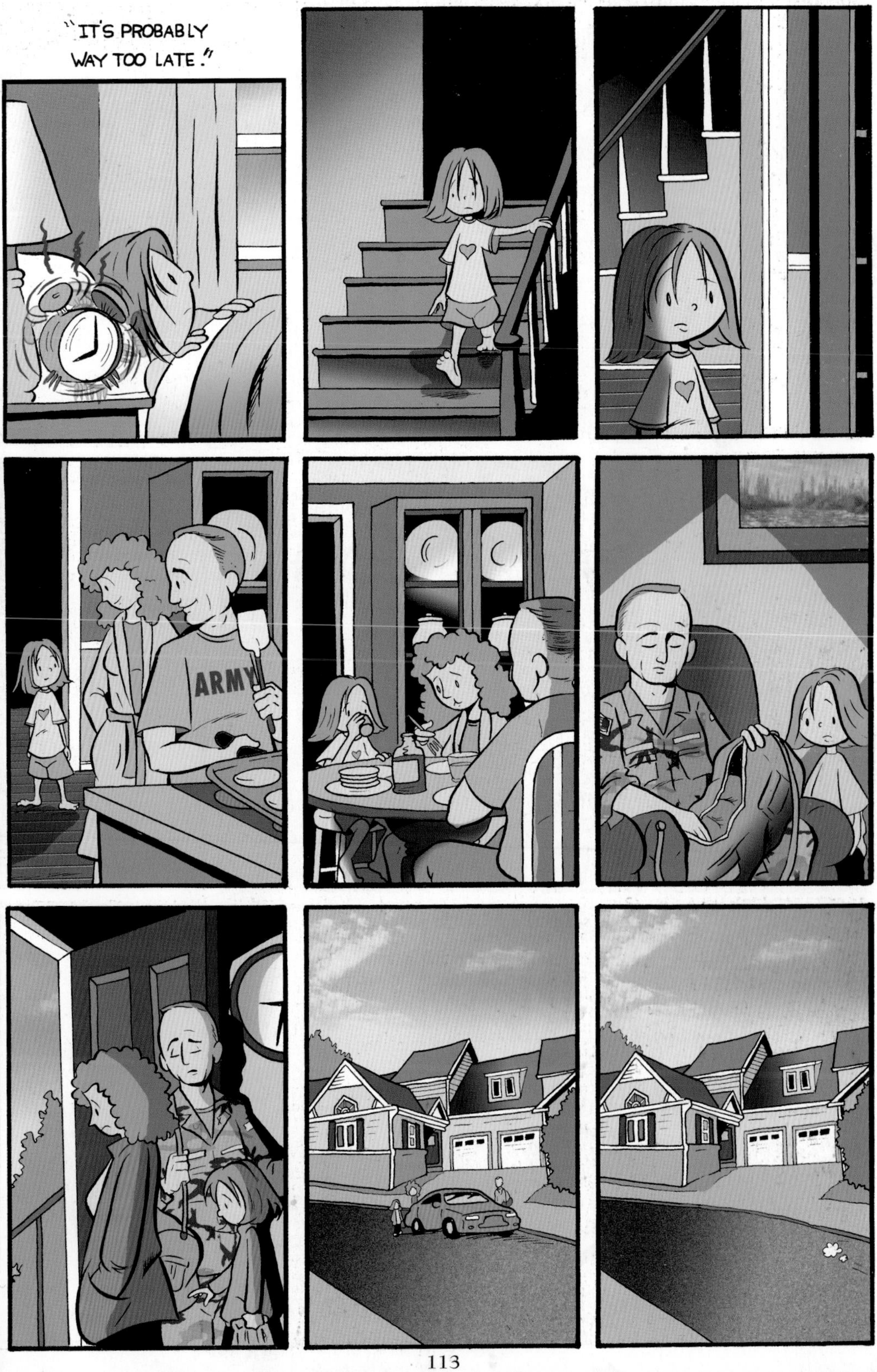
"IT'S PROBABLY WAY TOO LATE."
ARMY

115

PEOPLE THINK THEY KNOW HOW LONG A YEAR IS, BUT THEY DON'T.

I DO, THOUGH, I'VE DONE THE MATH.

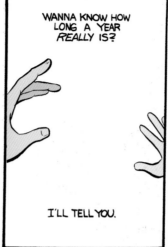

WANNA KNOW HOW LONG A YEAR *REALLY* IS?

I'LL TELL YOU.

THERE ARE 365 *DAYS* IN A YEAR.

THAT'S 8,760 HOURS.

THE HOURS ARE MADE UP OF 525,600 MINUTES...

WHICH EQUALS 31,536,000 SECONDS...

bye.

ONE- ONE THOUSAND...

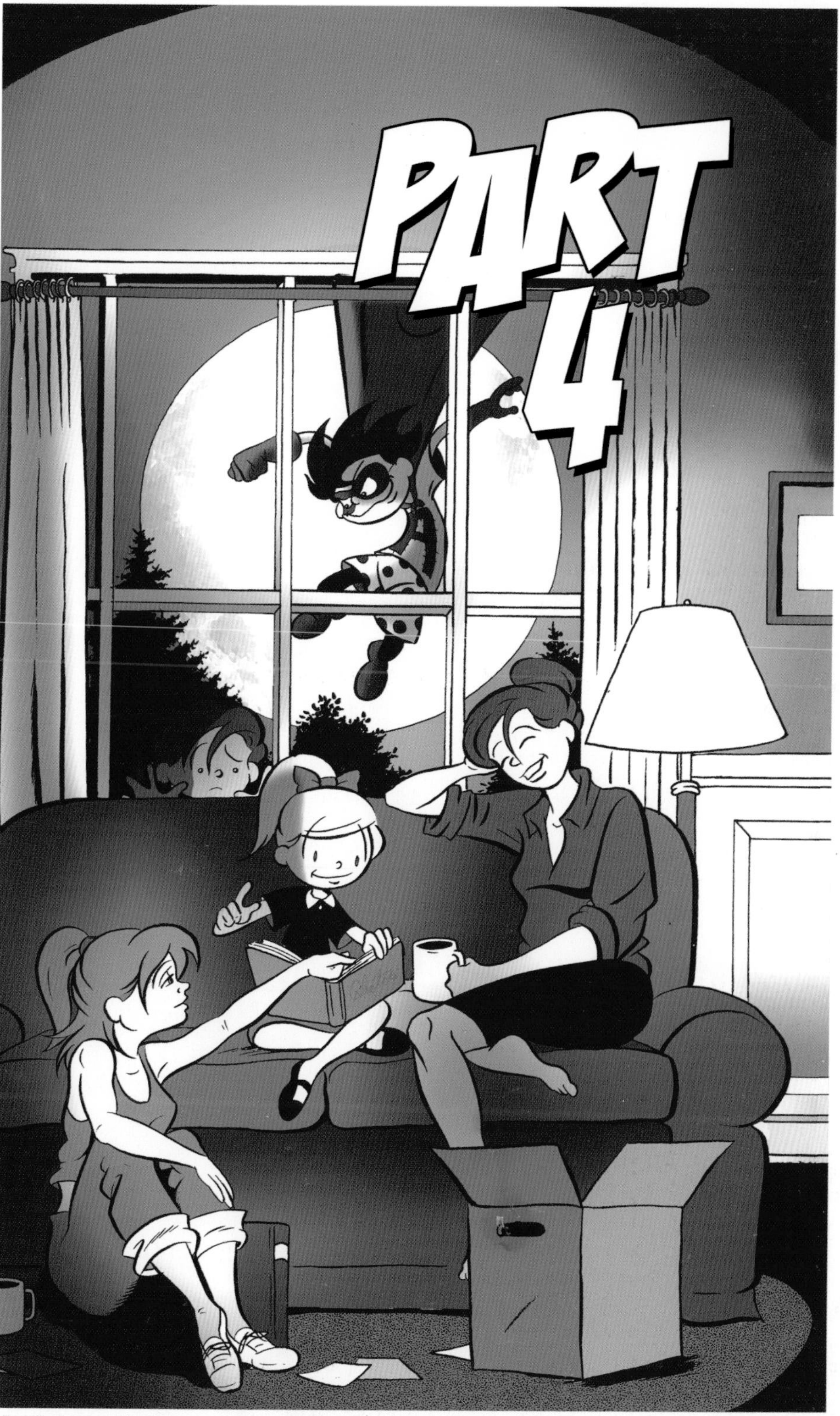
PART
4

"WHEN the PaST is a PRESENT"

Assemble the best athletes and brightest minds your town has to offer.

Failing that, just grab the usual group of knuckleheads you call friends.

Each player competes using only their wits, ingenuity...

and anywhere from two to four dollars, U.S.

(Which unfortunately eliminates SOME potential competitors immediately.)

The players then take turns barging into select convenience stores, racing frantically through the aisles, and choosing two completely unrelated items, such as:

LETTUCE and "GOLD BOND,"

or

"POP ROCKS" and SPAM

or

BACTINE and a "NOTDOG"

Then, breathlessly, and with panic in their eyes, the player races up to the clerk and shouts...

It's harmless, it's fun...

124

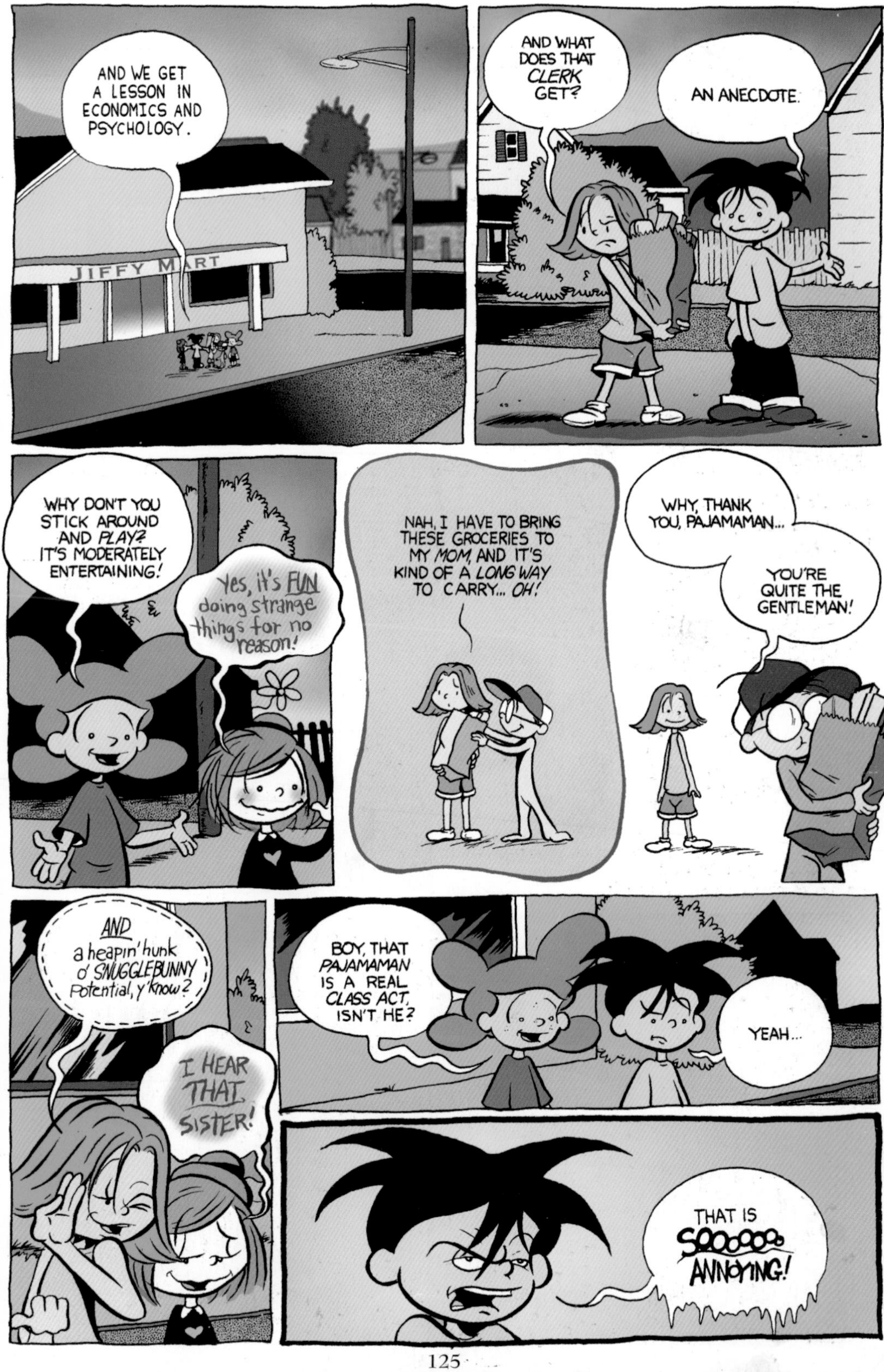
AND WE GET A LESSON IN ECONOMICS AND PSYCHOLOGY.
JIFFY MART
AND WHAT DOES THAT CLERK GET?
AN ANECDOTE.
WHY DON'T YOU STICK AROUND AND PLAY? IT'S MODERATELY ENTERTAINING!
Yes, it's FUN doing strange things for no reason!
NAH, I HAVE TO BRING THESE GROCERIES TO MY MOM, AND IT'S KIND OF A LONG WAY TO CARRY... OH!
WHY, THANK YOU, PAJAMAMAN...
YOU'RE QUITE THE GENTLEMAN!
AND a heapin' hunk o' SNUGGLEBUNNY Potential, y'know?
I HEAR THAT, SISTER!
BOY, THAT PAJAMAMAN IS A REAL CLASS ACT, ISN'T HE?
YEAH...
THAT IS SOOOOOO ANNOYING!

126

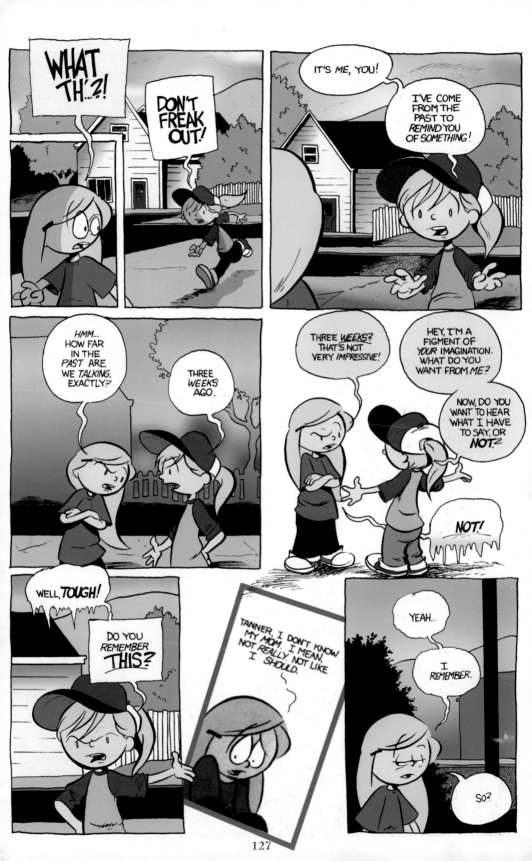

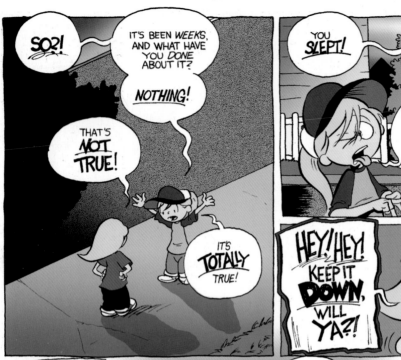

128

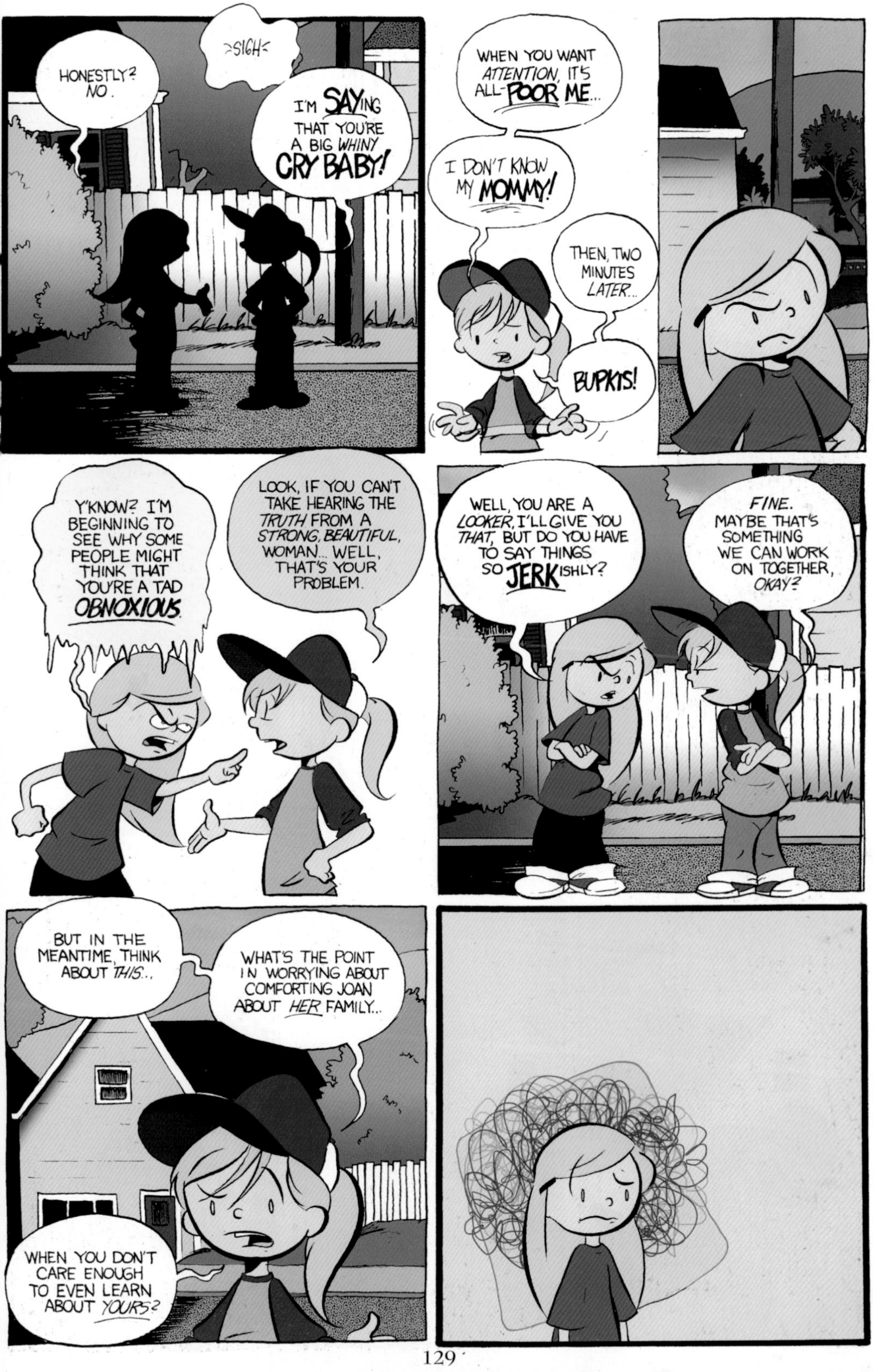
HONESTLY? NO.
SIGH
I'M SAYING THAT YOU'RE A BIG WHINY CRY BABY!
WHEN YOU WANT ATTENTION, IT'S ALL-POOR ME...
I DON'T KNOW MY MOMMY!
THEN, TWO MINUTES LATER...
BUPKIS!
Y'KNOW? I'M BEGINNING TO SEE WHY SOME PEOPLE MIGHT THINK THAT YOU'RE A TAD OBNOXIOUS.
LOOK, IF YOU CAN'T TAKE HEARING THE TRUTH FROM A STRONG, BEAUTIFUL, WOMAN... WELL, THAT'S YOUR PROBLEM.
WELL, YOU ARE A LOOKER, I'LL GIVE YOU THAT, BUT DO YOU HAVE TO SAY THINGS SO JERKISHLY?
FINE. MAYBE THAT'S SOMETHING WE CAN WORK ON TOGETHER, OKAY?
BUT IN THE MEANTIME, THINK ABOUT THIS...
WHAT'S THE POINT IN WORRYING ABOUT COMFORTING JOAN ABOUT HER FAMILY...
WHEN YOU DON'T CARE ENOUGH TO EVEN LEARN ABOUT YOURS?

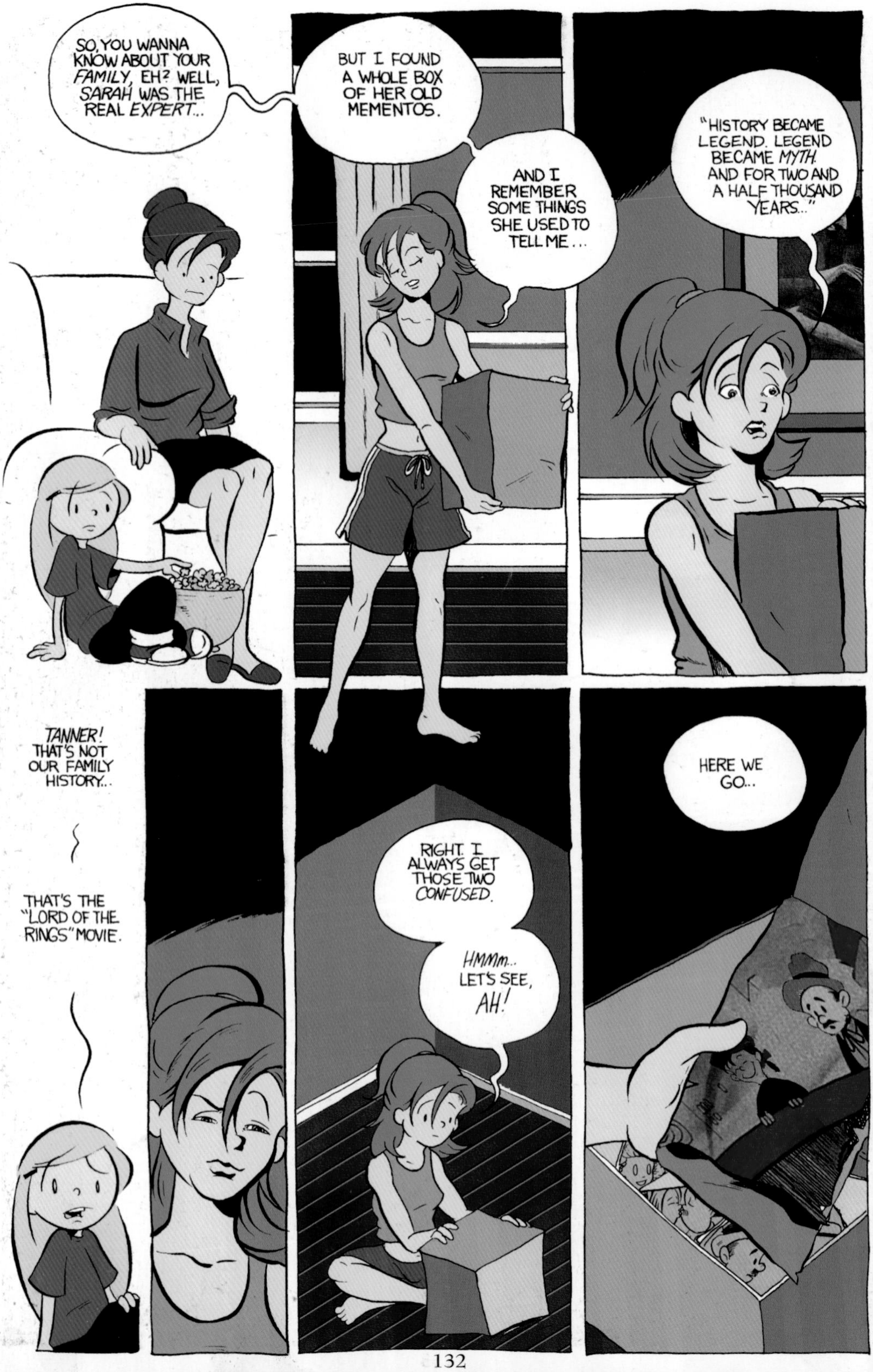
SO, YOU WANNA KNOW ABOUT YOUR FAMILY, EH? WELL, SARAH WAS THE REAL EXPERT...
BUT I FOUND A WHOLE BOX OF HER OLD MEMENTOS.
AND I REMEMBER SOME THINGS SHE USED TO TELL ME...
"HISTORY BECAME LEGEND. LEGEND BECAME MYTH. AND FOR TWO AND A HALF THOUSAND YEARS..."
TANNER! THAT'S NOT OUR FAMILY HISTORY...
THAT'S THE "LORD OF THE RINGS" MOVIE.
RIGHT. I ALWAYS GET THOSE TWO CONFUSED.
HMMm... LET'S SEE, AH!
HERE WE GO...

ARTHUR T. FLETCHER ARRIVES IN U.S.A.

Joined by new bride Louise.

We don't know much about the Clark side of the family, and if you want to know about the Irish McBrides you'll have to ask your dad.

But we know a lot about your grandmother's family, the Fletchers.

Arthur T. Fletcher grew up in England, the youngest child of George and Delores Fletcher. Now there were only two things Arthur wanted in the whole world: to marry his childhood sweetheart Louise and to move to America.

Unfortunately his entire family hated both Louise and the U.S. and made Arthur swear an oath that he would stay put and stay single (or at least marry someone more suitable).

So Arthur did what he believed was most sensible. He waited until everyone else in his family croaked and then did what he wanted.

So, as one century faded into the next, Arthur and Louise arrived in America.

FLETCHER'S FOLLIES

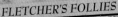

FLETCHER BUYS WIFE GIFT

Neighbors thrown into jealous rage.

Eventually the couple found themselves in Indiana, where a distant cousin of Louise owned a farm. Arthur was so happy to be in the land of his dreams and so grateful for the patience and devotion Louise had showed him that he bought her a present – a simple, delicate, and beautiful locket.

Louise kept the locket for the next 30 years until, on the day of her only son John's wedding, she passed it on to his bride Edna.

Now, Arthur had long since acquired his own farm, so John and Edna stayed on helping. By now, he and Edna had three children of their own: Jerome, Sarah, and Grace.

But try as he might, John just wasn't a farmer. So on the day of his tenth wedding anniversary, John Fletcher opened the "Family Valley General Store." No one but Edna believed it would succeed. Even John himself doubted it.

But somehow, against unbelievable odds, it did. It thrived through depression and war.

It even outlived John himself. It's still there today.

Unfortunately, during all the chaos and commotion of building the store, Edna lost the locket. Even though she searched and searched it never turned up.

One day, years after it was lost, Sarah found the locket in a field behind the store. She had no idea of the object's significance. It was weeks before she discovered that the little heart charm opened and she found a picture of her parents' wedding inside.

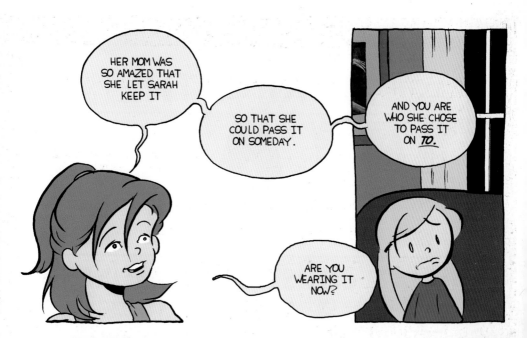

HER MOM WAS SO AMAZED THAT SHE LET SARAH KEEP IT

SO THAT SHE COULD PASS IT ON SOMEDAY.

AND YOU ARE WHO SHE CHOSE TO PASS IT ON *TO.*

ARE YOU WEARING IT NOW?

IT'S MY AUNT SARAH'S LOCKET.

INSIDE THERE'S A PICTURE.
I HAD SAM DRAW IT.

IT'S SUPPOSED TO BE YOU DRESSED AS PRINCESS TRISHARA.

DO... DO YOU LIKE IT?

UHH... NO.
IT... IT'S AT HOME.

SO, WHAT'S NEXT?

OH, I HAVE SOMETHING *INTERESTING*.

EXTRA DURING THE EXTRA

WAR!

Jerry enlisted in the Navy.

The oldest of the three children, Jerry, was just eighteen when he joined up. He got stationed on a destroyer, the USS Gainard. He never talked much about the war, but he would sometimes tell this one story.... One night, while on patrol in the Pacific, the alarm sounded that another ship, the Wadsworth, had been hit and was on fire and sinking fast. The Gainard was called to rescue the crew and Jerry was one of the men hauling injured sailors off the Wadsworth to safety on the Gainard.

I don't know why the one incident stuck in Jerry's mind more than any other, but it was really the only war story he ever told.

Anyway, one Christmas your father and I had a big dinner with both sides of the family at our place in New York. When Jerry met your grandfather McBride and found out that he too was an ex-Navy man, he told his story. The look on your grandfather's face was pure amazement. He was one of the injured men that Jerry had pulled to safety. We couldn't believe that all those years after the fact, these two men were reconnected through us.

WE THOUGHT ABOUT JERRY WHEN WE WERE HAVING YOU, AMELIA.

SOMEHOW, IT SEEMED LIKE BECAUSE OF THAT EVENT, EVERYTHING THAT CAME LATER WASN'T JUST AN ACCIDENT...

IT'S NOT JUST ABOUT THE ADVENTURE, THOUGH..

BOOM!

WHAT WAS THAT?!

SNEAK ATTACK!

IT WAS WHAT WAS MEANT TO BE.

After the war, Sarah and Grace grew up into beautiful young women...They both moved to New York, but only Sarah really liked it. She met Hugh, and, like I told you before, they never married, but did live happily ever after.

THE HEART OF SARAH FLETCHER

I CAN'T BELIEVE WE'RE HERE! OH, BUT I BET MOTHER IS MISSING US!

DON'T THINK OF THINGS LIKE THAT! WE'RE CITY GIRLS NOW!

REMEMBER, IT'S ALL ABOUT CONFIDENCE.

NOT JUST THAT, THOUGH.

IT'S ALL ABOUT THE CHOICES YOU MAKE...

HOW THEY AFFECT OTHER PEOPLE.

MEANWHILE... HMMM... FOXY LADIES!

HELLO, ANGEL. DID IT HURT WHEN YOU FELL DOWN FROM HEAVEN?

OH, NO! IS THIS ANOTHER DOOFUS? OR THE MAN OF MY DREAMS?

THE HEART OF SARAH FLETCHER

SO, DO YOU THINK SARAH WILL BE THRILLED WHEN I PROPOSE?

HMM... LET'S SEE... NO. NO I DON'T.

OH, YEAH?! WELL, WHAT DO YOU KNOW, ANYWAY?

I KNOW THAT YOU DON'T HAVE A CHANCE.

YOU'RE JUST SAYIN' THAT 'CAUSE YOU'RE JEALOUS!

YOU'RE JUST A BIG, DUMB, JEALOUS DOODY HEAD!

OH, NO!

HE'S FINALLY FLIPPED

So, anyway, Sarah stayed and became a famous writer. But Grace went home and became something even better... your GRANDMOTHER!

137

141

143

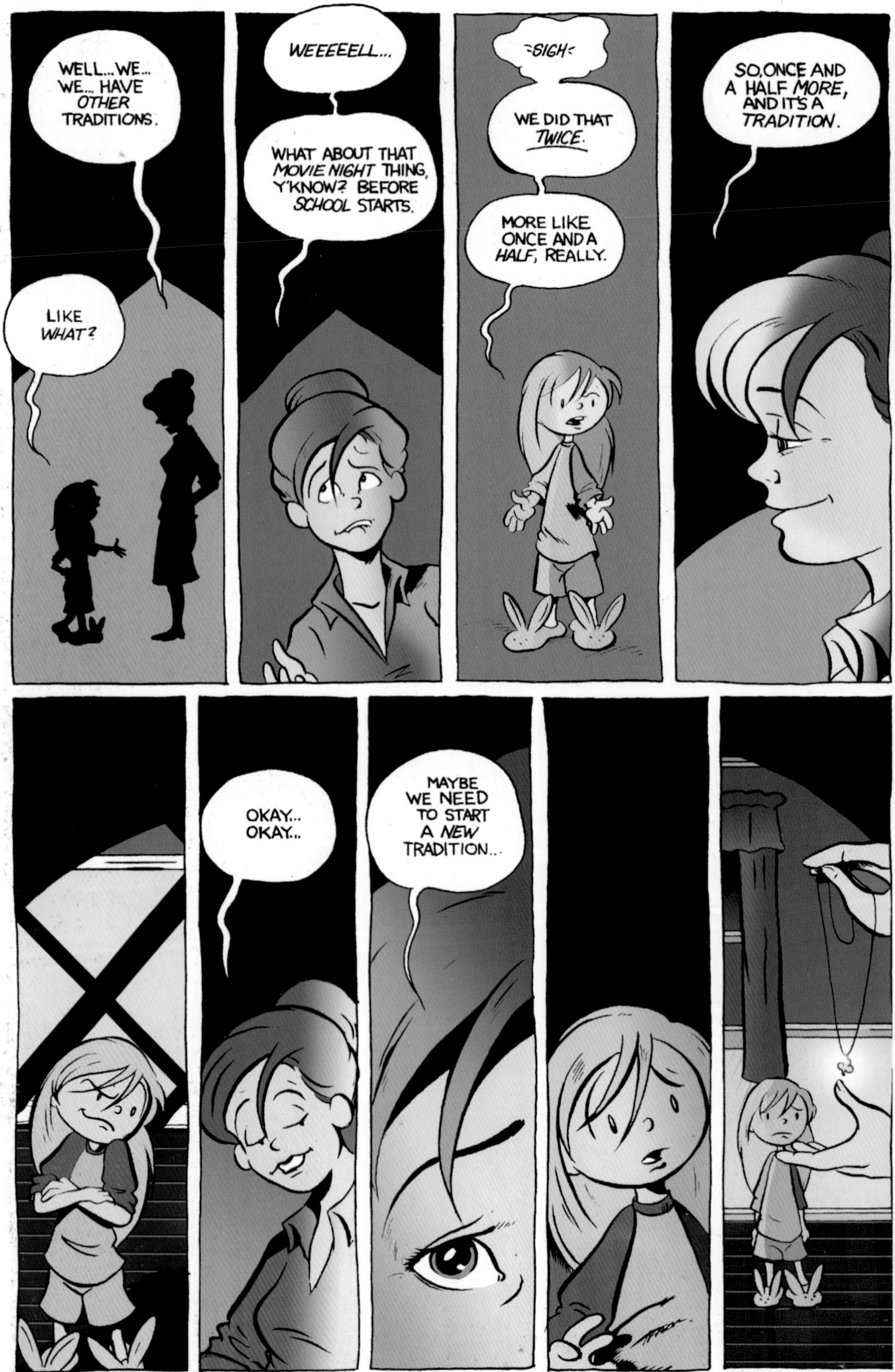
WELL... WE... WE... HAVE OTHER TRADITIONS.
LIKE WHAT?
WEEEEELL...
WHAT ABOUT THAT MOVIE NIGHT THING, Y'KNOW? BEFORE SCHOOL STARTS.
SIGH
WE DID THAT TWICE.
MORE LIKE ONCE AND A HALF, REALLY.
SO, ONCE AND A HALF MORE, AND IT'S A TRADITION.
OKAY... OKAY...
MAYBE WE NEED TO START A NEW TRADITION...

145

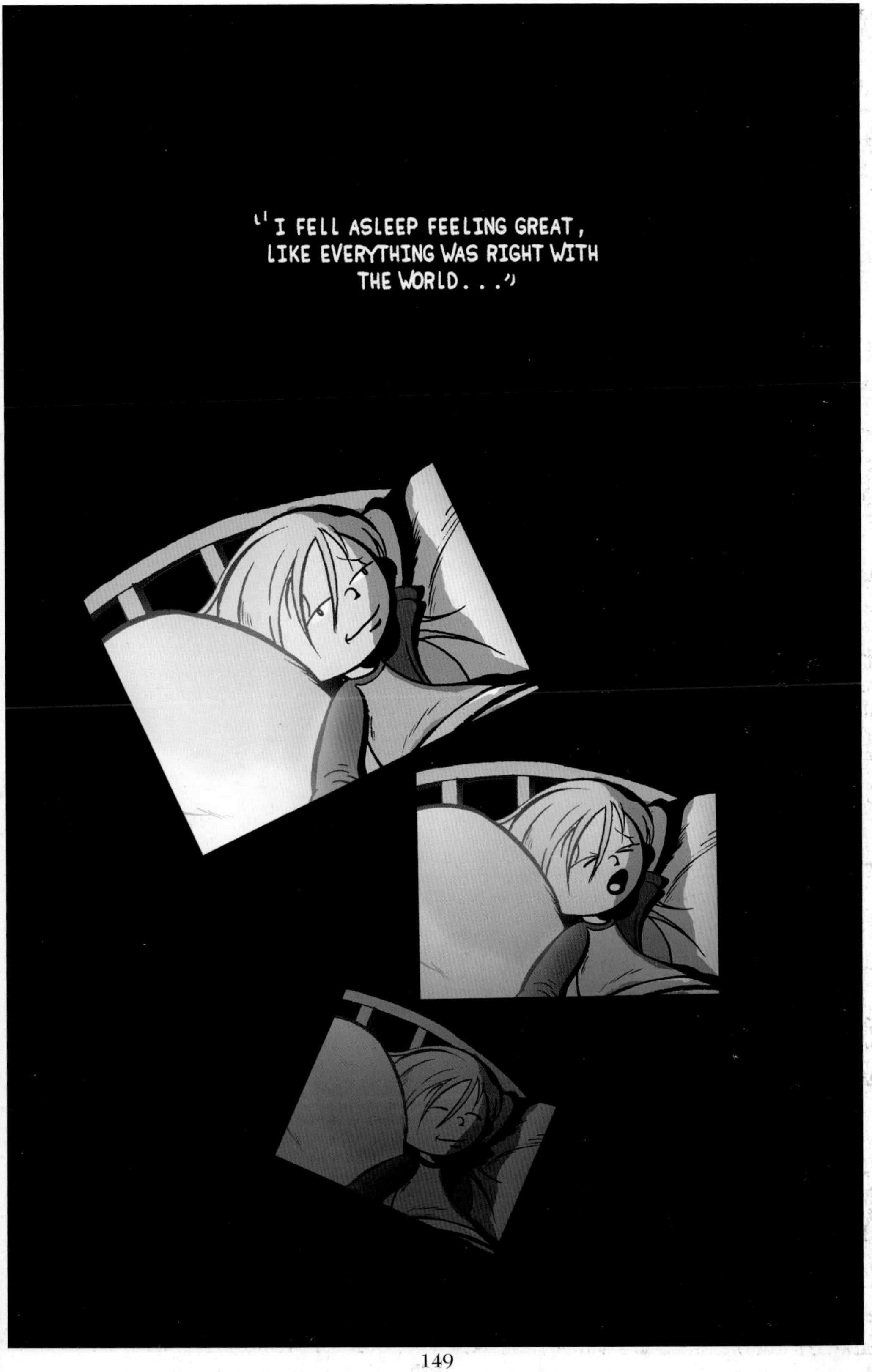
"I FELL ASLEEP FEELING GREAT, LIKE EVERYTHING WAS RIGHT WITH THE WORLD..."

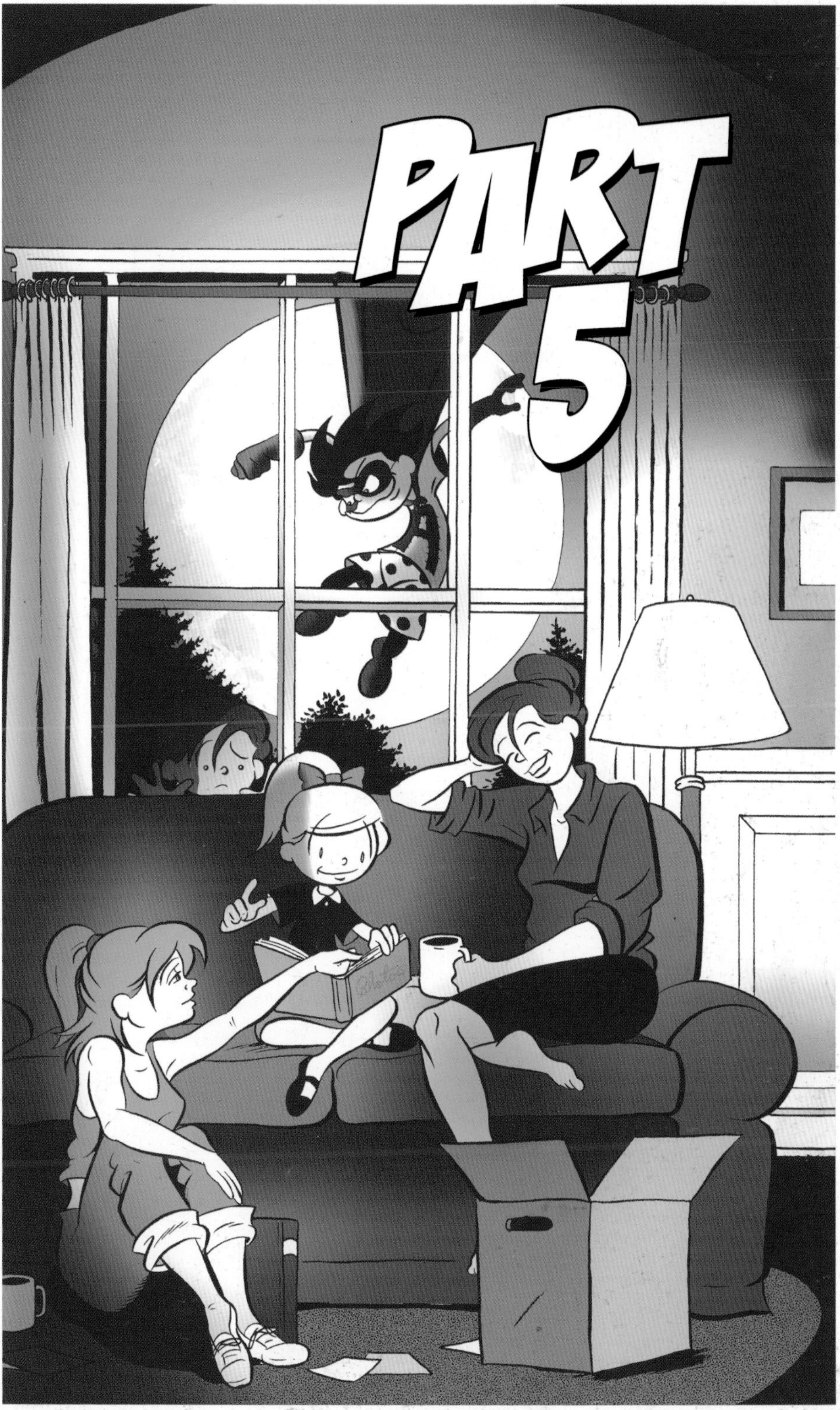
PART
5

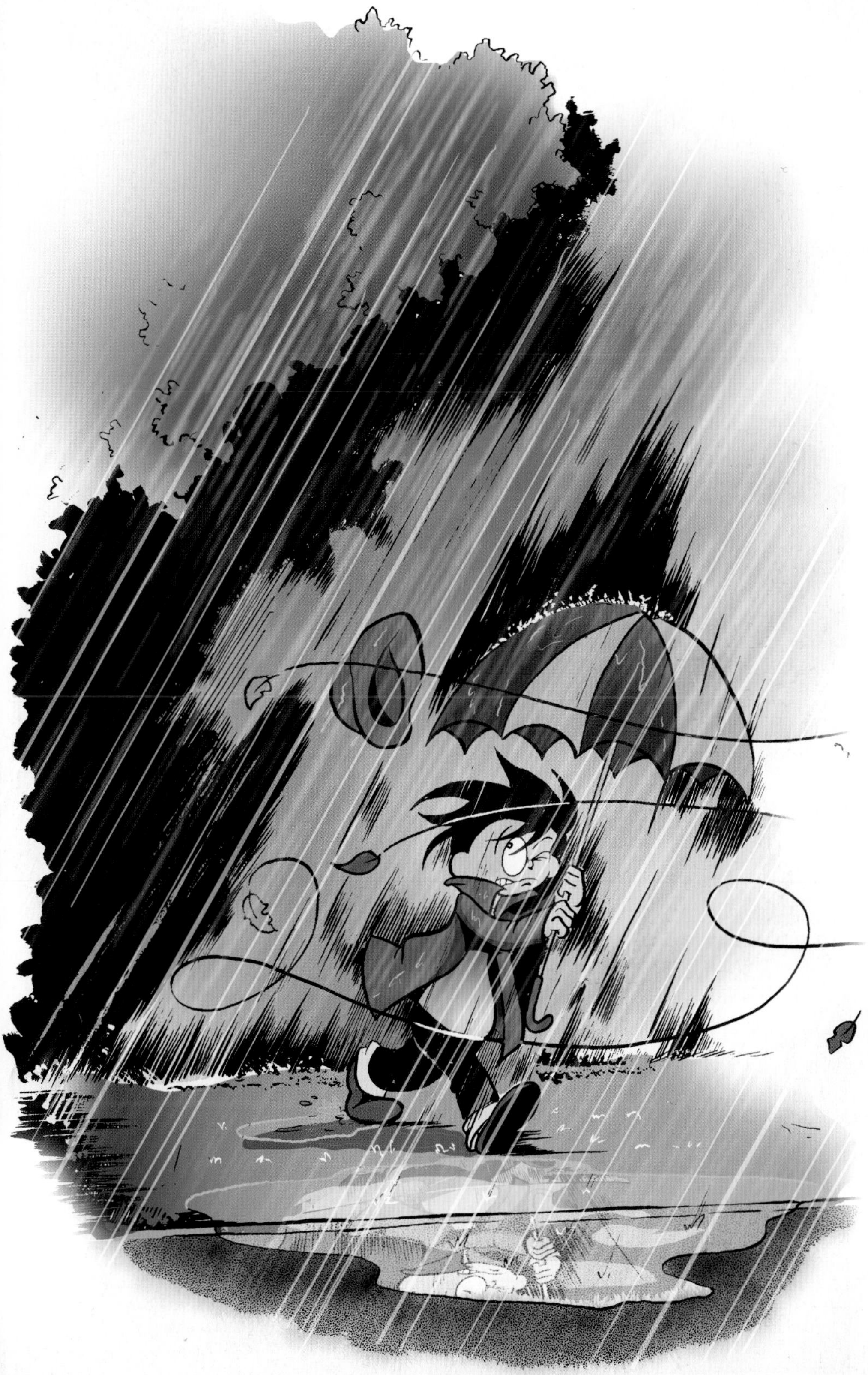

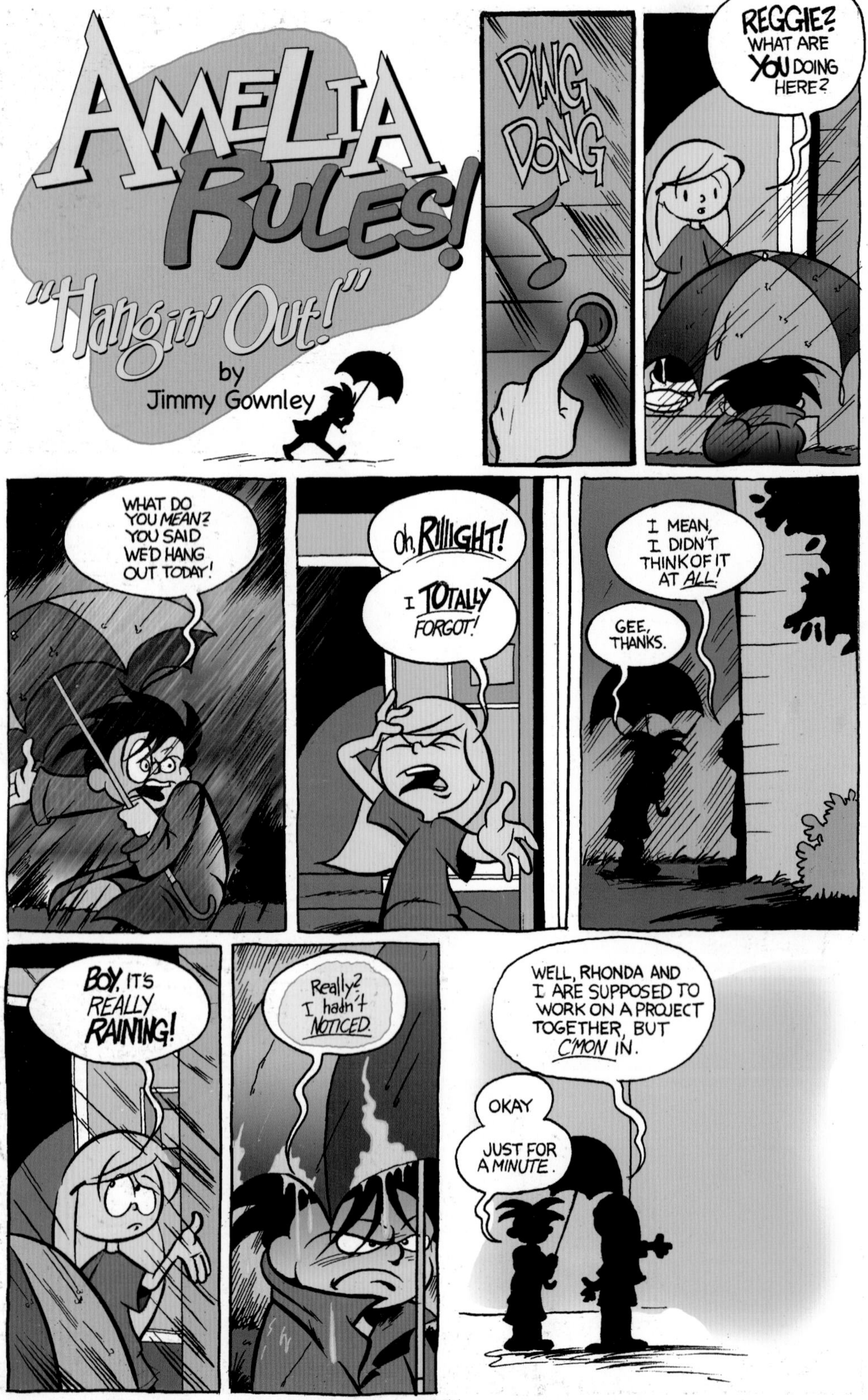
AMELIA RULES!
"Hangin' Out!"
by Jimmy Gownley
DING DONG
REGGIE? WHAT ARE YOU DOING HERE?
WHAT DO YOU MEAN? YOU SAID WE'D HANG OUT TODAY!
Oh, RIIIIGHT!
I TOTALLY FORGOT!
I MEAN, I DIDN'T THINK OF IT AT ALL!
GEE, THANKS.
BOY, IT'S REALLY RAINING!
Really? I hadn't NOTICED.
WELL, RHONDA AND I ARE SUPPOSED TO WORK ON A PROJECT TOGETHER, BUT C'MON IN.
OKAY
JUST FOR A MINUTE.

158

Hangin' Out

Hangtavious Outacus—More commonly known as "Hanging Out"—is a 20th Century American invention, in the vein of "Bummin' Around," or "Chillin'." Although Hanging Out at first appears rather simple, in fact, its rules are myriad.

(fig.1)

Hanging out cannot be done alone. That is called "moping" or "Being a Pariah," and neither one is particularly attractive. (fig. 1)

Any group containing two to five people may engage in Hanging Out, so long as doing nothing is the primary activity. For example, "Hanging Out and talking" is acceptable, while "Hanging Out and building shelters for Habitat for Humanity" is not. Snacks are not required, but are highly recommended. (fig. 2)

(fig.2)

There are strict restrictions on how many people may Hang Out, and how often the hanging may occur. For example, more than five people is now a Party, and while it may seem like you can Hang Out at a Party, you can't because the music is too loud, and let's face it, there's no way you like more than five people anyway. (fig. 3)

(fig.3)

(fig.4)

Here is where the slippery slope gets even slipperier.

More than five people more than once a month is no longer a party, but a club (fig. 4). This is fine, but you may be expected to pay dues or pretend to be interested in other people's boats and/or record collections. More than once a WEEK and it becomes a cult. It is definitely advisable NOT to join a cult, but if you feel you must, remember that it is better to be the leader than the guy who collects the fingers. (fig. 5)

(fig 5)

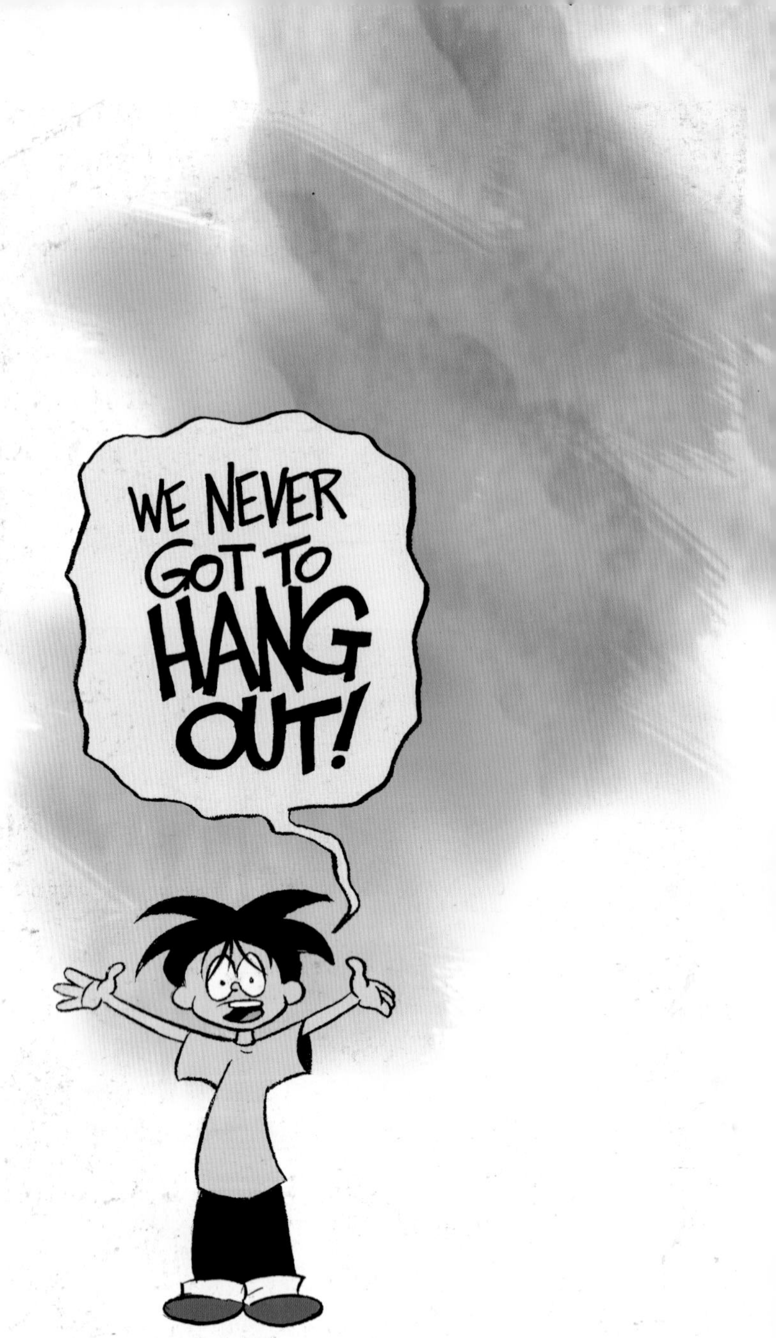
WE NEVER GOT TO HANG OUT!

Cartoonist Jimmy Gownley developed a love of comics at an early age when his mother read *Peanuts* collections to him. Not long after, he discovered comic books (via his dad) and developed a voracious appetite for reading any and all things comic-related.

By the age of 15, Gownley was self-publishing his first book, *Shades of Gray Comics and Stories*. The black & white slice-of-life series ran 16 issues and was recently collected by *Century Comics*.

The idea for *Amelia Rules!* came about several years ago while Gownley was still working on *Shades of Gray*. The goal was to create a comic book with comic strip sensibilities that both traditional and nontraditional comic book fans could enjoy. He also wanted to provide good, solid entertainment for kids that didn't talk down to them.

Since its debut in June 2001, *Amelia Rules!* has become a critical and fan favorite. It has been nominated for several awards, including the *Howard Eugene Day Memorial Prize*, the *Harvey Award* and the *Eisner Award*, and in 2006, the third volume of the series, *Amelia Rules! Superheroes*, received the *Cybil Award* for *Best Graphic Novel: Ages 12 and Under*.

Gownley lives in Harrisburg, Pennsylvania with his wife Karen and twin daughters Stella and Anna.